THE LOG CABIN

THE LOG CABIN

An American Icon

ALISON K. HOAGLAND

University of Virginia Press
CHARLOTTESVILLE AND LONDON

University of Virginia Press

Printed in the United States of America on acid-free paper

First published 2018
First paperback edition published 2019
ISBN 978-0-8139-4257-5 (paper)

1 3 5 7 9 8 6 4 2

The Library of Congress has cataloged the hardcover edition as follows:

Library of Congress Cataloging-in-Publication Data
Names: Hoagland, Alison K., 1951– author.
Title: The log cabin : an American icon / Alison K. Hoagland.
Description: Charlottesville : University of Virginia Press, 2017. | Includes bibliographical references and index.
Identifiers: LCCN 2017038820 | ISBN 9780813940861 (cloth : alk. paper) | ISBN 9780813940878 (ebook)
Subjects: LCSH: Log cabins—United States. | Collective memory—United States.
Classification: LCC NA 8470 .H63 2017 | DDC 728.7/30973—dc23
LC record available at https://lccn.loc.gov/2017038820

Furthermore:
a program of the J. M. Kaplan Fund

Publication of this volume was assisted by a grant from Furthermore: a program of the J. M. Kaplan Fund.

Cover art: "The Pioneer Cabin of the Yo-semite Valley," hand-colored Currier and Ives lithograph, ca. 1856–1907. (Library of Congress)

CONTENTS

List of Illustrations vii

Acknowledgments xiii

Introduction: Shelter and Icon 1

1. "The True Rustic Order":
Log Cabins in Time and Place 11

2. Presidential Timber:
The Log Cabin as a Symbol of Political Worthiness 50

3. Hovels and Cottages:
The Log Cabin as a Symbol of Poverty 78

4. Romancing the Wilderness:
The Log Cabin as a Symbol of the Pioneer 115

5. Twentieth-Century Leisure:
When a Log Cabin is Not a Log Cabin 148

6. "All the Pleasures of Primitive Living":
The Log Cabin on Vacation 173

7. Parks and Forests:
The Log Cabin as a Public Amenity 195

Epilogue:
The Log Cabin Today 227

Historiographical Note 235

Essay on Sources 239

Notes 243

Index 281

Color gallery follows page 126

ILLUSTRATIONS

1. "A Home in the Wilderness," Currier and Ives 3
2. Solo Mountain Shelter Cabin, Chisana, Alaska 5
3. Wickersham House, Eagle, Alaska 6
4. Interior, Wickersham House, Eagle, Alaska 7
5. "The Pioneer Settler," Orsamus Turner, 1849 12
6. "Second Sketch of the Pioneer," Orsamus Turner, 1849 12
7. "Third Sketch of the Pioneer," Orsamus Turner, 1849 13
8. "Fourth Sketch of the Pioneer," Orsamus Turner, 1849 14
9. "A design to represent the beginning and completion of an American Settlement or Farm," Thomas Pownall, 1761 15
10. "Log House in the Forests of Georgia," Basil Hall, 1827–28 17
11. "The Raising," 1848–49 19
12. Types of notching 22
13. Wollerton House, Chester County, Pennsylvania 23
14. Plan, Tyne Woody House, Cataloochee, North Carolina 26
15. Plan, McIntyre Log House, Charlotte, North Carolina 26
16. Plan, Alfred's Cabin, Hermitage, Tennessee 28
17. Plan, Tait Plantation House, Columbus, Texas 29

18. Elevations, Morehead-Gano Log House, Grapevine vic., Texas 31
19. "Wm. Robertson's house near his quarry on Aquia Creek," Virginia, Benjamin Henry Latrobe, 1806 33
20. Bertolet-Herbein Cabin, Oley Line, Pennsylvania 38
21. Plan, Bertolet-Herbein Cabin, Oley Line, Pennsylvania 39
22. El Dorado, California, ca. 1848–53 40
23. Gus Larson Cabin, Wiseman, Alaska 41
24. Interior, Gus Larson Cabin, Wiseman, Alaska 42
25. Creek House, 1791 44
26. Truchas, New Mexico, ca. 1940 45
27. Sitka, Alaska, 1827 47
28. Log cabin near Gheen, Minnesota, 1937 48
29. "General Harrison's Log Cabin March and Quick Step," sheet music, 1840 52
30. "Harrison and Reform" silk handkerchief, 1840 57
31. "Log Cabin, Hartford, Conn.," 1840 60
32. Cabin, Hodgenville, Kentucky, 1895 64
33. Dismantled cabin, College Point, New York, 1906 65
34. Abraham Lincoln Birthplace National Historical Park, Hodgenville, Kentucky 67
35. Lincoln Boyhood National Memorial, Lincoln City, Indiana 69
36. Lincoln Marriage Temple, Harrodsburg, Kentucky 71
37. Lincoln Tavern, Knob Creek, Kentucky 72
38. Lincoln's New Salem State Historic Site, Petersburg, Illinois 73
39. Living History Farm, Lincoln Boyhood National Memorial, Lincoln City, Indiana 75
40. Title page, Harriet Beecher Stowe's *Uncle Tom's Cabin,* 1852 80
41. Slave quarters, Will Crenshaw Plantation, Greenville, Alabama 83
42. George Walker property, District of Columbia, 1796 85
43. Unidentified log cabin with whitewash, 1900 86
44. Slave quarters, Sotterley, Hollywood, Maryland 88
45. Slave quarters, Hampton, Towson, Maryland 89
46. Slave quarters and kitchen, the Hermitage, Tennessee 90

47. Kitchen, Booker T. Washington National Monument, Franklin County, Virginia 93
48. Cabin, former Pettway Plantation, Gees Bend, Alabama, 1937 96
49. "Education," Harrogate, Tennessee, ca. 1906 98
50. Log Cabin Settlement, near Asheville, North Carolina 101
51. Log school building, Hindman School, Hindman, Kentucky 102
52. Log cabin, John C. Campbell Folk School, Brasstown, North Carolina 106
53. Weaving Cabin, Penland School of Crafts, Penland, North Carolina 107
54. "Travelog," 1933 108
55. Johnson Farm, Blue Ridge Parkway, Virginia, 1973 110
56. Johnson Farm, Blue Ridge Parkway, Virginia, 1996–97 111
57. Mountain Farm Museum, Great Smoky Mountains National Park, North Carolina 112
58. John Oliver House, Cades Cove, Great Smoky Mountains National Park, Tennessee 113
59. Walker Farm, Great Smoky Mountains National Park, Tennessee 114
60. Caroline Kirkland, 1852 118
61. Unpacking, from *A New Home: Who'll Follow?,* 1850 123
62. Log cabin under construction, from Laura Ingalls Wilder's *Little House on the Prairie,* 1953 126
63. Little House in the Big Woods, Pepin, Wisconsin, 1970s reconstruction 130
64. Little House on the Prairie, Independence, Kansas, 1970s reconstruction 130
65. Theodore Roosevelt in buckskins, 1885 132
66. Maltese Cross Cabin, Medora, North Dakota 133
67. Elkhorn Ranch, north of Medora, North Dakota 134
68. Hunter's Cabin, World's Columbian Exposition, Chicago, Illinois, 1893 137
69. Richard Proenneke Cabin, Twin Lakes, Alaska 146
70. New England Farmer's Home and Modern Kitchen, Centennial Exposition, Philadelphia, Pennsylvania, 1876 151
71. Log cabin, Plymouth, Massachusetts, 1921 153
72. Clubhouse, Craftsman Farms, Morristown, New Jersey 154
73. Detail of notching, Clubhouse, Craftsman Farms, Morristown, New Jersey 155

74. Log House, George Washington Birthplace National Monument, Colonial Beach, Virginia, 1938 158
75. Fort Rosalie gift shop, Natchez, Mississippi 160
76. Fort Ticonderoga gift shop, Ticonderoga, New York 161
77. Visitor information center, Ahmeek, Michigan 162
78. Visitor information center, Anchorage, Alaska 163
79. American Legion Hall, Fillmore, Utah 167
80. Boy Scout cabin, Woodlynne, New Jersey 167
81. Pell Playhouse, Ticonderoga, New York 168
82. Towle's Log Cabin Syrup advertisement, 1920 170
83. Theodore Roosevelt at the Grand Canyon, ca. 1913 171
84. Camp Sagamore, Raquette Lake, New York 175
85. "Cabin," in William S. Wicks's *Log Cabins: How to Build and Furnish Them,* 1889 176
86. Interior, Bagley Cabin, North Fork Club, Island Park, Idaho 179
87. Sprucewold Annex, Boothbay Harbor, Maine 180
88. Design for log house, Medford Lakes, New Jersey, 1927 181
89. "Pioneer Cabin in Minnesota Historical Society rooms," from Chilson D. Aldrich, *The Real Log Cabin,* 1935 183
90. Camp Ruthers, Lynchburg, Virginia 185
91. Bar BC Ranch, Jackson Hole, Wyoming 187
92. White Grass Dude Ranch, Jackson Hole, Wyoming 188
93. Painted Pony, Lake Luzerne, New York 189
94. Log Cabin Motel, Pinedale, Wyoming 191
95. Directors' cabins, Stratford Hall, Stratford, Virginia 193
96. Old Faithful Inn, Yellowstone National Park, Wyoming 197
97. Interior, Old Faithful Inn, Yellowstone National Park, Wyoming 198
98. Rangers' Club, Yosemite National Park, California 199
99. Interior, Paradise Inn, Mount Rainier National Park, Washington 203
100. Longmire Community Building, Mount Rainier National Park, Washington 204
101. Section, Longmire Community Building, Mount Rainier National Park, Washington 205

102. Yakima (now Sunrise) Administration Building, Mount Rainer National Park, Washington 207
103. Yakima (now Sunrise) Administration and Community Buildings, Mount Rainier National Park, Washington 208
104. St. Andrews Patrol Cabin, Mount Rainier National Park, Washington 209
105. Office building, Denali National Park, Alaska 210
106. Toklat River Patrol Cabin, Denali National Park, Alaska 211
107. Warehouse, Denali National Park, Alaska 212
108. Employees' residence, Denali National Park, Alaska 213
109. Douglas Lodge, Itasca State Park, Minnesota 215
110. Cabin 8, Itasca State Park, Minnesota 215
111. Old Timer's Cabin, Itasca State Park, Minnesota 216
112. Forest Inn, Itasca State Park, Minnesota 218
113. Plan, Cabin 6, Westmoreland State Park, Virginia 219
114. Cabin 6, Westmoreland State Park, Virginia 219
115. Cut Foot Ranger Station, Chippewa National Forest, Minnesota 221
116. Supervisor's Office Building, Chippewa National Forest, Minnesota 223
117. Plichta house, Little Traverse Bay, Michigan 228
118. Interior, Plichta house, Little Traverse Bay, Michigan 229
119. "Norway" plans and perspective, Hiawatha Log Homes 230
120. Schottler House, Old World Wisconsin, Eagle, Wisconsin 233

COLOR PLATES (FOLLOWING PAGE 126)

1. Caldwell-Hutchison Farm, Lowndesville, South Carolina
2. Campaign textile, 1840
3. Interior, Abraham Lincoln Birthplace National Historical Park, Hodgenville, Kentucky
4. Lincoln Logs
5. Notley Young property, District of Columbia, 1796
6. Slave quarters, Carter's Grove, James City County, Virginia
7. The Little House in the Big Woods, from Laura Ingalls Wilder's *Little House in the Big Woods,* 1953

8. Richard Proenneke building his cabin, Twin Lakes, Alaska, 1968
9. Richard Proenneke Cabin, Twin Lakes, Alaska, 1969
10. New England Coffee Shop (now El Comedor), Los Angeles, California
11. My Grandfather's House Antique Shop, McMinnville, Tennessee
12. Log cabin in Twitter offices, San Francisco, California
13. Camp Santanoni, Newcomb, New York
14. William Allen White Work Cabin, Rocky Mountain National Park, Estes Park, Colorado
15. Medford Lakes Lodge, Medford Lakes, New Jersey, 1962
16. Interior, Supervisor's Office Building, Chippewa National Forest, Minnesota

ACKNOWLEDGMENTS

As a book that draws so much on the work of others, this volume has incurred many debts. My first thanks goes to all those who have studied log cabins, some of whom are acknowledged in the end notes. During the course of the research for this book, I met many new people, some of whom I interviewed and others who introduced me to certain sites. I am indebted to Joe and Marcia Albright, Flat Creek Ranch, Wyoming; John Branson, Lake Clark National Park; Gary Bufe, Hiawatha Log Homes; Sueann Brown, Mt. Rainier National Park; Martha Carver, Tennessee Department of Transportation; Pamela Dobben, Morristown National Historical Park; Alicia Goehring, Wisconsin State Historical Society; Valerie Naylor, Theodore Roosevelt National Park; Alan Pape, Greenbush, Wisconsin; Barb Pahl, National Trust for Historic Preservation; the late Martin Perkins, Old World Wisconsin; Mark and Carol Plichta, Little Traverse Bay, Michigan; Douglass Reed, Mercersburg, Pennsylvania; Dan Watrous Sr. and Jr., Hancock, Michigan, American Legion; Thomas Windsor, Morristown National Historical Park; Katherine Wonson, Grand Teton National Park; and Bill Yourd, Chippewa National Forest. It was a pleasure to meet all of you, and I appreciate your generosity to me.

I also drew on the patience of many of my friends. I want to thank those who accompanied me on field trips to historic log cabins or provided lodging while I was in their part of the country: Arne Alanen, Betty Bird, Catherine Bishir, Lynn

Bjorkman, Dave Hoagland, Lucy Hoagland, Port and Louise Hoagland, Deb Hurtt, Jeanne Lawrence, Judy Lee, Barb Pettit, Jean Rodeck, Beverley Rowland, Mark Schara, and Michele Schara.

My Vernacular Architecture Forum colleagues were particularly gracious in giving advice, tips, and general wisdom. Among them, I would like to thank Sally Berk, Ken Breisch, Tom Carter, Betsy Cromley, Lisa Davidson, Claire Dempsey, Carter Hudgins, Richard Longstreth, Carl Lounsbury, Ann McCleary, Travis McDonald, Will Moore, Gigi Price, Roger Reed, Janet Sheridan, Michael Ann Williams, and Aaron Wunsch. Several scholars responded with valuable information to an email inquiry that I put out: Bob Craig, Stefani Evans, Cory Jensen, and Holly Taylor. And thanks to my former colleagues at Michigan Technological University, Carol MacLennan and Larry Lankton, for ongoing support.

Given the wide range of this book, assembling illustrations also required the help of many people. Thanks are due to Tom Carter, Brooke Childrey, Paul Davidson, Marilyn Ibach, Cory Jensen, Steve Ketcham, Margaret Kieckhefer, Jeff Klee, Carol Latti, Joan Lewis, Travis McDonald, Christi Mitchell, Janet Rankin, Margaret Westfield, and especially Mark Schara. Staff members at the Library of Congress and the Van Pelt and Opie Library of Michigan Technological University were also very helpful, as were those at a number of institutions mentioned in the captions. And thanks too to the whole crew at the University of Virginia Press.

Catherine Bishir offered advice and examples, accompanied me on a road trip from Colorado to Michigan, and provided valuable comments on an early draft of the manuscript. Al Chambers also commented on an early draft and referred me to certain sources. I am very grateful to them, both for their log cabin guidance and for their mentoring throughout my career. I can hardly imagine writing a book without consulting them at least once.

Given that I am a native of Delaware, the cultural hearth of the log cabin in America, and that my great-grandfather, Christopher L. Ward, wrote a history of the Swedes in Delaware, perhaps writing about log cabins was inevitable for me. But I think that the beginning of this book can be traced to the summer of 1982, when I was working for the Historic American Buildings Survey of the National Park Service and was sent to survey historic buildings, most of which turned out to be log cabins, in the newly established Lake Clark National Park and Preserve in Alaska. I would like to thank Bob Kapsch and Bob Spude for making that trip to

Alaska possible, as well as several subsequent ones. I would also like to thank Mike Tollefson and Clair Roberts for being such amiable hosts and expert guides at Lake Clark. As eye-opening as that trip was, I didn't fully comprehend the log cabins I found then. Many years later, I hope that this book brings a greater understanding to that most American architecture, the log cabin.

THE LOG CABIN

INTRODUCTION

Shelter and Icon

In 1850, William Cooper Howells moved with his wife, Mary, and their seven children into a log cabin near Xenia, Ohio. Having grown up in a log cabin, he wished to recapture that experience, if only for a year while a new frame house was under construction. The log cabin, probably fifty years old then, was a source of nostalgia to Howells; a "sore trial" to his wife, who cooked over an open fireplace for a time; and a repository of endless delight for his children, who were enraptured with the "cavernous maw" of the 6-foot-high, 3-foot-deep fireplace and the loft in which they slept, under shingles so cracked they could see the stars. Forty years later, one of those children, William Dean Howells, who had become a prominent novelist and editor, went back to the site, looking in vain for that log cabin. Although he had lived in the log cabin for only a year, it had a grip on his imagination.[1]

In 1940, Gus Larson built a log cabin in the remote Alaskan community of Wiseman. Located north of the Arctic Circle in the Brooks Range, Wiseman flourished in the early 1910s during the northernmost gold rush in the territory. The village, consisting of a few hundred people at its peak, dwindled in population through most of the twentieth century but attracted a few people who eked out a living trapping furs or mining gold. Gus Larson built his 12 by 14–foot cabin of round logs, saddle-notched at the corners, in this community of similar buildings.[2]

These two examples illustrate the simultaneous nature of log cabin as icon and shelter. In the first instance, the log cabin was an element of nostalgia for William

Dean Howells's father, who had lived in one in his youth, and for Howells himself, who attempted to visit the log cabin of his own childhood. In the second example, logs served as a practical and reasonable solution to a construction problem. In the mid-nineteenth century, even as Americans began to be sentimental about the log cabin, it was still serving as the best and most efficient building type in some parts of the country. That duality continued for a century, beginning in about 1840. The role of the log cabin as an object of nostalgia, or icon, occurred simultaneously with its role as a practical building, or basic shelter.

This book examines the log cabin in America as both icon and simple shelter. As a shelter, it is a straightforward structure, composed of local materials and harmonious with its surroundings. To many, it is a thing of beauty: weathered logs, crafted corners, shingled roof, forest setting. A link to preindustrial times, it can be made with hand tools. Part of its aesthetic appeal is this evocative connection to the past. And this history extended for four centuries. From almost the beginning of European settlement in North America in the late sixteenth century until well into the twentieth century, the log cabin was a reasonable option for a house.

The understanding of the log cabin is interwoven with the American past. The familiar image of intrepid settlers carving homes out of the wilderness, crafting a cabin out of the abundant resources of the land, exhibiting qualities of self-reliance and independence, has been complicated by later, more shaded interpretations of the past. The American wilderness was not really wild; it had long been settled by native peoples. Pioneers were intruders, not discoverers. Settlement across the continent was uneven and market-driven. Yet the imagined past outweighs more accurate interpretations when considering the iconic value of the log cabin.

Currier and Ives marketed this sentimentalized ideal in several lithographs produced in the mid-nineteenth century but clearly hearkening back to earlier times (fig. 1). In these, the one-story cabin has horizontal logs notched at the corners. Smoke curls out of the chimney, and often a mother and child stand in the doorway, conveying a domestic charm. This archetype will serve as a touchstone through this book as it examines the log cabin, whether a simple shelter or a more finished house. The reality of a log cabin as expedient, temporary shelter—dirt floors, glassless windows, wooden chimneys daubed with clay—gave way in the nineteenth century to a more acceptable domestic, even romantic, vision. While the Currier and Ives log cabins had their basis in historical reality, this was not always the kind of cabin that a pioneer would build at first. The metamorphosis of

Figure 1. "A Home in the Wilderness." Currier and Ives prints imbued the remote log cabin with domesticity, shown in this family scene in which the cabin of round saddle-notched logs and board roof is tidy and cheerful. (Currier and Ives, ca. 1870, Library of Congress)

the rough log cabin into a picturesque cottage is one aspect of the icon-making that surrounds the log cabin.

The story of the log cabin in America is replete with myths and nostalgia. It is no accident that the best-known book about log cabins is called *The Log Cabin Myth,* the myth being that English settlers brought the log cabin to this continent in the early seventeenth century.[3] Other narratives concern independent frontiersmen, who certainly built log cabins, but settlers with families also built them and made them homes. Self-reliant builders constructed cabins single-handedly, but more often communities, or at least a neighbor or two, pitched in. Cabins might have stood alone in the wilderness, but they also clustered into villages. For every well-crafted cabin with logs dovetailed at the corners for an impeccable fit, there were sloppily built ones that did not survive the first winter. But it is these counternarratives that make the log cabin such a complex icon of American experience.

Rather than a simple dichotomy of myth and reality, exploring the log cabin in terms of narrative and counternarrative reveals the complexity involved in this seemingly simple structure, as well as the subjectivity of experience with the log cabin. The counternarrative allows for an ambiguous interpretation. The log cabin's importance lies in the way that Americans have adopted these narratives, finding them more compelling than other interpretations. This book explores each of these narratives and counternarratives further.

Log cabins were a democratic building form. Part of the appeal of log cabins is that they are portrayed as a great equalizer. With a little bit of property and little to no cash, an enterprising individual could build a very cheap house from materials found on that land. It was the perfect first house, allowing a family to have an immediate shelter while amassing some capital through farming or trapping before building a more finished, more expensive house. But this progress narrative leaves little room for the poverty that is also associated with log cabins. Log cabins were not only the most common form of housing for enslaved people and rural whites; they also became a symbol of inadequate housing, frequently termed "hovels." As often as the log cabin was a step toward upward mobility, it just as often served as the only option for people trapped in poverty or in circumstances beyond their control.

Log cabins were masculine. Log cabins were often built by men, for themselves. In some periods, log cabins became a symbol of roughing it, of spurning modern-day conveniences for a hardier kind of living (fig. 2). But the image of log cabins as men's places is undercut by the fact that they were also homes, populated by families. Men on the move, such as explorers and frontiersmen, did not always build houses. It was the settlers, who intended to stay on the land and raise families, who built log cabins. Women, concerned with food preparation and child rearing, spent more time in their cabins than did men. Like most homes in the nineteenth century, log cabins were women's places. And later, amid the Colonial Revival and Arts and Crafts movements at the turn of the twentieth century, women became great proponents of log cabins.

Log cabins were built by English colonists. The identification of settlers with log cabins is strong, but a conflation of early seventeenth-century colonists and later settlers confuses the picture. English colonists may have built log cabins in the seventeenth century, but they did not introduce them to the American continent. Histories that concentrated on the English colonists who settled the East Coast fed this myth, but this long-held portrayal overlooked the contribution of Germans, Scotch-Irish, Swiss, Scandinavians, Russians, Spanish, and French, all of

Figure 2. Solo Mountain Shelter Cabin, Chisana, Alaska. The masculine image of log cabins alludes to independence, self-reliance, cowboys, and wide-open spaces. (Jet Lowe, photographer, 1982, Historic American Buildings Survey, Library of Congress)

whom erected log buildings. Many immigrant groups found that log cabins provided a good solution to the need for expedient housing.

Log cabins were cozy and home-like. The Currier and Ives image of a cozy cottage evokes the domestic bliss that a log cabin might provide. As Alaskan district judge James Wickersham enthused in a letter to his mother in 1900, after describing the log cabin he built on the Yukon River, "let the storms blow as they will, we'll be warm and comfortable still."[4] (figs. 3 and 4) A well-built, well-chinked log cabin with a wood stove might be as cozy as its occupants could wish, but many cabins were not so tight. Contemporary observers criticized dirt floors, leaky roofs, unglazed windows, and smoky fires. The log cabin could be cozy, but it could also be cold, wet, dark, and infested with vermin.

Log cabins were an escape from civilization. In the opening chapters of Mark Twain's *The Adventures of Huckleberry Finn,* Huck chafes at the Widow Douglas's attempts to civilize him, which meant that she expected Huck to wear starched clothes, attend school, sit in a chair, and sleep in a bed in her middle-class home. Huck's drunkard father appears and takes Huck to a log cabin in the woods, where the boy reverts to smoking, swearing, and skipping school. Huck prefers this uncivilized life, but his father's abusiveness causes him to saw his way out of the

Figure 3. Wickersham House, Eagle, Alaska. District Judge James Wickersham lived in this house between 1900 and 1903, when the court moved to Fairbanks. Shown leaning on his "Arctic entry," or storm shed, he exulted in the log cabin's warmth and coziness. (Alaska State Library, Wickersham State Historic Sites Photo Collection, P277-019-22)

cabin with an opportunely placed saw, fake his own death, then run away. While log cabins were sometimes positioned as the opposite of the civilized life, as in this example, they often symbolized it as well, being the first construction of a settlement, and thus the beginning of civilization, not its antithesis.

Log cabins were good breeding grounds for presidents. Abraham Lincoln stands as evidence that good presidents come from log cabins, but log cabins have more often simply produced good campaign slogans and political image polishing. The idea that humble birth is a desirable quality in American presidents is a recurring political theme, but in fact most U.S. presidents have been wealthier than the average Americans who have elected them. Politicians perceive that Americans confer nobility on humble birth, so they claim it for themselves. In the nineteenth century, birth in a log cabin served as a shorthand for modest origins, a desirable quality for presidents.

Figure 4. Interior, Wickersham House, Eagle, Alaska. The comforts of Wickersham's home included an iron bedstead, rocking chairs, and books, while the antlers, bearskin, and snowshoes reflected his current surroundings. (Alaska State Library, Wickersham State Historic Sites Photo Collection, P277-019-23)

Log cabins are harmonious with nature. This is part of their aesthetic appeal: they are made of the products of the land on which they stand. They are locally sourced, to use a twenty-first-century concept. They look appropriate to their surroundings because their material, texture, and color are found in that place. But some log cabins contain materials not found locally—window glass, fire bricks, or a waterproof layer in the roof. They also consume their place, requiring more timber to build than a comparable wood-frame house. That might not have been a consideration for settlers who had to clear the land of trees in order to farm it, but excessive timber usage is not usually harmonious with nature.

Log cabins are essentially American. Log cabins were built in northern and eastern Europe for centuries before they were built in America, and emigrants from that part of the world brought the building method with them. And log cabins were built in the forested parts of Canada just as they were in the United States. But what makes the U.S. identification with the log cabin so significant is the importance that the log cabin held in defining its citizens' conception of themselves. Nowhere else did the log cabin play a role in presidential elections. Nowhere else was the fundamental egalitarianism of society equated, in the public imagination, with society's origin in log cabins. And nowhere else was the log cabin such a protean symbol of an individual's character.

The appropriation of the log cabin as an icon of individualism, democracy, masculinity, and so on—even with all the caveats noted above—reveals something about Americans. The willingness to find meaning in a humble dwelling reflects beliefs in individualism and self-reliance, in egalitarianism and democracy, in wilderness and opportunity. The meaning Americans have found there has varied, of course, depending on who they were and what they were looking for, and it has varied, just as the log cabin has, depending on time and place. The story of the log cabin is ultimately one that is more about American values and perceptions than about the building itself.

This book explores the log cabin as both icon and shelter, across the United States and through nearly four centuries. The book moves through time and to various regions of the country, while considering a number of narratives and counternarratives associated with the log cabin. Beginning with an examination of the log cabin as shelter, the first chapter defines and describes the log cabin, discussing its characteristics, its ubiquity by 1800, and how it changed over time and across the continent. Although log construction also served for a wide range of other buildings—barns, churches, stores, and so on—this book remains focused on domestic use.

The remainder of the book explores the overlap of perceptions of the log cabin as icon and shelter from 1840 to roughly 1940. Chapters 2, 3, and 4 look at the perceptions of the log cabin in the nineteenth and early twentieth centuries. Chapter 2 examines two particularly iconic uses of the log cabin, those associated with presidents. William Henry Harrison and his Log Cabin Campaign tapped into a nostalgia for the log cabin that was already widespread in 1840. The campaign used Harrison's occupation of a log cabin as a symbol of his masculinity, modesty, earthiness, and frontier experience. Abraham Lincoln's identification with having been born in a log cabin—an association that again implied a man-of-the-people background—became even more significant several generations after his death, when midwesterners in particular found the log cabin an apt form of commemoration. As Americans moved farther away from personal associations with the man, exhibitions of Lincoln's several log cabins underwent phases that included providing tangible connections to him, building shrines to a sanctified personage, and developing educational settings to learn about his life.

After this glorification of humble birth, chapter 3 explores how a building perceived as a "hovel" becomes a "cottage" in the eyes of early twentieth-century reformers. This chapter studies the log cabin as housing for the poorest: slaves in the South and whites in Appalachia. Housing for enslaved people became part of the arguments about the institution of slavery—how well did plantation owners care for their slaves? The interpretations of the log cabins as places where most slaves were housed echoed the discussions about the morality of slavery and the humaneness of their treatment. Discussions about Appalachian people's poverty often cited their log cabins as both evidence of their destitution and as symbols for their possible redemption. By the early twentieth century, reformers saw log cabins as worthy representations of their pioneer past and their expertise in handcraft.

Chapter 4 takes a more personal approach to the log cabin, examining four popular authors who wrote about living in log cabins in the wilderness. This chapter looks at the log cabin in the West, along with the shifting definition of what the West or wilderness is, according to its occupant. The authors provide insights into building and inhabiting log cabins, uniquely informed by their genders, age, and status. Each of them also uses the log cabin to support an argument in favor of his or her lifestyle, so once again the log cabin reinforces a larger world view.

The final three chapters, 5, 6, and 7, look at the more self-conscious iterations of the log cabin in the twentieth century. The Colonial Revival and Arts and Crafts movements, combined with the mobility provided by the automobile, resonated with tourists who found log cabins to be the perfect combination of the familiar and the exotic. With this new view of log cabins, they became popular for uses other than primary residences. Chapter 5 examines leisure-time functions such as tea rooms, gift shops, antique shops, and clubhouses, roles in which the log cabins' different or even outlandish appearance helped attract patrons.

Chapter 6 explores log cabins that were built as vacation lodging—second homes, camps, dude ranches, and motels. The combination of rustic surroundings and modern-day conveniences made the log cabin an appealing leisure-time residence, removing the vacationer from the familiar but still offering comfort. The tourist industry invoked log cabins as suitable symbols of olden times or the West, to people who were far removed from both.

The popularization of the log cabin, as found in public places, is the subject of chapter 7. In the early twentieth century, the federal government built log cabins not only because they were compatible with sylvan settings but also because they reminded the public of a romanticized past. In national and state parks and national forests, log cabins served park and forest personnel as housing and offices, while tourists were often directed to visitor centers and accommodations in the form of log cabins.

The epilogue briefly considers log cabins in the twenty-first century. A flourishing industry in log cabin production provides stock plans and milled logs for homeowners who want their own large, comfortable log home. At the same time, local historical societies across the country display log cabins as tangible representations of a community's past. Log cabins continue to appeal to Americans as rational building solutions and as symbols of their past, real or imagined, as artifacts and icons. They also continue to appeal to scholars, as discussed in the Historiographical Note following the epilogue in this volume.

For all the discussion of the meaning and interpretation of log cabins, one aspect should not be overlooked: they worked. The log cabin was the best solution for a wide range of conditions, over nearly four centuries, across a continent, for people of vastly different backgrounds. It could be cheap and expedient. Surviving historic cabins, which tend to be better than average quality, or well-equipped twentieth-century incarnations lead to an underestimation of the essential nature of the log cabin as the most basic form of housing. That it was the right building for so many situations contributes to its iconic status.

1

"THE TRUE RUSTIC ORDER"

Log Cabins in Time and Place

In 1849 Orsamus Turner, a newspaperman in New York State, published a sequence of drawings depicting pioneer settlement in his *Pioneer History of the Holland Purchase.* The first image depicts a small clearing in a large forest (fig. 5). In the foreground, a man is trimming an already felled tree. In the center is a small log cabin with icicles at the eaves and smoke pouring out of its chimney-less roof. Large round logs, notched at the corners, form the walls. The author informs us that "the roof of his house is of peeled elm bark; his scanty window is of oiled paper. . . . The floor of his house is of the halves of split logs; the door is made of three hewed plank[s]—no boards to be had—a saw mill has been talked of in the neighborhood, but it has not been put in operation." A woman stands in front of the cabin, feeding chickens and pigs in the yard. The labor of carving this homestead out of the forest is evident in the stumps scattered around the yard and the size of the trees. But Turner reassures us: "The task before him is a formidable one, but he has a strong arm and a stout heart, and the reader has only to look at him as he stands in the foreground, to be convinced that he will conquer all obstacles."[1]

The second drawing depicts the same scene, but in the following summer (fig. 6). A stick chimney has been added to the house, the clearing is much larger, and a fence surrounds the yard. The wife has planted flowers and vines, and she holds a baby. This scene shows the same level of development, evidence of hard work, and pioneer fortitude as the Currier and Ives print "A Home in the Wilderness" (see

Figure 5. "The Pioneer Settler." Orsamus Turner included a sequence of drawings in his 1849 *Pioneer History of the Holland Purchase of Western New York* that depicted the progress narrative of the log cabin. (J. A. Ayres, delineator, Turner, *Pioneer History,* opposite p. 562)

Figure 6. "Second Sketch of the Pioneer." By the following summer, the pioneers have added a stick chimney and flowers by the door. Their neighbors are helping them clear land through a "logging bee," which occurs in the background. (Turner, *Pioneer History,* opposite p. 564)

fig. 1). The third image depicts the scene ten years later (fig. 7). A hewn-log house with multipaned windows and a masonry chimney has been added to the original log cabin, because the farmer "has had too much reverence for his primitive dwelling to remove it." A framed barn and extensive fields and fencing demonstrate the family's prosperity. The log schoolhouse in the far left distance indicates that the settlers are no longer alone but are part of an organized community. Finally, by the fourth image, depicting the homestead forty-five years after the first drawing, the original log cabin has been demolished and a fashionable Greek Revival house stands in its place, the farmer's reverence for the log cabin apparently forgotten (fig. 8). The forests are no longer in the picture; cultivated fields stretch off into the distance, along with a small village on the far right. Our farmer has achieved success: "He has more than comfortable farm buildings, orchards, and fruit yards; the forest has receded in all directions; he is prosperous in the midst of prosperity."[2]

The sequence of images depicts the progress narrative of brave pioneers settling in hostile and isolated surroundings, gradually civilizing the land around them and making a good living for themselves and their progeny. The role of the log cabin is literally front and center; it is the building that both reflects its surroundings, by

Figure 7. "Third Sketch of the Pioneer." Ten years later, the pioneers have added a large hewn-log section onto the original round-log cabin, and they have cultivated and fenced the land. (Turner, *Pioneer History,* opposite p. 565)

Figure 8. "Fourth Sketch of the Pioneer." Forty-five years after the first settlement, the pioneers have replaced their log cabin with a fashionable Greek Revival house. Cultivated land stretches into the distance. (Turner, *Pioneer History,* opposite p. 566)

being constructed of the material that dominates the first image, and enables the transformation, by being an inexpensive, expedient, and temporary form of building. One compelling idea about the log cabin was that it was part of a transformative process, perhaps not intended to last forever or even into the next generation, but enabling a family to take root (fig. 9).

Movement characterizes the log cabin in several ways. One is this idea of sequence, a family moving from a log cabin to a better house. A second form of movement is change over time and space. Called "the architecture of migration," log cabins as a building type suited migrating peoples. They were built of local materials with relatively little effort, utilized trees that had to be cleared anyway, and could be easily left behind.[3] As the architecture of first settlement, the log cabin crops up in different places as settlement spreads. *Where* first settlement occurs varies along with *when*—generally moving westward from the East Coast

Figure 9. "A design to represent the beginning and completion of an American Settlement or Farm" shows a log cabin on the left, behind the mill, and a two-story frame house across the river. This 1761 drawing is one of the earliest depictions of the progress associated with the log cabin. (Paul Sandby, delineator, from a drawing made by Governor Thomas Pownall, Library of Congress)

in the seventeenth and eighteenth centuries, but also northward, southward, and eastward, not reaching interior parts of Alaska and the West until the twentieth century. The forms of log cabins reflect their places, responding to hot climates or heavy snowfalls in different ways. In the nineteenth and twentieth centuries, technological innovations also affected the log cabin.

This chapter begins by defining and describing the log cabin and its characteristics. Next comes a short discussion of its origins and diffusion, followed by an assessment of its dominance on the built landscape, as a type that housed probably half the population in 1800. The chapter concludes with an account of how the log cabin varied through the centuries and across the country.

DEFINING THE LOG CABIN

In its examination of the log cabin, this book focuses on buildings with horizontal logs notched at the corners. There were other ways to lay logs, of course. Various forms of vertical log construction were popular among French colonists. *Jacal,* another form of log construction, in which vertical poles were lashed together and daubed with mud, was common in the Southwest. Palisade walls were familiar to Native Americans as well as European colonists. Short lengths of logs laid transversely created a stovewood wall, a form of building that required a great deal of mortar.[4] Logs could also be laid longitudinally, yet not notched at the corners. Instead, other methods would join the logs to vertical posts: mortise and tenon, nailing the logs to the posts, or nailing vertical pieces to the posts to hold the logs in place. Yet it was the notched, horizontal logs that dominated log construction in the United States, both in actuality and in the public mind.

The "cabin" part of a log cabin also requires some explanation. Fortunately, Thaddeus Mason Harris, a Unitarian minister, provides a fine distinction between a log cabin and a log house in his description of an 1803 journey in southwestern Pennsylvania:

> The temporary buildings of the first settlers in the wilds are called *Cabins.* They are built with unhewn [i.e., left in the round] logs, the interstices between which are stopped with rails, calked with moss or straw, and daubed with mud. The roof is covered with a sort of thin staves split out of oak or ash, about four feet long and five inches wide, fastened on by heavy poles being laid upon them. 'If the logs be hewed [i.e., squared]; if the interstices be stopped with stone, and neatly plastered; and the roof is composed of shingles nicely laid on, it is called a *log-house.*' A log-house has glass windows and a chimney; a cabin has commonly no window at all, and only a hole at the top for the smoke to escape. After saw-mills are erected and boards can be procured, the settlers provide themselves more decent houses, with neat floors and ceiling.[5]

Harris's description nicely dovetails with Orsamus Turner's drawings: a log cabin is crude, window-less and chimney-less, built of round logs without nails or sawn lumber (fig. 10). A century later, the same temporary function of a round-log cabin persisted. In the Appalachian community of Hollybush, Kentucky, "pole houses"

Figure 10. "Log House in the Forests of Georgia" pictures a log cabin with round saddle-notched logs, few if any windows, no foundation, and a board roof supported by purlins. (Basil Hall, *Forty Etchings, from Sketches made with the camera lucida, in North America, in 1827 and 1828* [Edinburgh, 1829], Library of Congress)

of round logs laid directly on the ground were perceived as provisional shelters, replaced within a year or two by hewn-log houses supported by stone foundations.[6]

A log structure that a builder intended to last a while—which Harris called a house—was constructed more carefully, maybe with a stone foundation, hewn logs, and dovetailed notching. Log buildings that needed to be secure, such as jails, garrison houses, and storehouses, were constructed even more carefully, with tightly fitted logs that could not be breached. Log houses survived at a greater rate than cabins, so Americans often remember the basic log cabin as being more finished than it usually was. As both Harris and Turner pointed out, it also could be upgraded over the years, turning the cabin into a house.

The appellation "cabin" gradually became applied to more than the minimal, window-less and chimney-less building. As *cabin* took on more romantic connotations, as explored in this book, the building also took on a window and a chimney and other features, so that the log cabin of popular memory resembles the Currier and Ives version (see fig. 1) more than the Orsamus Turner one (see fig. 5). In the nineteenth century, as long as people were building their cabins out of necessity, they tended not to call them cabins, which had derogatory connotations. Only in retrospect, perhaps, would the log building acquire the name *cabin* with romantic, even desirable, associations.

The decision to build in log resulted from many factors, with availability of trees and familiarity with the form chief among them. Simply stated, log cabins were built where there were trees. Because of the weight of the logs, if they had to be moved any distance to a cabin site, it was easier to saw them and build a wood frame. And once settlement spread westward to the treeless Great Plains, log construction was no longer the best option. If trees were available, a builder might consider log construction if there were no sawmill or if he had no cash with which to purchase sawn lumber. It was, of course, possible to produce sawn lumber without a sawmill. Whipsawing or pit sawing, involving two people pulling a long saw down a length of timber, could produce planks. The work was difficult, however, and the log cabin avoided the necessity. Also, the use of a sawmill was usually predicated on money, so cash-poor homesteaders found the log cabin an expedient solution. There were always home builders who preferred log construction, despite the option of a sawmill, because it was solid, durable, and energy efficient.[7] There were also reasons to build log cabins that had nothing to do with practicality, and subsequent chapters consider these more romantic and nostalgic associations.

The debate over the amount and kind of labor needed to build a log cabin has often overlooked its varying complexity. The log cabin could be built by just one or two people, if the logs were fairly short and the notching was simple. Help in the form of a work party was always desirable, though (fig. 11). In that case, preparing the logs on the ground and notching them was done ahead of time; then neighbors were brought in to hoist them into place in the walls. In this way, a log cabin could be "built" in a day, but the day included only erecting the walls and roof framing; a great deal of work before and after that one day was necessary. Hewing the logs square would involve additional time and labor, but perhaps only a few days' worth. The expertise inherent in some notching types suggests that professionals were required. Some accounts describe "corner men" preparing the notches at each corner as other men helped hoist the logs into place; other observers argue that the similarity of the notches on a building indicates a single craftsman. One account of building a log house intended for vacation use in the 1930s describes the pride taken in a tight-fitting notch: "There was one old and grizzly, stoop-shouldered fellow who took exceptional pride in notching the logs at the corners. He always addressed me as 'Boy.' When he got the notch in the log cut to his satisfaction he

Figure 11. "The Raising." A crew of men hoists a log to the top of a wall, where an axeman is notching the corners. (B. F. Ells, ed., *The Western Miscellany* [1848–49], 342, Library of Congress)

would call out to me, 'Boy, come over here and watch her go into place!' The two notching logs would fit perfectly, and he would back up a few feet, take a proud look, and say, 'Ain't she a beaut?'"[8]

The number of tools required also suggested the level of expertise. One study of log houses in southern Indiana suggested that seventy-six tools were required—far more than a farmer would have owned. A craftsman with specialized tools and knowledge would have been involved. An account from northeastern Texas described this process: "such men will be readily procured. . . . a plain log hut, eighteen feet square, with a rough wooden floor" could be built by two men in two days, while a dogtrot—two rooms separated by a covered passage, open at both ends—of hewn logs would take three men three days.[9]

Other accounts relate far fewer tools for much simpler buildings. Revolutionary War soldiers building quarters at Morristown, New Jersey, in the winter of 1779–80 were allotted thirty-three different tools to build their 14 by 16–foot log cabins, but three of these were files and grindstones, and eight concerned alignment (compass, chalk, chalk line, etc.). Shovels, spades, and picks related to site preparation; mason trowels and hammers served for any stone construction. Cutting tools included narrow axes, broad axes, cross-cut saws, handsaws, augers, adzes, froes, and drawing knives. Chisels, gouges, mauls, and wedges rounded out the list, along with fifty pounds of nails. Army officials did not assume that there were any professional builders among the soldiers; rather, they assumed that soldiers knew how to house themselves. More simply, an account written in the 1830s stated, "the axe, auger, froe, drawing knife, broad-axe, and crosscut saw are the only tools required in constructing these rude edifices." A basic round-log cabin could be built with even fewer tools: a felling axe to fell the tree and shape the notches and a hand saw or crosscut saw to cut logs to length. If hewn logs were desired, a broad axe would be required.[10]

Most essential to a log cabin were, of course, the log walls. The type of wood depended on what was available; chestnut, white oak, cedar, poplar, pine, and fir were preferred due to their length and straightness. Builders could leave logs in the round—even with the bark on for a very expedient structure, usually an outbuilding—or hew them square for a more permanent dwelling. They could also hew logs in part, which was often called "shaped": either hewing the sides for a more finished look or to enable cladding to be put on, or hewing the top and bottom, for a tighter fit. When builders hewed or sawed the logs so that they were only two to six inches wide, this was often known as plank construction.[11] In the twentieth century, builders used circular saws to square logs.

A Presbyterian clergyman humorously described the architectural scene in Indiana in the 1820s:

> Our cabin was in truth a cabin of the Rough Order; for, reader, the order[s] of the cabin architecture are various like those of the Greek; for instance, *The Scotched Order.* In this, logs are hacked longitudinally and a slice taken from one side, the primitive bark being left on the other sides. The scotching, however, is usually done for pastime by the boys and young women, while the men are cutting or hauling other timbers. *The Hewed Order*—in which logs, like the stone for Solomon's Temple, are dressed on purpose. *The Stick-out-Corner Order*—the logs left to project at the corners, and the reverse of this, *the Cut-off-Corner Order.* I might name, too, the *Doubtful or Double Order.*

> In this, two cabins are built together, but, until the addition of chimneys, it is doubtful whether the structure is for men or brutes; and also the *Composite Order*—i.e. loggeries with stone or brick chimneys.[12]

The notching—the method of joining the logs at the corners—depended on a variety of factors, including the shape of the logs (fig. 12). Round logs were usually saddle-notched, a simple form of scooping out to fit the log below, while hewn logs were often dovetailed, an intricate joint that sloped in several directions for a very secure fit. (The names of these notches are not necessarily contemporary with their use, but are helpful for this discussion.) Some notches, such as a simple lap joint or square notch, hardly locked at all. Others seemed to combine notching forms, such as the V-notch, which was a pointed form of the saddle notch. The double notch, most familiar to those with experience with Lincoln Logs, was essentially a squared saddle notch. More complicated notches included the tooth or keyed notch, which had an L-shaped tenon. In the saddle, V-, and double notches, the logs extended past the notch itself. This was also possible in some of the other notches, but less likely. While type of wood and cultural tradition of the builder sometimes affected the selection of the notch, time was also a factor.[13] The time-consuming dovetailed notching virtually disappeared in the twentieth century.

Some builders used pins to hold the courses of logs in alignment. They placed these cylinders—initially wooden pegs, later metal spikes—vertically in long walls. Sometimes they pegged just the top log in the eave wall, because it would bear the pressure of the rafters. At the door and window openings, where there was no notching, the builder further secured the logs, usually by pegging or nailing them into a vertical piece at the opening, which functioned as a jamb.[14]

The amount of chinking between the logs depended on the shape of the logs as well as the intent of the builder. Most logs needed some chinking, though, because they were laid while still green, and they shrank across the grain. Round logs needed chinking because they could not fit tightly, and the taper of the log would create a space. In some shaped log construction, the logs were scribed, or grooved lengthwise, to fit tightly over the log below, so only minimal chinking was required. In some cases, it appears that builders intended hewn-log buildings with large spaces between logs and flush corners to be covered with siding. Clapboards, stucco, or, in the nineteenth century, bricks were employed.[15]

Chinking in a minimal log cabin consisted of moss, wood chips, or straw, cov-

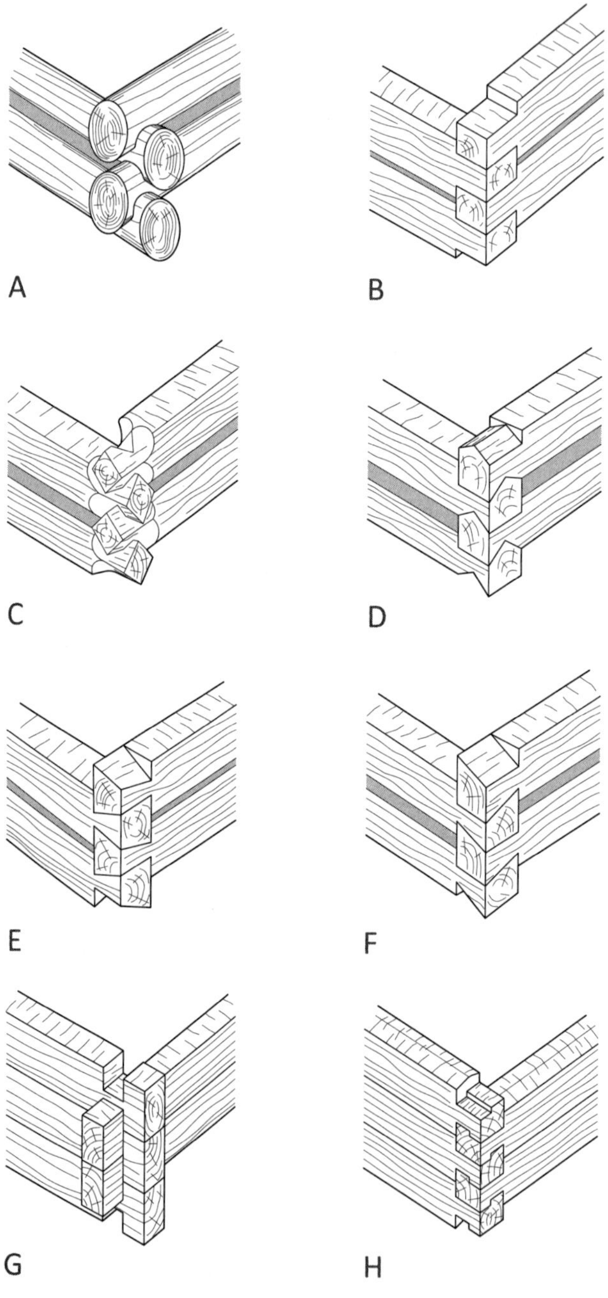

Figure 12. Types of notching: A, saddle notch; B, square notch; C, diamond notch; D, V-notch; E, dovetail; F, half dovetail; G, double notch; and H, tooth notch. (Drawing by Paul Davidson)

Figure 13. Wollerton House, Chester County, Pennsylvania. The diagonal stones shown on this 1770s log house are one of the more elaborate types of chinking. (Ned Goode, photographer, 1958, Historic American Buildings Survey, Library of Congress)

ered with mud; in a more finished house, chinking might be stones and plastered (fig. 13). Rather than daubing, which had to be patched periodically, some builders covered the chinking with thin strips of wood or even metal. In some warmer regions, chinking was removed during the summer to increase ventilation.[16]

Chinking, or lack of it, caused a great deal of discussion among observers. Frederick Law Olmsted, who toured the South in the 1850s, remarked on houses with no chinking: "The logs are usually hewn but little; and, of course, as they are laid up, there will be wide interstices between them—which are increased by subsequent shrinking. These, very commonly, are not 'chinked,' or filled up in any way; nor is the wall lined on the inside. Through the chinks, as you pass along the road, you may often see all that is going on in the house and, at night, the light of the fire shines brightly out on all sides." In 1845 a missionary visited a cabin in what is now West Virginia and noted, "many of the spaces between the logs were wide enough for the dogs and cats to pass out and in at pleasure." Architect Benjamin Henry Latrobe, while spending the night in a log building in Virginia in 1806, found a book of Arabian tales in the "chasm of the Logs" near where he was sleeping. He took the book out and read it.[17]

Like the finish of the logs, foundations also indicated the builder's intentions for the cabin. The builder could lay logs for the walls directly on the ground, in which case the floor would probably be dirt. A dirt floor might be wetted down periodically and swept to create a hard-packed surface. Direct contact with the earth was not a permanent solution, though; the base logs would rot fairly rapidly. The builder could elevate the sill logs on wood posts or on piers of brick or stone or, most elaborately, on a perimeter masonry foundation. Elevating the cabin would mean that a floor was required; it also implied that the builder intended for the building to last. Without a sawmill or laborious handsawing to create planks, a builder could split logs in half, creating puncheons. The builder would lay them flat side up to create floors.[18] If sawn lumber was available, though, flooring would be a priority for it.

Without sawn lumber, a builder constructed a roof by building up the gable ends of logs, notching purlins into them, and crowning them with a ridgepole (see fig. 10). The purlins could hold puncheons, clapboards split from logs, or bark, as in Turner's example, laid transversely. John S. Williams, who as a child lived in Belmont County, Ohio, explained the difference in an article he wrote in 1843: "Clapboards are such lumber as pioneers split with a frow, and resemble barrel staves before they are shaved, but are split longer, wider, and thinner; of such our roof and ceiling were composed. Puncheons were planks made by splitting logs to about two and a half or three inches in thickness, and hewing them on one or both sides with the broad-axe. Of such our floor, doors, tables, and stools were manufactured."[19]

A builder created a roof by placing ever-shorter logs in the gables; as one contemporary account had it, "the roof is formed by shortening each end log in succession til one log forms the comb of the roof. The clapboards are put on so as to cover all cracks, and held down by poles or small logs." A 1767 inventory of Lord Baltimore's property in western Maryland defined "cabbin roof" as "made by splitting trees into thin pieces which they lay up on one another for a cover. It saves the expense of nails and is said to be as tight as Clapboards." In Alaska, builders laid tightly spaced branches laterally and placed sod or grasses on top to provide an extra layer of insulation. Generally, a "cabin roof" applied to any log-supported roof. As with floors, though, builders valued sawn lumber for roof decking, with shingles on top. If builders used sawn members to frame the roof, they lap-jointed, mortised, and pegged the rafters together; they built the gables of vertical studs covered with clapboards or board-and-batten siding.[20]

The log cabin is by definition a one-room space, often called a "pen." A pen refers to the space enclosed by the log walls; it could be partitioned within and still be a single pen. The plan, then, was simple. There were two variables in the arrangement of this space—heat source and entrance. Until the mid-nineteenth century, wood-fueled fireplaces usually provided the heating. As noted by Turner, one option was to have no fireplace at all, but to hope the smoke rose directly to, and through, the roof, without smoking out the occupants. While Scandinavians favored a large fireplace in the corner of the dwelling and Germans in the center, English settlers preferred a fireplace in the center of the gable end, a convention that the others soon adopted. In 1748 Swedish traveler Peter Kalm found that corner fireplaces were rare in the mid-Atlantic region. Masonry fireplaces were difficult to place in end walls, because of the shrinkage of green logs. Often, the fireplace and chimney were built of logs or sticks and lined with mud. The fireplace in the end wall limited the size of the cabin to about 24 feet long by 20 feet wide, if the heating were to be effective.[21]

Entrance was usually in the center of the long side of the dwelling, where the eaves were low. This side-gable form (i.e., the gables are on the sides of the dwelling) seems nearly universal among survivors that date from before the mid-nineteenth century, but there is ample evidence that the front-gable form was employed as well.[22] In the mid-nineteenth century, the entrance shifted to the gable end, for reasons that are discussed later.

Two major plan types characterized log cabins in the southern Appalachians. One was square, or close to it, and derived from English precedent (fig. 14), while the other was a rectangular plan with Scotch-Irish origins (fig. 15). Both had gable roofs and exterior chimneys in gable ends. The rectangular cabins tended to have doors on opposing long walls, while the square cabins had just one door. Either plan might be partitioned, usually into just two rooms. In southern Indiana, where the buildings that survived to the mid-twentieth century were either shaped-log or hewn-log construction, about two-thirds were single rooms with a sleeping loft, typically 18 feet by 24 feet. The fireplace was in the center of one of the short walls;

Figure 14. Plan, Tyne Woody House, Cataloochee, North Carolina. The main part of this log house shows a square plan, although in this case the rear ell was part of the original 1893 construction. (Drawing by Paul Davidson, after Charles S. Grossman, delineator, 1937, Historic American Buildings Survey, Library of Congress)

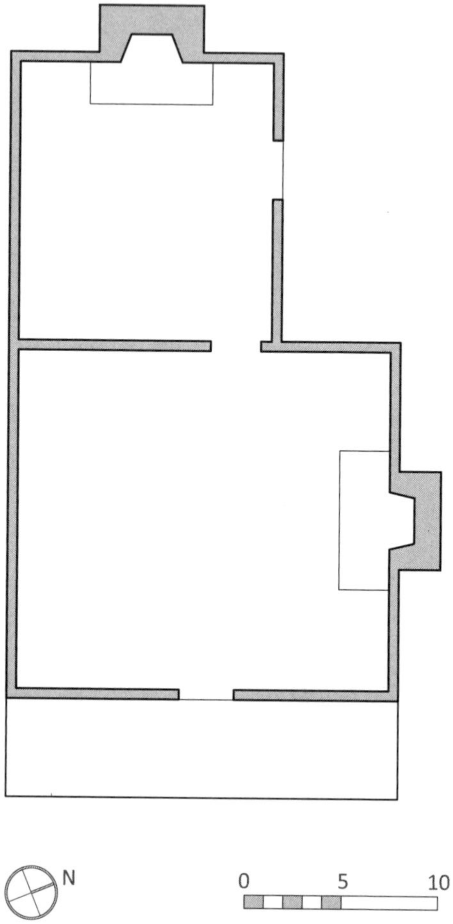

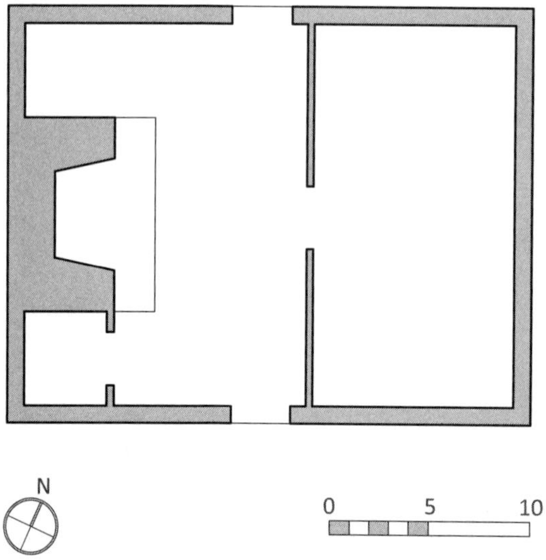

Figure 15. Plan, McIntyre Log House, Charlotte, North Carolina. Built in 1726 and demolished in 1941, this house had two rooms and a loft in a rectangular plan. (Drawing by Paul Davidson, after Warren Mobley, delineator, 1934, Historic American Buildings Survey, Library of Congress)

doors and windows were in the long walls, with the doors centered. The staircase was in a corner next to the fireplace. This plan enabled the room to be heated by a single fireplace, and it could be cross-ventilated in summer.[23]

Single-pen houses could also be subdivided, both physically and conceptually, without interior walls. In an 1820s description of an Indiana log cabin, the occupants subdivided the 17 by 19–foot space to accommodate multiple family members by stringing carpets and buffalo robes to create "rooms." Even when homeowners did not subdivide a single-pen house physically, they subdivided it conceptually. Cooking, eating, and socializing took place around the hearth, while sleeping was relegated to the opposite end of the cabin. This intricate system of maintaining privacy in what seemed like a very public space enabled multiple generations of family members to live and sleep in one room. The common name for these single-pen cabins in western North Carolina, "the big house," referred not to their size but to the multiplicity of activities within.[24]

The interior surfaces of the logs, even if originally laid round, could be hewn over time. One reminiscence of prospecting in Alaska in 1888 included the humorous account of Howard Hamilton Hart, "a member in good standing of the 'Don't Worry Club.'" A late sleeper, he would arise to find his firewood stolen, "so he took his axe and hewed enough wood from the log walls of his cabin to make a fire to cook breakfast." This happened so often that soon "he had his cabin all hewed on the inside," and then started on the outside. Before he left it for the summer, "his cabin was well hewed both inside and out, in some places being not more than two inches thick." When asked what he was planning to do for firewood next winter, Hurt replied, "'Well . . . next winter has not come yet.'"[25]

The interior might be whitewashed or painted directly onto the logs; one hewn-log house in northern Michigan, probably built in the 1880s, showed evidence of bright blue and red walls before a later generation of residents lathed and plastered them. Newspapers and magazines also covered walls of log cabins (plate 1). William Dean Howells recalled that the cabin he occupied in 1850 had newspapers pasted onto plastered walls. He also noted that this must have been typical, as it caused no comment from neighbors. In an early twentieth-century community in Appalachia, newspapers, magazines, and catalogs covered walls that had first been lined with cardboard. The printed matter was carefully arranged and could even be instructive; one resident memorized poems from the papers and could recite them years later.[26]

A single room had its limitations, though, and homeowners often subdivided and added onto log cabins. Commonly, a homeowner added a loft for sleeping space or storage. A builder could construct partitions of sawn lumber within the dwelling. Sawn or slabbed lumber, the rounded, outside pieces of a log that were discarded when the log was sawn into planks, could serve for a shed, not intended to be heated, surrounding the entrance. In warmer climates, a builder might erect a separate kitchen building, especially once the cook stove made separation of heating and cooking viable.[27]

Log construction was especially ill-suited, though, for major additions. The difficulty of notching into logs that have already been laid meant that any addition would find the connection point difficult. One solution was to build another four walls of logs and connect the two pens with a roof. If the new pen was on the other side of the gable-end fireplace and shared the chimney, the plan is known as a saddlebag (although, as with the notching, the names of these plans are not necessarily contemporary) (fig. 16). If the new pen was at the opposite end of the cabin and separated by a breezeway ranging from three to ten or more feet wide, the plan is known as a dogtrot (fig. 17). The dogtrot became a popular log building form, especially in the South, with some log houses being built originally in this way, not additively. As one observer noted in the 1820s: "Almost all these forest houses in the interior of the State of Georgia consist of two divisions, separated by a wide,

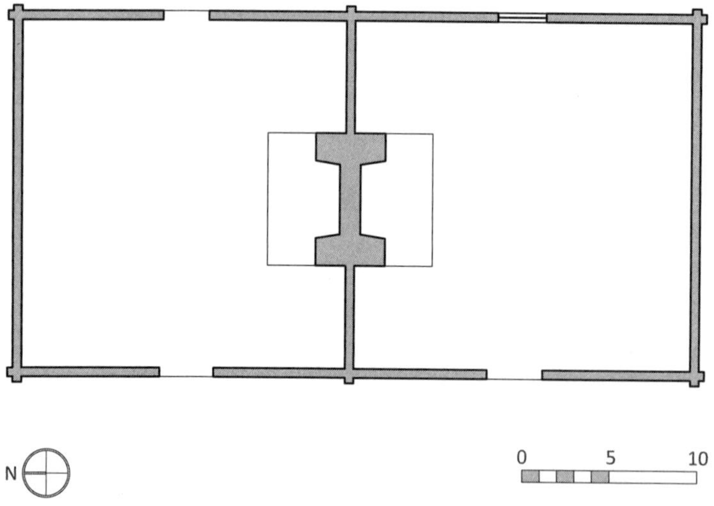

Figure 16. Plan, Alfred's Cabin, Hermitage, Tennessee. This log cabin for slaves, built in 1843, had a saddlebag plan, in which the two rooms shared a central chimney. (Drawing by Paul Davidson, after Naomi Hernandez and Mark Schara, delineators, 1999, Historic American Buildings Survey, Library of Congress)

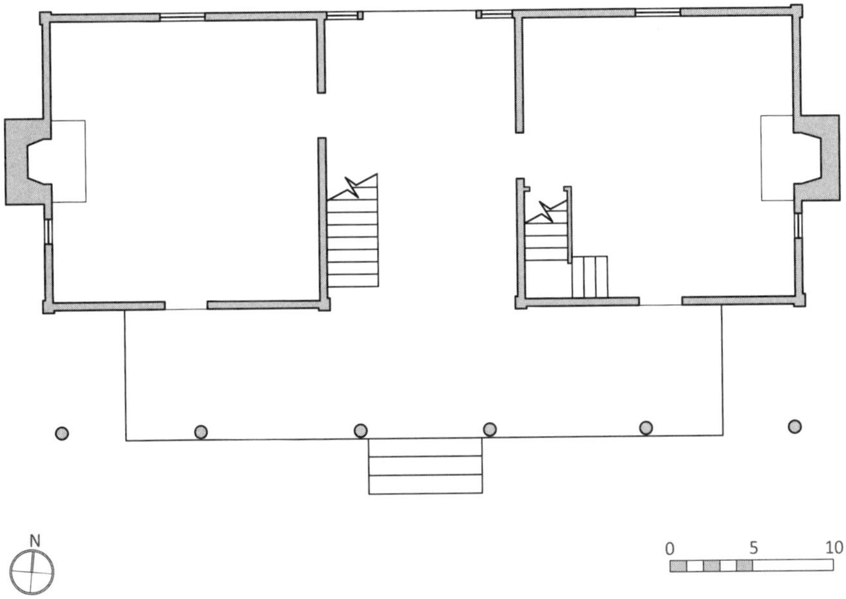

Figure 17. Plan, Tait Plantation House, Columbus, Texas. This log house, built in the 1840s, illustrates the dogtrot plan, in which two rooms are separated by a wide space that is covered but not enclosed. (Drawing by Paul Davidson, after Gerald R. Rogers, delineator, 1936, Historic American Buildings Survey, Library of Congress)

open passage, which extends from the front to the back of the building. They are generally made of logs, covered with a very steep roof, I suppose to carry off the heavy rains. The apartments, at the ends of these dwellings, are entered from the open passage which divides the house in two, the floor of which is raised generally two or three feet from the ground. This opening being usually ten or twelve feet wide, answers in that mild climate the purpose of a verandah, or sitting-room, during the day."[28]

Most importantly, log cabins changed throughout their lives. While the evolution might not be as smooth as the progress narratives would have it, homeowners could upgrade their dwellings so that a cabin became a cottage, or even a house. Homeowners replaced sill logs or added foundations to lengthen the lives of their cabins. To expand them, they added sheds, or whole other buildings, as in the Turner example. And they enclosed dogtrot openings and added a second story. To upgrade their dwellings, they covered cabins with clapboard so their logs disappeared (fig. 18). In the mid-twentieth century, as new attitudes about log cabins arose, homeowners removed the cladding and exposed the logs. Homeowners could also downgrade their log cabins, using them for animals or crop storage when they moved their families to wood-frame houses. In short, homeowners transformed their log cabins to accord with their needs and circumstances.

A LANDSCAPE OF LOG CABINS

The largest settlement of log cabins ever built in North America was surely the Continental Army's encampment at Valley Forge, Pennsylvania, eighteen miles west of British-held Philadelphia. On December 19, 1777, General George Washington's twelve thousand troops arrived and immediately set about building two thousand log cabins. They endured a cold winter, poorly supplied and fed, and suffered severe casualties due to disease and exposure. Reinforced with new recruits in the spring, the army moved out of the cabins in June 1778 and resumed fighting.

Although no buildings, images, or reliable descriptions of the encampment survive, documents indicate its character. Washington issued General Orders on December 18, 1777, governing construction of the cabins, termed "huts": "The Soldier's huts are to be the following dimensions, viz.: fourteen by sixteen each, sides, ends and roofs made of logs, and the roof made tight with split slabs, or in some other way; and sides made tight with clay, fireplace made of wood and secured with clay on the inside eighteen inches thick, this fireplace to be in the rear of the hut; the door to be in the end next the street; the doors to be made of split oak-slabs, unless boards can be procured. Side-walls to be six and a half feet high."[29]

Because of a shortage of tools in the camp, especially axes—as one surgeon's mate wrote, he and his cabinmates "have one Dull ax to build a Logg Hutt"—it is likely that the logs were left in the round. The huts went up rapidly, and the entire army was housed within a month. Thomas Paine exaggerated when he described the construction as taking only a few days, but he gave a flavor for the scene: "I was there when the army first began to build huts. They appeared to me like a family of beavers, everyone busy; some carrying logs, others mud, and the rest plastering them together. The whole was raised in a few days and it is a curious collection of buildings, in the true rustic order."[30]

The roofs caused Washington some concern because "boards, for covering, may

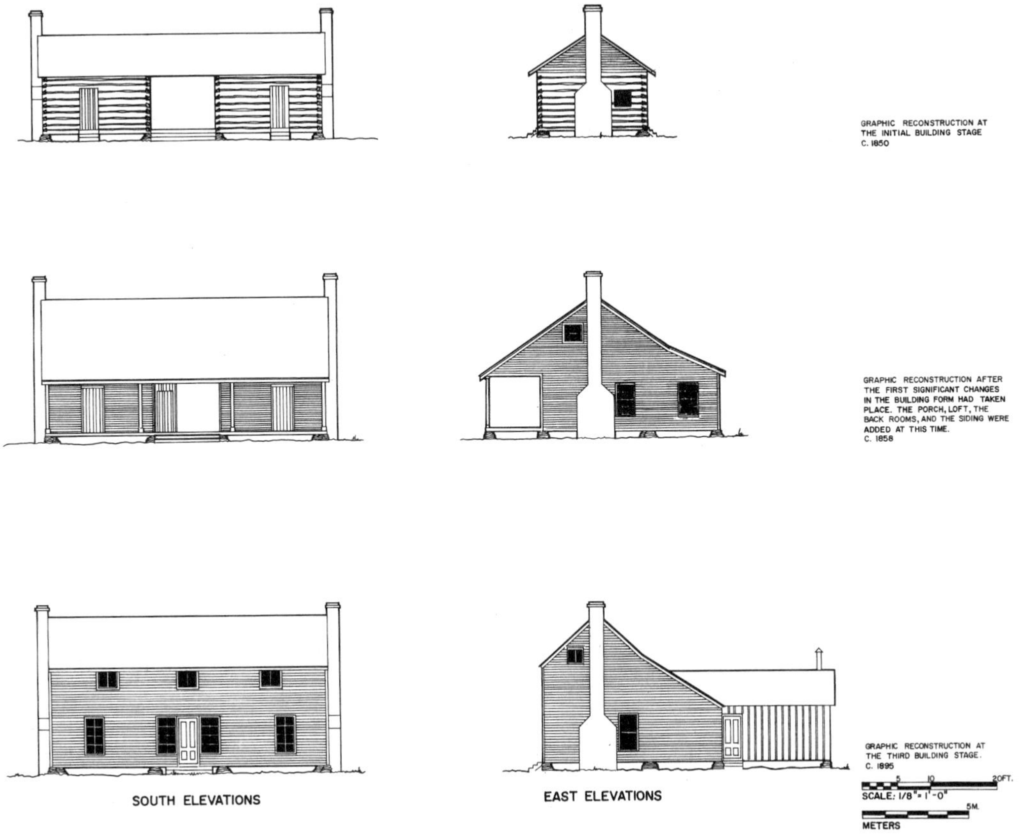

Figure 18. Elevations, Morehead-Gano Log House, Grapevine vic., Texas. These drawings illustrate the probable growth of this house, from its original dogtrot form in about 1850, to its later 1850s additions of a front porch, rear wing, and siding, to its late nineteenth-century addition of a second story, more windows, and longer rear wing. (Anthony Crosby, delineator, 1974, Historic American Buildings Survey, Library of Congress)

be found scarce and difficult to be got." He offered $100 to any officer or soldier who could come up with a "cheaper and quicker" solution, but it is not known if anyone claimed the prize. Two contemporary descriptions recount the use of turf and dirt on the roofs. The use of sawn lumber was limited to doors for officers' quarters.[31]

Washington ordered the fireplaces to be put in the end wall, but archeological evidence suggests that some appeared on side walls and in corners.[32] Doors were to be in the wall opposite the fireplace, in what seems to be a front-gable design. This arrangement was probably intended as the best way to accommodate the bunks of the twelve men who lived in each hut. It is also quasi-urban, with the narrow ends of the buildings facing the "streets," which also had to be laid out.

After the soldiers left Valley Forge in June, the army used part of the encampment for the next few years, but within a few decades the cabins had completely disappeared. The following year, 1778–79, the army was divided among several places, including Middlebrook, New Jersey, and Redding, Connecticut, where soldiers also built log cabins. In Morristown, New Jersey, in 1779–80, soldiers built 1,200 log cabins and withstood a particularly brutal winter.[33] Clearly, log cabin construction was common enough that Washington was able to prescribe it with very little instruction, other than how big the cabins should be. His soldiers must have brought experience with log cabins to their army life, and if they did not, they learned about log buildings while there. At the end of their enlistments, they returned to all parts of the new republic with this knowledge.

Log cabins were widely known in America in 1700 and ubiquitous by 1800 (fig. 19). The federal tax taken in 1798 was the first to document building materials, as well as size and condition, of dwellings. The surviving tax lists are incomplete, and census takers described building materials inconsistently, but historians have extrapolated from extant lists to conclude that the building stock was overwhelmingly wood and most often log. More than half of the dwellings were valued at less than $100, and thus not taxable. The basic log cabin, small and windowless, undoubtedly dominated that category. Of the houses valued at more than $100, log also dominated except in the long-settled portions of New England. Nine percent of the enumerated dwellings were in cities, where log construction was not common. Among older small towns and rural communities, log construction varied widely according to region, but among newer small towns and rural areas, log construction was more common, reaching 99 percent in some places.[34] Probably half of Americans lived in log dwellings in 1800.

The quintessentially American log cabin was an import. Swedes colonizing the Delaware River valley beginning in 1638 were the first to introduce the log cabin to the continent. When their colony fell to the Dutch in 1655, it numbered just 400 settlers, at least half of whom were descendants of Finns who had migrated

Figure 19. "Wm. Robertson's house near his quarry on Aquia Creek," Virginia, August 21, 1806. When architect Benjamin Henry Latrobe toured the United States, sketchbook in hand, in the early years of the nineteenth century, he depicted many log cabins. (Courtesy of the Maryland Historical Society, Item 1960.108.1.9.11)

to Sweden several generations earlier. The Dutch lost the colony to the English in 1664. Despite the changes in governance, many Swedes remained in the area, and others continued to immigrate. By 1697 an estimated 1,200 Swedish speakers populated the former New Sweden. Without any contemporary images or descriptions, or first-generation survivors of Swedish buildings, it is impossible to know what these buildings looked like. Slightly later descriptions, though, indicate that the Swedes were building in log. Two Dutchmen, Jasper Dankers and Peter Sluyter, described a journey they took in 1679–80. They spent one night at a house near Burlington, New Jersey, identifying it as "being made according to the Swedish mode," which they characterized as "block-houses, being nothing else than entire trees, split through the middle, or squared out of the rough, and placed in the form of a square, upon each other, as high as they wish to have the house; the ends of these timbers are let into each other, about a foot from the ends, half of one into half of the other. The whole structure is thus made, without a nail or a spike."[35] Log structures did not appear in Dankers and Sluyter's account until they reached the Swedish area, further confirming that it was a Swedish import.

The log cabin spread rapidly. English colonists were building occasional log structures in Virginia and Maryland by the 1650s and in New England by 1662. In the mid-seventeenth century, Edmund Plowden visited America to scout for a site for a new settlement and published *A Description of the Province of New Albion,* the site he found in New Jersey. In the second edition, published in 1650, he described six forms of houses in the New World, including "a log house of young trees 30 feet square notched in at corners."[36] He had probably learned of this form from the Swedes in the Delaware valley; his mention of it confirms its acceptability to the English.

By the late seventeenth century, the log cabin was known over all the colonies. Although occasionally singled out as a Swedish style, by that time nearly every immigrant group was constructing log buildings in all parts of the East Coast colonies. The suitability of hewn-log structures for garrison houses, blockhouses, jails, and storehouses meant that they were commonly built as such. The suitability of round-log structures for expedient housing, able to be built without nails or sawn lumber, meant that they too were commonly built, particularly in the back country. William Byrd, while surveying the line between Virginia and North Carolina in 1728, observed, "Most of the houses in this part of the country are log-houses, covered with pine or cypress shingles, three feet long and one broad. They are hung upon laths with pegs, and their doors too turn upon wooden hinges, and have wooden locks to secure them, so that the building is finished without nails or other iron work."[37]

In the mid-eighteenth century, new immigrants from countries with long experience with log construction brought the log cabin with them. Between 1730 and 1783, about a hundred thousand Germans, mostly from the Rhine Valley, immigrated to Pennsylvania; by the end of that period, one-third of Pennsylvania's population spoke German. The buildings they created were overwhelmingly log. As the duke of La Rochefoucauld-Liancourt traveled west from Lancaster, Pennsylvania, in the 1790s he observed, "We met with scarcely any but log-houses; every where we observe German farms, small houses, and large barns." The Germans were soon joined by the Scotch-Irish, Protestants from Northern Ireland, who quickly adopted the log building and disseminated it, as they spread westward and south. The Scotch-Irish may not have been familiar with logs initially, but they were certainly familiar with cabins—small, simple, impermanent dwellings. As Swedish traveler Peter Kalm reported from the former New Sweden in 1748, "Formerly the houses of the Swedes were all of wood, with clay smeared between the logs, like those now being built by the Irish." The Germans and Scotch-Irish settled in about half the territory east of the Mississippi.[38] The influx of immigrants familiar with log construction, the ready adoption of it by others, and the expanding settlement of the back country led to the dominance of log buildings by 1800.

A significant portion of the population knew of no buildings but log. Joseph Doddridge described an experience during his childhood in the 1770s around the western Virginia and Pennsylvania border: "The tavern at which my uncle put up, was a stone house, and to make the change still more complete it was plastered in the inside, both as to the walls and ceiling. On going into the dining room I was struck with astonishment at the appearance of the house. I had no idea that there was any house in the world which was not built of logs; but here I looked round the house and could see no logs, and above I could see no joists; whether such a thing had been made by the hands of man, or had grown so of itself, I could not conjecture."[39]

Doddridge's complete unfamiliarity with anything but a log building is complemented by accounts from foreign visitors who felt compelled to explain log construction to people back home who had never seen such a thing. Laurence Butler wrote to an English friend in 1791 about his visit to one of the mineral springs in the Alleghenies: "Our lodgings was in Logg Cabins . . . I suppose you do not know what kind of a house is meant by Logg cabbin. Therefore I must describe it to you," which he then proceeded to do:

> They are generally about 20 feet long and about 16 feet wide, with . . . round logs piled upon each other . . . and after they get them up about seven feet high they keep laying them up and drawing them in, which forms a roof after this they cover it with slabs or boards of about four feet without the help of a nail. Then they lay a plank floor and then they sop the body of the house between the loggs with mud to keep the air out. After this gets dry they generally whitewash the whole house inside and out, in each of these cabins there's

generally about three people lodges and thus we are accommodated at the Sweet Springs.

During an 1802 trip, Frenchman François André Michaux differentiated buildings geographically but still noted the predominance of log: "At Philadelphia the houses are of brick; but in the other towns, and even in the fields which surround them, the half, and frequently the whole of the houses are of shingles; while between seventy and eighty miles from the sea, in the Middle and Southern States, but particularly in those that lie to the westward of the Allegany Mountains, seven tenths of the inhabitants live in *log-houses.*" He then described the construction material as "trunks of trees from twenty to thirty feet long, and about four or five inches in diameter" and noted that they were "placed one above the other," as opposed to the vertical placement more common among the French. He also identified dovetailed corner notching and log gables.[40]

The decline in log construction in the East seems to have happened fairly rapidly during the first few decades of the nineteenth century. In New York State in 1855 there were about 33,000 log buildings, mostly located in the northern and western corners of the state, but nowhere did they form even a quarter of the building stock in a county. They composed only 6 percent statewide. By 1875 the total number had declined to 12,659.[41] The increased density of the population in the East, greater prosperity, and the proliferation of sawmills contributed to the growing dominance of wood frame, while urban construction was increasingly masonry. The parts of the country, particularly the West, that were sparsely populated in the mid-nineteenth century experienced a boom in log construction in the last half of that century. The ubiquity of log construction moved in time as well as place.

TIME AND PLACE

The universality of log buildings did not mean that they all looked alike. Within a broad similarity, regional differences in log construction can be discerned. Sometimes these differences are due to the environment, such as weather, trees, and topography; sometimes to historical factors, such as the availability of sawn lumber or cast-iron stoves; or sometimes to the origin and experience of the builders themselves. No immigrant group imported its building traditions wholesale;

they were influenced by environment, technology, and other cultural traditions, so that log cabins were all transformed by time and place. The understanding of the differences among log cabins of varying times and places is dependent on the work of many fieldworkers and researchers and is by no means comprehensive, but rather suggestive of the many forms the log cabin could take.

French colonists in the Mississippi Valley brought various forms of log construction. Their most common was a timber frame with squared logs set vertically, sometimes as much as eight feet apart, then infilled with masonry and covered with a mud-clay mixture or wood siding. The logs might be set into sills, in which the form was known as *poteaux sur sole* (posts on a sill), or in the ground, as *poteaux en terre* (posts in the ground). The same heavy timber frame might also be infilled with logs stacked horizontally and tenoned into the vertical posts; this form was known as *poteaux en coulisse* (grooved posts). French colonists also built with both hewn logs with dovetailed corners and saddle-notched round logs. When Henri Joutel, traveling with French explorer René-Robert Cavelier, Sieur de La Salle, described the buildings erected in 1685 at the outpost La Salle established on the Gulf of Mexico in present-day Texas, he identified the hewn logs with dovetailed corners as Canadian: "the first one was built in the manner of Canada, and the other almost in the same way . . . since the pieces of the latter were very straight and thick, they fit better; all of the pieces were fastened in a dovetail at the corners." Horizontal log construction was commonly used in Quebec by the middle of the seventeenth century and was the predominant form throughout the province by the late eighteenth century.[42]

Poteaux en coulisse were particularly important as Canadians moved west. The Selkirk settlement on the Red River in Manitoba, founded in 1813, used this construction form, probably due to French Canadian builders who worked for the North West Company and the Hudson's Bay Company. Spread rapidly among fur traders and settlers of French descent, not only across Canada but also in the northern United States, this technique became known as the Red River frame or the Hudson's Bay style, acknowledging its connection to fur traders.[43] Unlike the common American log cabin, it was of hewn logs, not round and not notched at the corners. For a hewn-log style, though, it was expedient; logs could be shorter, complex joinery was not required, and it was easier to add onto.

Germans who immigrated to Pennsylvania in the eighteenth century built

Figure 20. Bertolet-Herbein Cabin, Oley Line, Pennsylvania. German immigrants built this log cabin sometime between 1737 and 1745. (Cervin Robinson, photographer, 1958, Historic American Buildings Survey, Library of Congress)

homes of logs in a distinctive form: a central chimney, three-room plan (figs. 20 and 21). The kitchen across one end had a large masonry fireplace. Doors in front and back provided access to the kitchen. The rest of the first floor was divided into two rooms. By the nineteenth century, though, this distinctive plan faded as Germans adopted a more "English" mode of end chimneys and passageways separating rooms.[44] One aspect of German log construction that was apparently not picked up by the Scotch-Irish was horizontal hewn logs tenoned into corner posts. Similar to the form used by the French and others, this corner-post technique did not spread as widely or as readily as notched corners.

Scotch-Irish immigrants, who came in great numbers in the mid-eighteenth century, settled in the same general places as Germans and, arriving without a log-building heritage, quickly followed the Germans' examples of log construction. The Scotch-Irish built in a traditional plan, though, often one room with an exterior gable-end chimney. Both Germans and Scotch-Irish migrated west and south-

Figure 21. Plan, Bertolet-Herbein Cabin, Oley Line, Pennsylvania. The cabin has a typically German three-room plan with a massive central fireplace. (Drawing by Paul Davidson, after J. Michael Everett, delineator, 1958, Historic American Buildings Survey, Library of Congress)

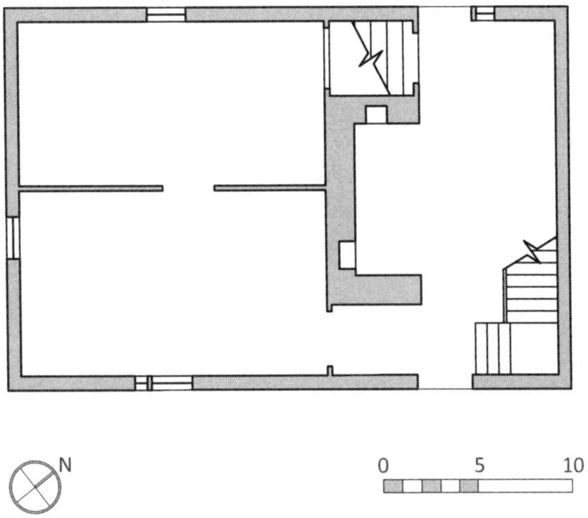

west. The preponderance of half-dovetail, V-notch, and saddle-notched cornering marked their immigration routes.[45]

In the Deep South builders adjusted the log cabin to the climate, often raising it a few feet off the ground and giving it porches. Plank walls, logs hewn to five or eight inches thick, were most often half-dovetailed or V-notched.[46] The openness of the dogtrot made it particularly popular in the South.

West of the Mississippi, the log cabin was also common, especially in forested regions. The settlement of the West, contingent on removal or appeasement of the Indians, was driven by the search for riches as well as new opportunities. The mineral rushes in particular attracted Euro-Americans, so much so that they settled in mountain areas as well as on agricultural lands along the Pacific Coast. Between 1840 and 1860 about three hundred thousand people followed the overland trails to the West Coast. These prospectors, for whom the log cabin was an essential element of survival, might not have stayed long enough in one place to build a community, but they were effective in spreading a thin population over a large area. The transient settlements that resulted from mining booms were suitable for the log cabin, being expedient and temporary in nature (fig. 22). One contemporary description echoed those from a century earlier and even made an explicit comparison. Naturalist Ernest Ingersoll described a Colorado mining community in 1873, before the introduction of stoves or sawn lumber:

Figure 22. El Dorado, California. Men mine for placer gold in the foreground, with a large log cabin visible in the background. (Ca. 1848–53 photograph, Library of Congress)

> The miners hastily throw up little log cabins, six or eight logs high, covered with a roof of poles and dirt, and having nothing better than the hard-tramped earth for a floor. In one end is the fireplace (the chimney is outside, like that of a negro's hut in the South), and at the other end are rough bunks, where the owner stuffs in some long grass or spruce boughs or straw, and spreads his bed or blankets. These rude little cabins are packed close together up and down the sides of the gulch, so as to be as near as possible to, and yet out of the way of, the mining, and they give a very pretty look to the wild scenery of these mountains.[47]

Ingersoll's mention of their picturesqueness suggests the growing romance associated with log cabins.

As Euro-Americans moved into the vast space between the Mississippi and the Pacific, those who farmed settled the prairies around the Missouri River and into the Great Plains. These settlements might have originated with basic log cabins, but people intent on establishing communities soon replaced them with more elaborate log and frame houses. Even in the sparsely forested Great Plains, where the sod house was seen as the most practical solution, settlers built log cabins when possible and then built more permanent dwellings.[48]

One critical feature differentiated the western log cabin from those in the East: the front-gable entry (figs. 23 and 24). This form was not unknown in the East, having been mandated at Valley Forge and appearing in other places. Conversely, the side-gable entry was also found in the West, particularly in Mormon communities. The front gable's predominance in the West is striking, though, with several possible explanations. In an area where timber is scarce, entrance in the gable end meant that the longer side walls could be shorter in height, requiring fewer logs.

Figure 23. Gus Larson Cabin, Wiseman, Alaska. Entrance is into the front gable, through the storm shed on the right, in this log cabin built in 1940. Flattened five-gallon fuel cans compose the metal roof. (Jet Lowe, photographer, 1984, Historic American Buildings Survey, Library of Congress)

Figure 24. Interior, Gus Larson Cabin, Wiseman, Alaska. One man could live comfortably in this 12 by 14-foot cabin. Tony Tomsich, pictured here, was the owner at the time of the photograph. (Jet Lowe, photographer, 1984, Historic American Buildings Survey, Library of Congress)

And in an area of heavy snows, the gable entrance offered protection from sliding snow; the ridgepole and purlins could even be extended and covered, providing additional shelter.[49] Comparing East and West, though, involves different time periods. By the time pioneers were building in much of the West, cast-iron, and later sheet-iron, stoves were popular alternatives to labor-intensive fireplaces and chimneys. A stove would be more likely to be placed in the center of a one-room dwelling, so an entrance in the center of the long side would bring the visitor to the stove in a few steps. Entrance on the narrow end would permit better circulation around the stove.

Generally, notching types became simplified as settlers moved west. Surveys of surviving log buildings in the West document the popularity of round logs, which lend themselves to saddle notching. But particularly of note in the West is the frequency with which square notching was employed.[50] This form, a simple lapped joint, does not naturally lock, so nails or spikes are required to hold the notch. Again, the popularity of this notch type reflects the later settlement of the West, with the greater availability of metal fasteners in the late nineteenth century. Similarly, the appearance of raftered roofs is a reflection of time. While ridgepole-andpurlin roofs were found throughout the West, the raftered roof prevailed where sawn lumber was available. Sawmills appeared early in mining communities, desirable for building both sluices for small-scale operations and stamp mills for larger facilities. Although technological changes caused western log cabins to differ from those built a century earlier in the East, log cabins still served the essential purpose of being an expedient first dwelling.

One of the more intriguing instances of internal diffusion is that of the forced migration of the "Five Civilized Tribes" to the Indian Territory, composing most of present-day Oklahoma, due to the Indian Removal Act of 1830. These Indians—Cherokee, Chickasaw, Choctaw, Creek, and Seminole—had adopted log construction in their home regions of the Southeast in the eighteenth century (fig. 25). The naturalist William Bartram traveled among the Cherokee in North Carolina in the 1770s. As he described their typical dwelling, it resembled the common Euro-American log cabin: "one oblong four square building of one story high; the materials consisting of logs or trunks of trees, stripped of their bark, notched at their ends, fixed one upon another, and afterwards plaistered well, both inside and out, with clay well tempered with dry grass, and the whole covered or roofed with the bark of the chesnut tree or long broad shingles." This rectangular house would be divided into three aligned rooms. When the government dispossessed these Cherokees and others of their homes and property and forced them to move west, they built of the same material in their new land. Although few of these houses survive, researchers for the Works Progress Administration in the 1930s interviewed nineteenth-century residents of Oklahoma, including dozens of Indians who described their houses. Log walls were most commonly shaped or hewn; round logs were rare. The type of notching was only rarely described, but the dogtrot was the most common plan.[51] The Indians, who had adopted log construction from Euro-Americans in the Southeast, introduced it to the Indian Territory in the West.

In New Mexico, Mexican settlers built log buildings in the highland regions by the early nineteenth century. The appearance of log construction was closely tied to elevation. Adobe, commonly identified with the American Southwest, was widely used on lower-elevation lands. Between about 4,500 and 7,000 feet in elevation, pinon and juniper trees were used for construction, but their rapid taper and gnarled trunks made them suitable only for the vertical log construction known as *jacal*. Above 6,000 feet, the Ponderosa pine provided a suitable material

Figure 25. Creek House, 1791. Native Americans also adopted the log cabin. (J. C. Tidball, delineator, in Henry Rowe Schoolcraft, *History of the Indian Tribes of the United States*, 1855, 5:130, Library of Congress)

for horizontal log construction (fig. 26). Outbuildings were overwhelmingly log and houses less so but, in a familiar pattern, often the first building on a site was log, then the homeowner converted it to an outbuilding and built a larger, more permanent house. Homeowners often covered log houses with adobe clay, making them difficult to identify as being basically of log construction.[52]

Mexican houses in highland New Mexico departed from Anglo-American precedents. Hispanic log construction used only two types of notching: double and saddle. Hispanic builders placed the fireplace in a corner, in contrast to the Anglo placement in the center of a wall. Hispanic builders hewed their logs square in about half of the surviving examples, and when using round logs they always peeled the bark. Anglo roof construction of low gables and ridgepoles, covered with shingles, was unknown to the Hispanics, who preferred a flatter roof as being more suitable to the climate. While Anglos placed the door in the center of the gable end, which they did in the West, Hispanics placed it in the center of a long wall. And Hispanics did not adopt frame construction, even when it became available.[53]

Due to all these differences, and to the fact that New Mexican log construction predated the arrival of Anglo-Americans, the origins of log construction in New Mexico lie elsewhere. The Spanish brought no experience with logs to the New World, but they did bring foreign missionaries, including fifty-three German Jesuits to Mexico between 1678 and 1767. Foreign missionaries were usually assigned to distant regions such as the Sierra Madre in northeastern Mexico. Another possible source was German mining technicians, engaged in mining in the Sierra Madre as early as the sixteenth century. And from this region Mexicans migrated into New Mexico, with an especially large influx in the early nineteenth century. A third possibility is German miners who appeared in Sultepec, on the western coast of Mexico, in 1536. Native laborers at the mines might have taken the construction techniques to central Mexico, and from there it moved northward.[54] However the technique of log construction arrived in Mexico, it seems to have been carried from there into New Mexico, where it differed markedly from Anglo-American

Figure 26. Truchas, New Mexico. Log structures populated New Mexican villages in higher elevations, such as Truchas, which is at an elevation of 8,000 feet. (John Candelario, photographer, 1940?, courtesy Palace of the Governors Photo Archives [NMHM/DCA], neg. no. 165816)

log construction coming from the East. Anglo-American settlers moving into New Mexico in the latter part of the nineteenth century brought their own log building tradition, which soon dominated.

Russians, who colonized Alaska beginning in 1741, brought their own form of log construction to the New World. Although initially their settlements were few, by the early nineteenth century, when their colonial population included a significant number of Finns, they began constructing villages with an eye toward permanence and effect. Illustrations show both round- and hewn-log structures with steep hipped roofs, very blocky in appearance (fig. 27). The most impressive survivor is the two-story Russian Bishop's House in Sitka, built in 1842–44 to accommodate a school on the first floor and the bishop's quarters on the second. The hip-roof building has a broad, 64-foot front with numerous glass windows, symmetrically placed; galleries, or stair towers, on either end extend the front to 90 feet. Builders covered the front log walls with horizontal planks. They hewed the logs to a width of 8½ inches and a height of 10 to 19 inches, and grooved them on the bottoms so that they fit snugly over the log below.[55]

Russia's architectural impact on North America was limited to Alaska, with one exception. In northern California, the Russians built an outpost to aid their fur-trading empire. Founded in 1812, Fort Ross had a handful of buildings constructed of hewn logs with dovetailed corners, protected by a stockade wall and blockhouses. The settlement was not a success, however, and the Russians sold the fort to John Sutter in 1841, before the great influx of Anglo-Americans from the East.

One of the later immigrant groups that brought a distinctive form of log cabins to America hearkens back to one of the first. The Finnish, Swedish, and Norwegian immigrants to the Upper Midwest who arrived between 1890 and 1920 settled mostly in agricultural regions. These Northern Europeans built with logs hewn to a width of about five to eight inches, then grooved lengthwise on the bottom to fit tightly over the log underneath. The fit was so tight that no chinking was required, although moss or other material might be used for insulation. The double notch was the most common form of joinery, extending beyond the joint; dovetailed notching was also used (fig. 28). Both of these were fashioned with a ripsaw—again, a technological change that facilitated a structural one. Among Finnish immigrants, the most common plan was a one-story, two-room house divided with a log wall.[56]

This Northern European construction form also appeared among Mormons in

Figure 27. Sitka, Alaska. An octagonal Russian Orthodox church stands out in this drawing, but other buildings of various sizes are also of round, saddle-notched logs. F. H. von Kittlitz, delineator, 1827. (University of Washington Libraries, Special Collections, NA3954)

Utah. About thirty thousand Scandinavian immigrants arrived in Utah by 1900, bringing with them log construction. The longitudinal groove and tightly fitting logs were common, joined with the double notch, dovetail, and the tooth notch. Despite Brigham Young's explicit discouragement of log buildings—as he said in 1860, "log buildings do not make a sightly city, we should like to see buildings that are ornamental and pleasing to the eye"—immigrants nonetheless built of log. As Norwegian carpenter Oluf Larsen recalled of his house in Circleville, Utah, after immigrating in 1862: "I now planned to build a house on the front of my lot as soon as possible. I hauled out logs and hewed them to a thickness of six inches, building them into the house as I hauled them. When the house was finished it was the best in Circleville as it was dovetailed and grooved together as they build log houses in Norway."[57]

While log cabins varied across the United States, the greatest variant was not spatial, but chronological. The shift that occurred between 1900 and 1930 was marked. Hewn-log buildings with dovetailed corners almost ceased to be con-

Figure 28. Log cabin near Gheen, Minnesota. The double notching characteristic of Scandinavian construction in the early twentieth century is visible here. (Russell Lee, photographer, 1937, Farm Security Administration, Library of Congress)

structed, while uniform round logs, saddle-notched at the corners, became widespread. Part of this shift was due to an increase in construction of log cabins for recreational purposes—vacation homes at the lake or in the mountains—and reflected a class shift; no longer were log cabins the housing of the poor. The popularity of log cabins as self-conscious statements about wilderness and self-reliance is explored in subsequent chapters. But log cabins also changed for those who had no other place to live. Entry into the cash economy meant that neighbors were less available or inclined to help with construction. The craftsmanship required to hew logs and make dovetailed corners disappeared, and construction became more hurried. Beginning in about 1900, hewn logs were replaced by shaped logs, with the tops and bottoms left in the round, and then by round logs. Coal-burning stoves replaced wood-burning fireplaces. Windows became more numerous. After about 1935, metal roofs replaced riven boards. Speed in construction became more important than appearances.[58] Milled lumber was more available, and many chose to build of frame.

Today, Americans continue to build log cabins, but out of choice more than necessity. The new houses are flagrantly log—left in the round, often of huge dimensions, with carefully sawn ends projecting beyond the saddle notches or butt joints. That Americans should continue to build log cabins, even as the original need for them has dissipated, illustrates the tenacious hold that log cabins continue to have on the American imagination.

2

PRESIDENTIAL TIMBER

The Log Cabin as a Symbol of Political Worthiness

An intriguing feature of American democracy is that so many presidential aspirants have claimed that they were born in or lived in log cabins. Candidates today have to prove that they are men (or women) of the people, that they understand the concerns of the middle class, and that they do not look down their noses at those less educated or less wealthy. In the nineteenth century, as presidential candidates confronted an expanding electorate, they realized that the common touch would benefit them, and the log cabin helped them accomplish this. Birth in, or subsequent occupation of, a log cabin signified modest origins, ability to overcome adversity, strength of character, and lack of pretension.

Two presidents' associations with log cabins stand out. William Henry Harrison was the first to tap into the marketing possibilities of his log cabin, contrasting it with the supposedly opulent lifestyle of his opponent, Martin Van Buren. The Log Cabin Campaign of 1840 employed the log cabin as an image, a meeting place, and a rhetorical shorthand to appeal to voters suffering financially from his opponent's policies. Abraham Lincoln's association with the log cabin has persisted most strongly to the present day. His reputation as a rail-splitter dominated his campaign, providing associations of masculinity, hard work, and rural life, but his birth in a log cabin has proved to be a timeless reference to humble origins and impressive achievement. The log cabin helps promote a core ideal of democracy—that anyone can grow up to be president.

While Harrison and Lincoln are most readily identified with log cabins, these modest structures also served as the birthplaces of at least five other presidents, and at least four others subsequently lived in them.[1] The first president who can be conclusively identified to have been born in a log cabin is Millard Fillmore, born in upstate New York in 1800, and the last was James A. Garfield, born in Ohio in 1831. The president who first mobilized the common man as a political force, Andrew Jackson, may have been born in a log cabin, but his exact birthplace is uncertain. (He subsequently lived in a log cabin, discussed in the next chapter.) The log cabin became such a credential that some politicians bemoaned the fact that they had not been born in one. Daniel Webster, while campaigning on Harrison's behalf in 1840, said, "Gentlemen, it did not happen to me to be born in a log cabin; but my elder brothers and sisters were born in a log cabin, raised amid the snow-drifts of New Hampshire at a period so early that when the smoke first rose from its rude chimney and curled over the frozen hills there was no similar evidence of a white man's habitation between it and settlements on the rivers of Canada. Its remains still exist. I make to it an annual visit. I carry my children to it, to teach them the hardships endured by the generations which have gone before them." Webster was among the first politicians to claim humble birth, a phenomenon that continues to the present day.[2]

Although Americans may not believe that one's original station, or class, in life, is one's destiny, they do seem willing to believe that the accident of birth shapes character; how people start out in life holds significance. The way that presidential candidates used the log cabin in their campaigns, and how the public subsequently associated cabins with political figures, shows that the log cabin resonated as a statement about political worthiness.[3] The stories of William Henry Harrison and Abraham Lincoln, both particularly identified with log cabins, illustrate the power of the humble log cabin.

WILLIAM HENRY HARRISON

The presidential campaign of 1840 is known for many things. Whig William Henry Harrison challenged the incumbent, Democrat Martin Van Buren, in a hard-fought, highly visible campaign that engaged the masses and relied on spectacle and emotion as much as policies and reason (fig. 29). The election generated the third-largest voter turnout in American history, at a little more than 80 percent of

Figure 29. "General Harrison's Log Cabin March and Quick Step." William Henry Harrison's 1840 presidential campaign used the log cabin as a vivid image, including as a representation of sheet music. (Library of Congress)

eligible voters.[4] Harrison was the first presidential candidate to give speeches on his own behalf. For the first time, women played an active role in the campaign, despite their inability to vote. Campaign songs, newspapers, and artifacts appeared for the first time. And the Log Cabin Campaign introduced an architectural element to presidential politics.

In 1840 Martin Van Buren hoped to be elected to a second term. Although Henry Clay had been the Whig candidate in 1832 and attempted to assume the role again in 1840, William Henry Harrison, a sixty-seven-year-old retired general and farmer from Ohio, won the party's nomination. Harrison was an amiable man, but not one of the party's theorists; as John Quincy Adams said of him, he had a "lively and active, but shallow mind." Born into wealth in Virginia, Harrison served in the army from 1791 to 1798, attaining the rank of captain. He then became secretary of the Northwest Territory, the territory's first delegate to Congress, and then governor of Indiana Territory from 1800 to 1812. In 1811 he led an army against Shawnee leader Tecumseh, emerging victorious at the Battle of Tippecanoe. During the War of 1812, Harrison commanded the Army of the Northwest and engaged combined British and Indian forces at the Battle of the Thames, resulting in the death of Tecumseh. After resigning his commission in 1814, Harrison returned to his farm in North Bend, Ohio. He owned his farm but was deep in debt; his detractors charged that he sought public office in order to secure a steady income.[5]

To some extent, the campaign served as a delayed referendum on the policies of Andrew Jackson. Elected in 1828, Jackson had dismantled the central bank, causing a severe depression that plagued the presidency of his protégé, Martin Van Buren. Beginning in 1837, unemployment rose, wages declined, foreclosures increased, and bank closures multiplied. Accordingly, economic policies loomed large in the 1840 campaign. The Whigs favored a national bank, protective tariffs, and government-funded transportation systems, while the Democrats held to Jacksonian principles of decentralization and states' rights.[6]

The Whig Party did not adopt a platform at its convention, preferring generalities and platitudes to articulated positions. Harrison followed suit; his enigmatic presentation earned him the nickname "General Mum." Democrats teased that their opponents "have carried their barbarous caution so far as actually to shut up the old gentleman in an iron cage, finding they could not entirely prevent his making indiscreet disclosures."[7] Provoked by these insults, he began making speeches—the first time a candidate had done so on his own behalf. Harrison made twenty-three speeches, most of them two or three hours in length. Part of the strategy was to show that the elderly Harrison was healthy and vigorous, and most newspaper reports commented on his physical capability.

The enthusiasm and emotional investment in this campaign made it memorable in American history. Harrison and his running mate, John Tyler of Virginia, earned the jovial sobriquet "Tippecanoe and Tyler Too!" Thousands of supporters turned out for rallies and conventions. Newspapers, aided by cheaper printing technology, fanned the flames of partisanship. Supporters wrote campaign songs for the occasion and published them in songbooks. Women took a strong interest in the election, attending rallies and speeches, hosting political meetings, and acquiring campaign-related paraphernalia. In the general frenzy and public participation that accompanied this campaign, historians have identified a connection to the evangelicalism that was also engaging Americans in this period. Harrison made a deliberate effort to appeal to this moral, temperance-adhering, and Sabbath-observing segment of the electorate.[8]

Other voters were more interested in drinking and carousing. A Whig reporter wrote that a Democratic newspaper "sneered at the idea of electing Gen. Harrison" by saying, "Give him a barrel of HARD CIDER, and settle a pension of two thousand a year on him, and my word for it, he will sit the remainder of his days in his LOG CABIN, by the side of a sea-coal fire, and study moral philosophy." With that, the opposition handed the Whigs the perfect symbol. They embraced the image that was intended to be a slur; "*Log Cabins* and *Hard Cider* were spontaneously adopted as the emblem and the watchword."[9] Hard cider played a role in the campaign as less of an image and more of an excuse for conviviality, but the log cabin proved to be a symbol onto which partisans could place various meanings, all of them positive.

Harrison did not claim, nor did his opponents allege, that he was born in a log cabin. He was not; he was born into Virginia aristocracy at Berkeley, the Harrison family plantation. When he became governor of Indiana Territory, he built a two-story brick house in Vincennes. But when he returned from the War of 1812 he moved to his property in North Bend, Ohio, where a log cabin already existed. He added onto it extensively, turning what had been a three-room log cabin into a clapboarded, seventeen-room Palladian mansion with a two-story main block. Although the interior was lathed and plastered, his granddaughter remembered him fondly showing off the logs that remained exposed in one closet.[10]

At first, Harrison claimed only that part of his house was a log cabin; as he said in Columbus, Ohio, in June, 1840: "the unlucky wight who put me in a log cabin was a little nearer the truth than he probably supposed himself to be. It is true that part of my dwelling-house is a log cabin, but as to the hard cider—" at which point the crowd's laughter drowned out the speaker. But a few months later his house had become more modest: "I would have preferred to remain with my family in *the peace and quiet of our log cabin at the Bend,* rather than become engaged in political or other disputes." The house itself became a partisan issue, with Democrats emphasizing its luxury and Whigs its humbleness. One of his supporters described a visit: "The General's house is far from being a log cabin, and it is also far from being a palace. It is a large, plain, two story, frame house—probably 80 or 100 feet front. . . . He is not wealthy, it is very true; but he owns the farm where he resides, and a very beautiful farm it is." An opposition paper published a sarcastic description: "*Definition.—'Log Cabin'*—A large, elegant, white framed house, 'from 80 to 100 feet in front, with numerous out-houses,' in the midst of one of the most beautiful farms in the state of Ohio."[11]

Harrison's campaign used the log cabin to identify the candidate with people who lived in modest circumstances, particularly in the West, which at that time was understood to mean the former Northwest Territory. Calling Harrison poor, a Whig paper noted that "the poor man is as much entitled to the honors of the office and the confidence of the People as the haughty aristocrat with his hoarded millions" and that "Every 'Log Cabin' beyond the mountains and throughout the mighty West will rush to the contest in support of a gallant soldier and veteran statesman." Representative Patrick G. Goode of Ohio defended Harrison in Congress:

> The real secret is, that all the early settlers in the Western country once resided in '*log cabins*.' They were often destitute of chimney or hearth. Sometimes they had windows without glass, and doors that could not be shut, except, perhaps, by a blanket. They often sat upon stools constructed by the help of an axe and an auger, and ate their frugal meals from a plank split from the body of a neighboring tree. They suffered many inconveniences and privations unknown to later emigrants. At that early day, Gen. Harrison was in the Western country. He, too, encountered the same privations. He associated with our people, and in all respects was one of them. Our population at that day were hardy, intelligent, virtuous, and brave. . . . The early settlers of the Western country regard Gen. Harrison as their associate and companion in the hardships and privations of former days.[12]

Goode's defense also reveals that nostalgia for the log cabin dates from as early as 1840. He went on:

> To the ears of those men, the term '*log cabin*' has a sort of charm. At its very mention, a thousand pleasing recollections rush upon the mind; old associates are brought to remembrance, and an enthusiasm is awakened, which can only be appreciated by those who have experienced it. . . . While reading accounts of some of those enthusiastic meetings lately held in our 'Buckeye State,' I have found my mind unconsciously carried back to the days of youth and of '*log cabins*'; to the days of hunting, and 'of youthful sports and buoyant pleasures;' to my associates of that day; and, in short, to all the ten thousand recollections to which the memory clings with a fondness and enjoyment that may be felt but not described.

Goode perceived the success this nostalgia had in generating enthusiasm for the campaign: "It is to these feelings that we are in some degree indebted for those enthusiastic demonstrations of the Western States, and the display of '*log cabins*' with all the paraphernalia of skins, rifles, traps, &c., which were only known to the early settlers of that country." He then appealed to a reverse snobbism: "I am aware that these representations call forth sympathies and feelings hostile to those who treat the pioneers of the West with sneering and contempt."[13]

According to the Harrison campaign, the log cabin also had an illustrious history. As Harrison's supporters claimed, "Log Cabins were the early homes of all of the first settlers of every state in the Union," as well as Puritans fresh off the *Mayflower,* settlers at St. Mary's and the James River, and "the pioneers of the mighty West." This history instilled in Harrison, through his log cabin, "the lessons of wisdom, moderation, and courage." Despite their association with "olden time," log cabins were still very much a viable building form in 1840. Contemporary newspapers include references to log cabins, such as an advertisement published in a Columbus, Ohio, newspaper that offered to lease land in return for the tenant building an 18 by 20 or 22–foot log cabin and other improvements.[14]

The Whigs portrayed Van Buren as an aristocratic, effeminate dandy. In a speech in the House that stretched over three days and, when printed, ran to thirty-two pages, Rep. Charles Ogle of Pennsylvania analyzed every expenditure for the White House and grounds over the previous twelve years and found that the Democratic administration had spent excessive amounts to furnish a house (or "palace," in Ogle's terminology) that had been fully furnished after it had burned in 1814. Ogle's purpose was not to eliminate the $3,665 appropriation proposed for the president's house and grounds, but rather to contrast the aristocratic Van Buren with the down-to-earth Harrison. Ogle charged that Van Buren maintained an imperial presidency, not only in accoutrements but in behavior. Whig supporters insisted that Harrison was unfailingly hospitable, inviting passersby into his home and offering them hard cider. "This is more than they can get out of Mr. Van Buren, who has nothing in his palace but Champagne, old hoc, Madeira, sherry, and 'prime Havanas,' and these choice things are only dealt out to his 'silk stocking and ruffle shirt friends.'"[15] The regal palace versus the log cabin vividly expressed that polarity.

The log cabin proved to be a versatile symbol, effective in various media: as a label, a drawing, or a three-dimensional object (plate 2, fig. 30). It also marked a

Figure 30. "Harrison and Reform." Silk handkerchiefs produced in 1840 carried the image of the log cabin as a recognizable symbol of the presidential candidate. (Library of Congress)

shift from allegorical symbols of the early republic to those that were more familiar to a less educated electorate. As Philip Hone, a New York Whig, noted in his diary:

> Now on all their banners and transparencies [translucent paper cylinders or boxes lit from within] the temple of Liberty is transformed into a hovel of unhewn logs; the military garb of the general, into the frock and shirtsleeves of a laboring farmer. The American eagle has taken his flight, which is supplied by a cider-barrel, and the long-established emblem of the ship has given place to the plough. Hurrah for Tippecanoe! Is heard more frequently than Hurrah for the Constitution! . . . Thus is it that our opponents have, by their silly, disparaging epithets applied to the Whig candidate, furnished us with *weapons, the use of which is understood by every man in our ranks; who would not understand the ship, and eagle and Temple of Liberty* and, whatever may

be the result of this election, the hurrah is heard and felt in every part of the United States.[16]

Harrison's campaign consistently termed him the "Log Cabin Candidate." The image of a log cabin appeared everywhere: on banners and transparencies, on handkerchiefs and mugs, on buttons, fans and fire screens. A "rustic" chair made in Paris, "ornamented with a representation of General Harrison's reception of an old soldier at his log cabin," was offered for sale. One newspaper described a meeting in Harrisburg, Pennsylvania: "At an early hour a transparency representing Gen. Harrison's 'log cabin,' on one side—the battle of the Thames on another—the flag of the Republic on a third—and the motto of 'DEMOCRACY, REFORM, AND ONE PRESIDENTIAL TERM' on the fourth, was introduced; and it was then that the full hearts of the country people broke loose with all the wild joyous acclamations that their lungs could give vent to." One enterprising distiller, E. C. Booz of Philadelphia, developed a glass bottle in the shape of a log cabin and filled it with "Old Cabin Whiskey." Allegedly, his name became a slang term for alcohol that is still used today.[17]

As images, log cabins were portrayed not identically, but surprisingly consistently. Unlike the images of Harrison, invariably showing his face in three-quarter profile, which were so similar as to indicate that they derived from the same depiction, the many representations of log cabins were not identical. They were not based on a real thing, as Harrison's log cabin was too well hidden to serve as a model. Instead, artists were free to interpret "log cabin" as they wished, and they chose a fairly consistent image: a small building of round logs saddle-notched at the corners with a gable roof. Entry was either in the end or side; windows, if shown, were small. Chimneys were interior, either in the center or at one end. The overall consistency of the log cabin images demonstrates what a powerful image it was, easily understood by all, and that a consensus had arisen around what a log cabin should look like.[18]

Miniature log cabins also appeared on wagons, used as floats in parades. A partisan paper described the Whig convention in Ohio in breathless terms, noting the hordes of people pouring into the capital: "The procession is *two miles* in length. Hark! that shout—louder than the thunders of the Olympiad. The *Log Cabin,* drawn by four horses, is coming. The implements of the early pioneer are hanging around it. There is the gun, the axe, the deer skin—the spoils of the huntsman.

Again, and again, the shout goes up to the vaulted roof of high heaven." In Lynchburg, Virginia, Marian Cobbs reported in a letter that an acquaintance "traveled 40 mils in a log cabben drawn by splendid horses, the cabben was decorated with coon skins redpaper brooms a live coon live chickens in a coop which was attached to the back of the cabben, when ever the cheering for *Harrison the hero of Tippacanoe* commenced the chickens would all commence a loud crowing. What well trained whigs, you may think, though a whig I think it very ridiculous. The orators were all very complimentary in their speeches to the ladies. As we love flattery that was quite suffienct to make us whigs." Daniel D. Brockway, during a journey from Michigan to New York State in the summer of 1840, reported to his father seeing "a log cabin in almost every town, and even the steamboats on the lakes have built a cabin on their upper decks." He also saw "a cabin built upon wheels, with a caldron of pork and beans, and hogshead of hard cider," as well as forty passengers, all drawn by eight horses.[19]

Full-sized log cabins also served as three-dimensional billboards. Local groups supporting Harrison built log cabins on vacant lots in the centers of towns to function as campaign headquarters or "council houses," as they called them. In Washington, DC, supporters built a log cabin on Pennsylvania Avenue, just north of Central Market. The 40 by 50–foot cabin, marked by a 107-foot-high Liberty Pole with a banner hailing "Harrison and Tyler," served as a meeting room for the Tippecanoe Club of Washington. In Connecticut, "at a meeting of the Whigs of Hartford, on Tuesday evening, it was voted to build a Log Cabin, 33 by 75 feet on the vacant lot, corner of Asylum and Trumbull streets. This lot is owned by Joseph Pratt, Esq. and has been generously offered by him for the purpose" (fig. 31). The process of building the log cabin was a communal activity that brought Whig supporters together. As a Whig paper said, "Log Cabins are the order of the day. . . . Every whig city and hamlet is erecting its log cabin council house." Another said that log cabin council houses "will soon become as common in the country as Tippecanoe Clubs and patriotic songs are popular." One log cabin suffered a mock attack from former Democrats dressed as Indians, who immediately "surrendered" and declared themselves Harrison men. They were invited into the cabin and treated to hard cider.[20]

Besides advertising, the log cabins provided a site to rally around, a place where men could drink hard cider, and a large room for an occasional party. One correspondent attended a Log Cabin Ball in Tontawanta, New York. "When I arrived

Figure 31. "Log Cabin, Hartford, Conn." Harrison supporters built log cabins to serve as "council houses," such as this one in Hartford, dedicated on July 4, 1840. (Library of Congress)

I found an actual log cabin 115 feet long, with walls 12 feet high, and of a suitable width.... The cabin was literally crowded with a numerous and respectable company—six hundred at least were in attendance, embracing the farmers, mechanics and their wives, sons and daughters of the surrounding country.... [E]very eye beamed with joy and every bosom was warm in devotion to the illustrious patriot in honor of whom they had assembled." Partaking of corn bread and hard cider, the writer reflected that "the political *supper* hereafter is likely to consist of corn bread and cider, to be served up in a log cabin . . . and the opponents of

Harrison, I trust, will rue the day when they taunted and sneered at the brave Harrison as an occupant of a log cabin and a drinker of hard cider."[21]

The fervor created by the Log Cabin Campaign succeeded in getting unprecedented numbers of people to the polls. With 80.2 percent of the electorate casting votes—the highest turnout the country had yet seen, an increase of more than half over the previous election—Harrison won nineteen of the twenty-six states. But his presidency is remembered more for its brevity than anything else; Harrison died a month after his inauguration. Some attribute his two-hour inaugural speech, outdoors on a bitterly cold day, to the pneumonia he contracted two weeks later.[22]

The introduction of the log cabin as a campaign symbol sheds light on its meaning at the time: as a symbol of humble status, as a reference point for nostalgia for simpler days, as a reminder of a war hero's actions on the frontier, as a sign of the candidate's lack of pretension, and as a place for conviviality and domesticity. The use of the log cabin as a political symbol also differentiates it as an American icon. While other countries might have had many more log cabins, in none was it heralded as a symbol for a political leader, effectively branding him as a man of the people.

ABRAHAM LINCOLN

Americans celebrated the 1909 centennial of Abraham Lincoln's birth across the nation. In Chicago, two million people turned out for events around the city. One, in the Dexter Pavilion at the stockyards, drew twenty thousand attendees. Described as "an enthusiastic and good natured, if somewhat unruly, crowd," they could not hear the speakers, but they reacted to the pictures. Organizers projected stereopticon views, beginning with a cathedral in Norwich, England, where Lincoln's family had originated. But it was not until a picture of Lincoln's log cabin birthplace appeared that the crowd erupted. The newspaper said that it "was recognized by the audience immediately and was the signal for applause and shouting."[23]

Abraham Lincoln is probably the president most associated with the log cabin, due not only to his birth in one but also to the subsequent association of him with that fact over two centuries. Linking him to the virtues of humble background, hard work, and overcoming adversity, the log cabin image burnishes the reputation of a president also credited with saving the nation and emancipating the slaves. Because he is one of the most popular American presidents, visitors flock to historic sites associated with him, and most of those sites involve log cabins.

Lincoln's early life involved several log cabins. He was born on February 12, 1809, in a log cabin near Hodgenville, Kentucky. When he was two years old, his family moved ten miles northeast, to a log cabin near Knob Creek, where they lived until 1816. Then, apparently frustrated with his inability to secure legal title to land in Kentucky, Abraham's father, Thomas, moved with his family to a log cabin near Little Pigeon Creek, Indiana, where Abraham's mother, Nancy Hanks Lincoln, died in 1818. Thomas soon remarried and eventually moved the family to yet another log cabin, this time in Decatur, Illinois, in 1830. Abraham, then twenty-one years old, left his parents and moved to New Salem, Illinois, in 1831, where he worked as a storekeeper, studied law, and boarded in several log cabins. From there, his fortunes improved. In 1837 he moved to Springfield, the state capital, and lived in several wood-frame buildings until 1844, when he and his wife, Mary Todd, moved into a handsome two-story frame house.[24] From there he was elected to serve in the White House.

All of these buildings, and more, have attracted the notice of a public that is fascinated by Lincoln. The way that organizers have presented the buildings in response to that interest indicates the changing ways that Lincoln is held in the public memory. Initially, exhibitors treated cabins with Lincoln associations as curiosities, then as shrines, and later as educational tools.

By the time of the 1860 presidential campaign, Lincoln's log cabin roots were well known. His image as a rail-splitter, though, is what first caught the public imagination. Promotional pieces in newspapers noted that he and his cousin, John Hanks, split three thousand rails in 1830, when Lincoln was twenty-one. Republican clubs became known as Rail Splitters, just as Log Cabin Clubs for Harrison had been popular two decades earlier. The rail-splitter identity arose from the actions of Hanks and a friend, Richard Oglesby, at the Illinois Republican Convention in Decatur in 1860. The two men went out to the Decatur farmstead where Lincoln had split rails for fencing in 1830, picked up two of the rails and carried them triumphantly into the convention hall. Lincoln said that "though he could not swear he had split these exact rails, he had split many like them."[25] "Rail-splitter," connoting a life of hard work and manual labor, became an attractive association for Lincoln.

Once in office, Lincoln tried to shed reminders of his humble origins, hoping to be perceived as more dignified and statesmanlike. After his assassination, the "regal" image persisted, resulting in several grand statues and paintings. One of the few early references to his log cabin birth came from Oglesby and Hanks, his supporters in Illinois, who returned to the Decatur farmstead. They assured the public that the log cabin on the site was the one that Lincoln had built; then they dismantled it, reassembled it, and exhibited it at the Great Sanitary Fair in Chicago in May 1865. Promoters also exhibited the cabin at the Barnum Museum in New York and on the Boston Common before it disappeared.[26]

By and large, though, Lincoln's log cabin associations were not flaunted in the nineteenth century. Even Lincoln, as a revered former president, was not as popular as he would become in the early twentieth century. The public focused instead on George Washington as a great man to be admired and emulated, and the first president retained his hold on the public through the 1890s. The publication of Ida Tarbell's popular biography *The Early Life of Abraham Lincoln,* first serialized in *McClure's* in 1895, began to shift public opinion. Tarbell set out to destroy the conception "that Abraham Lincoln came from a home similar to those of the 'poor white trash' of the South." She pointed out that there was no shame in living in a log cabin "when there was scarcely anything else in the state."[27] This reading of the log cabin—that it marked not only how far he had come, but also conferred some normalcy, even nobility, on it—may have fed the early twentieth-century obsession with Lincoln's various log cabins. It also occurred at a time when many Americans were only a generation or two removed from log cabins themselves.

Also in the mid-1890s, Alfred Dennett, a New York restaurateur, bought Lincoln's birthplace, Sinking Spring Farm, near Hodgenville, Kentucky, with an eye toward memorializing Lincoln there. Although the cabin in which Lincoln had been born had probably not survived until his presidency, Dennett, through his agent, James W. Bigham, found a neighbor who asserted that the cabin had been moved to a nearby site. Dennett acquired that building and erected it on the original farm site in November 1895 (fig. 32). At that time, the building was one story, measured 16 by 18 feet, and had an incomplete wood chimney, mud chinking, a roof of log purlins and wood planks, one central door, and one unglazed window.[28]

Over the next eight years, Dennett and Bigham dismantled and reerected the cabin several times. They displayed it at the Tennessee Centennial Expo in Nashville in 1897, along with Jefferson Davis's birthplace cabin. They stored both cabins

Figure 32. Cabin, Hodgenville, Kentucky. The cabin heralded as Lincoln's birthplace, as it appeared in 1895. (Glass Lantern Collection, National Park Service)

in the basement of a New York City Bowery mission that Dennett operated in 1899, displayed them at the Pan-American Exposition in Buffalo in 1901, and in 1903 stored them on Long Island. By this point, the logs of Lincoln's cabin had intermingled with those of Davis's.[29]

The next owner of the logs was the Lincoln Farm Association, formed in February 1906. Robert J. Collier, publisher of *Collier's Magazine,* had bought the Sinking Spring Farm at auction and donated it to the new organization, which also acquired the logs of Lincoln's birth cabin. The new organization advertised widely, encouraged contributions as small as 25 cents, and received tens of thousands of donations, managing to tap into a populist wave of enthusiasm for Lincoln. The Lincoln Farm Association aimed to make the site into a national park with "wider and broader inspiration" than Civil War battlefields. "It is not to be a park to commemorate our lamentable differences but a park to commemorate our unity, harmony, prosperity, and high citizenship," a promotional newspaper article stated.

Consistent with other commemorations of Lincoln at this time, his role as the savior of the Union outweighed his reputation as the president who freed the slaves.[30]

The association defined its purpose: "to restore to its original place the log cabin in which Abraham Lincoln was born." This was an impossible task; if the cabin had even survived into the 1890s—which is unlikely—its logs were now hopelessly indistinguishable from those of Jefferson Davis's birth cabin. For its advertising, the group used a photograph of the cabin taken in 1895, when it had been temporarily erected on Sinking Spring Farm before beginning its travels across the country.[31]

With as much fanfare as it could muster, the association shipped the logs from New York to Kentucky in a heralded tour (fig. 33). A large crowd turned out to see them off from New York. Employees of John Wanamaker's department store decorated the flatcar with bunting, American flags, and portraits of Lincoln. Kentucky militiamen, who guarded the logs at every moment, were successful

Figure 33. Dismantled cabin. Workmen in College Point, New York, load the logs from the dismantled cabin in 1906, sending it on its final trip back to Kentucky. (Library of Congress)

in "thwart[ing] the efforts of souvenir seekers to take away parts of the cabin." The logs made stops in Philadelphia and Baltimore and a host of smaller cities so that legions of admirers could see and even touch them. When the association reassembled Lincoln's cabin temporarily in Louisville, though, it had grown markedly and displayed two doors and two windows. The logs now seemed to have emanated from three different sources: one marked by carved roman numerals, one marked with black paint, and one unmarked.[32]

Lincoln's birthplace cabin was not the only Lincoln cabin in circulation. Besides the one from Decatur, Illinois, that traveled in the 1860s, there was also one with an even more tangential relationship to Lincoln, which had been built in Goose Nest Prairie, south of Charleston, Illinois. Although Thomas Lincoln probably built it in 1837, after his son had left for Springfield, legend had it that he erected it in 1831 with Abraham's help. At any rate, Thomas Lincoln died in Goose Nest Prairie in 1851 and his wife, Abraham's stepmother, in 1869. Lincoln was known to have visited his stepmother there, so the cabin's more certain claim to fame was that Lincoln slept there. The Chicago-based Log Cabin Association bought the cabin in 1891 and dismantled it. After exhibition at the 1893 Chicago World's Fair, it disappeared.[33]

These three mobile cabins point to the ease with which log cabins can be dismantled and reconstructed—particularly if the concern is not with chinking, roofing, or anything but the logs. The visible construction of log cabins makes them easy and apparently enticing to deconstruct. Their travels also reflect how enthusiasts accommodated the desire to bring historical objects to the public, which was easier to do with log cabins than with most other types of buildings. Before people were able to travel easily to historic sites, it was much more efficient to bring the objects to them. The log cabins were displayed as curiosities at fairs, alongside technological achievements, exhibits of manufactured goods, and entertainments for the masses.

The second phase of cabin exhibition—creating shrines—began with the birthplace cabin, once it had completed its journeys and was "back home" in 1906. The Lincoln Farm Association decided to enshrine the reerected cabin in a classical temple, hiring architect John Russell Pope to design the new building (fig. 34). The granite building with a Doric portico stood at the top of fifty-six wide steps, one for every year of Lincoln's life. The formal, Beaux-Arts presentation was the polar opposite of the rough log cabin housed inside, representing to some visitors the

Figure 34. Abraham Lincoln Birthplace National Historical Park, Hodgenville, Kentucky. John Russell Pope designed the temple that enclosed the much-traveled log cabin. The shrine was dedicated in 1911. (Photograph by the author, 2012)

dichotomy of Lincoln's memory: both master statesman and man of the people, both stately and humble.[34]

Before its enshrinement, the appearance of the birthplace cabin had continued to change. President Theodore Roosevelt attended a cornerstone-laying ceremony to observe the centennial of Lincoln's birth, February 12, 1909, in Hodgenville. When the association erected the cabin for this event, it more closely resembled the 1895 incarnation, with one door and one window (although the association added glass panes and muntins). The association dismantled the cabin soon afterward and built the classical temple but when it came time to reerect the cabin inside, the cabin proved to be too large. Undeterred, the Lincoln Farm Association sawed the ends off of the logs, reducing the cabin several feet in both dimensions to 12 by 17 feet (plate 3).[35]

The authenticity of the cabin was obviously less of a concern than that there be some representative object, an icon. That the temple did not adequately accommodate the building it was sheltering reflects this lack of concern.[36] In the first decades of the twentieth century, historic sites associated with Lincoln were more concerned with commemoration and worship than with historical explanation. The construction of a temple was a deliberate choice. Lincoln was close enough in public memory that he was still mourned. The presence of the log cabin was not to show how he lived so much as to provide a tangible link to the great man.

A second shrine connected to Lincoln began as a commemoration of his mother, Nancy Hanks. A marble headstone and cast-iron fence erected in 1879 marked her grave near the site of the log cabin on Little Pigeon Creek in southern Indiana. Nancy Hanks Lincoln's reputation began to be redeemed by Ida Tarbell in her Lincoln biography of 1895. Although Nancy Hanks was illiterate and some biographers had claimed her birth was illegitimate, Tarbell described her, on very little evidence, as a "fair and delicate" woman "who had ideas of refinement" and a "sensitive nature."[37] The sanctification of Lincoln's mother continued apace; the public endowed her with all the maternal virtues of Victorian America. Her posthumous deification was also due in part to the unpopularity of Mary Todd Lincoln, Abraham's widow. In Nancy Hanks Lincoln, Americans constructed the sweet, supportive woman that they thought Abraham deserved.

In 1909 the State of Indiana acquired her gravesite and built a road marked with an iron fence and gateposts surmounted by statues of gold-painted concrete lions. Responding to the continuing concern over the upkeep of the site, in 1926 the state established the Nancy Hanks Lincoln Memorial Park. The Indiana Lincoln Union, a citizens group, undertook a fund-raising campaign to assist the project. Prominent landscape architect Frederick Law Olmsted Jr. designed a memorial plaza and a long allée leading up the hill to Nancy Lincoln's gravesite. Olmsted's goal was to create a quiet and contemplative site; he even referred to the cabin site and graveyard as the "Sanctuary."[38]

The nearby site of the Lincolns' cabin had also been identified, so in 1933 the state allocated funding for a bronze memorial there. Without any evidence of the original appearance of the cabin, Thomas Hibben's design was deliberately suggestive, not literal. He cast the cabin's sill logs and hearth stones in bronze and laid them on site, surrounded by a limestone wall (fig. 35). He wrote: "The log sill is chosen as appropriate to mark the outline of the cabin; the hearth and fireplace are chosen because they have been, since time immemorial, the altar of the home, the center around which all life moved. The entire conception is cast in bronze in order that it may be durable and that it may not in any way seem a reconstruction of the original cabin. The entire purpose of the design is intended to be a symbol

Figure 35. Lincoln Boyhood National Memorial, Lincoln City, Indiana. The site of the cabin in which the Lincolns lived while Abraham was a boy was marked with a bronze outline, designed by sculptor Thomas Hibben, in the 1930s. (Photograph by the author, 2012)

of the hearth and home of the Lincoln family." In a similar vein—that references to buildings were compelling associations—the Indiana Lincoln Union laid out a Trail of Twelve Stones, a half-mile-long path lined with pieces from a dozen buildings of significance in Lincoln's life, each explained by a bronze plaque. A newspaper article described the stones as "shrines," with benches "where pilgrims might rest." At the foot of the hill, at one end of Olmsted's allée, the state constructed a large memorial building that incorporated a re-creation of an early nineteenth-century church, with pews and altar, and a "cloister," with five bas-relief sculptures depicting phases of Lincoln's life.[39]

Yet a third shrine to Lincoln—or on Lincoln's behalf—commemorated his parents' marriage. Soon after Lincoln's assassination, his former law partner, William H. Herndon, began gathering material for a biography. Although it was not published until 1889, Herndon lectured and shared his material with other biographers. Intrigued by Lincoln's own vagueness about his family and unable to find a marriage certificate for his parents, Herndon questioned the legitimacy of Lincoln's birth. Although the Lincolns' marriage certificate was discovered before Herndon's biography was published, he disclaimed his assertions only reluctantly.[40]

For several decades after his death, Lincoln's legitimacy remained in question—a blot on the reputation of a great man.

Thomas Lincoln and Nancy Hanks were married on June 12, 1806, near Beechland, Kentucky. In 1911, the owner of the logs of the cabin in which they were wed donated them to the Harrodsburg Historical Society, which erected the cabin in Harrodsburg. Because of the questions about the legitimacy of Lincoln's birth, the cabin in which his parents were married—the physical representation of his legitimacy—was treated as a Lincoln shrine. As the editor of the *Harrodsburg Herald* wrote in 1922, evidence of his parents' marriage "removed the stigma on the birth of the Great Emancipator that hung like a shadow over him until the day of his death." Perhaps jealously regarding the success of Hodgenville in displaying Lincoln's birthplace, Harrodsburg residents also built a shelter for it. Unlike the birthplace temple, the Harrodsburg shrine resembled a brick Federal church (fig. 36). The building even contained an altar and pulpit so that couples could be married in the shadow of the Lincoln Marriage Cabin, as it was called. The temple opened on June 12, 1931, with the day being declared a state holiday. Students from Transylvania College in Lexington reenacted the wedding ceremony in elaborate proceedings.[41]

The religious symbolism is clear: two temples, a "sanctuary," a church interior, a trail with Stations of the Cross, and a passion for architectural relics, or pieces of the True Cross. In the period from the centennial of Lincoln's birth in 1909, through the dedication of the Lincoln Memorial in Washington, DC, in 1922, the publication of Carl Sandburg's popular biography in 1926, and until after World War II, Americans worshiped Lincoln. People visited sites to pay their respects to a great man, someone whom their parents or grandparents might have revered.[42]

Despite the presentation of these historic sites as shrines, commercialism pervaded them. Within sight of Lincoln's Birthplace, in 1928 James Richard Howell built the Nancy Lincoln Inn, a large log structure, accompanied by four smaller log cabins that served for lodging. The inn reflected the growth of automobile tourism, which contributed to the success of the birthplace, which received twenty thousand visitors in 1927. One of the more popular souvenirs from the inn was a miniature log cabin, based on Lincoln's birthplace as enshrined nearby, whittled by local men and women who sat on the inn's front porch.[43]

Similarly, at the site of Lincoln's second home, the Knob Creek, Kentucky, cabin, which had been destroyed in the early 1870s, Howell's sister, Hattie Howell

Figure 36. Lincoln Marriage Temple, Harrodsburg, Kentucky. This shrine, built in 1931, shelters the log cabin associated with Lincoln's parents' marriage. (Photograph by the author, 2012)

Howard, built a log tavern with gas pumps in front in 1933 (fig. 37). The facilities served tourists who visited a reconstructed cabin, built from logs from a nearby cabin that was alleged to have stood at the same time as the Lincolns' cabin. For the reconstruction Howard and her husband relied on the memory of Robert Thompson, who had been born nearby in 1841 and was familiar with the Lincolns' house. Accordingly, the cabin was heavily altered in the reconstruction to accord with his memory.[44]

Initially, commercialism also affected the reconstruction of Lincoln's last log cabin home. New Salem, Illinois, founded in 1829 and the location where Lincoln had worked as a shopkeeper and studied law, was a short-lived community. By 1840 all of its residents had moved away, either taking their buildings with them or allowing them to deteriorate. Interest in the site revived due to Tarbell's biography,

Figure 37. Lincoln Tavern, Knob Creek, Kentucky. Hattie Howell Howard built this log tavern and gift shop in 1933 to serve visitors to the nearby reconstructed cabin, intended to reference another chapter in Lincoln's boyhood. (Photograph by the author, 2012)

which included a map of the village drawn according to former residents' recollections. In 1917 the Old Salem Lincoln League formed to further interest in the site; it raised funds to reconstruct five log buildings there (fig. 38). The league's enthusiasm, which included the performance of pageants, convinced the State of Illinois to assume ownership in 1919. The state initially prioritized tourism at the site, placing a parking lot in the middle of the reconstructed buildings and emphasizing the recreational aspects of the park.[45]

These accommodations for tourists might seem jarring today—preservationists would call them "intrusions"—but at the time creating a historic landscape was not the consideration. In the first half of the twentieth century, visitors were more concerned with getting close to something associated with Lincoln than with understanding the way he lived. The setting was less important than the object itself, even if the object had only passing associations with Lincoln.

The third phase of exhibit strategy for Lincoln's log cabins flourished after World War II, when the Lincoln sites underwent a fundamental shift from hagiography to biography, as the interpretations of the cabins began to show how Lincoln

Figure 38. Lincoln's New Salem State Historic Site, Petersburg, Illinois. Beginning in 1917, nonprofit, state, and federal agencies reconstructed a village of log cabins at the site where Lincoln first lived as an adult. (Photograph by the author, 2012)

lived. For people several generations removed from anyone who knew Lincoln, his ability to command reverence was ebbing. Visitors to historic sites wanted to learn and to experience, not just worship or pay respects. And the philosophy of exhibiting historic sites was changing as well.

This shift dramatically redefined the interpretation at the Lincoln Boyhood National Memorial—the name it assumed when the National Park Service took over the Nancy Hanks Lincoln Memorial Park near Little Pigeon Creek, Indiana, in 1962. As the first park service superintendent explained, "the decision has been made to concentrate on life not on death."[46] So besides the name change, the site that included Nancy Hanks Lincoln's gravesite, the bronze foundation of a cabin, and the Trail of Twelve Stones received two significant additions. The memorial building, now seen as inadequate to the task of explaining the site, received a large addition for exhibit space. One of the exhibits was a furnished log cabin interior.

Secondly, in 1968, on top of the hill, near the cabin site, the National Park Service re-created a pioneer farm, complete with log cabin, outbuildings, farm animals, and costumed interpreters (fig. 39). The living history interpretation contributed to "a vivid picture of life as Lincoln lived it," according to a recent park publication.[47] This accorded with a National Park Service push in the 1960s toward providing living history at all suitable sites. By 1974, 114 national parks offered living history programs. The farm, which seems a discordant addition to a site originally focused around a grave, reflects the evolution from commemorating angelic motherhood to explaining a well-known heroic man. It also demonstrates the evolution from passive, worshipful visitors to active groups of schoolchildren. Nor is it the only living history farm associated with Lincoln. In Goose Nest Prairie, Illinois, at the site of the log cabin that went to the Chicago World's Fair and did not survive, the state operates a living history farm.

At Lincoln's birthplace near Hodgenville, Kentucky, the shift in interpretation was less abrupt. True to the Lincoln Farm Association's original plan, the federal government acquired the birthplace in 1916, and the War Department operated it as a public historic site; the National Park Service assumed control in 1933. Today the National Park Service interprets the cabin as "symbolic," declining to claim that it has any historical link to Lincoln. The visitor reaches the temple by climbing the fifty-six steps, a dramatic approach, and then enters through the rear door, a much less dramatic entrance. The temple, cool and dark, is plain and rather severe, with the log cabin as its focal point. The National Park Service removed four explanatory marble plaques, original to the building, in 1959 and has not reinstalled them, due to debates over the wording.[48] All explanation is left to the visitors center, constructed five hundred feet away in 1959, where exhibits include a furnished cabin interior. Again, the impulse is to show how Lincoln lived, to fill in the blanks between an empty, much-traveled log cabin and its temple setting, with artifacts that illustrate a way of life. The aim now is to explain a life, not just evoke it.

The National Park Service is not the only agency to use log cabins to explain Lincoln's life. At New Salem the State of Illinois also shifted its interpretation, beginning with the reconstruction of more log buildings to give a better sense of the village. In 1932 the state funded construction of a dozen buildings, all hewn log. Two years later a concentrated effort by Civilian Conservation Corps workers began, resulting in seven more buildings, rail fences, and landscaping. The interpretation changed as well. Administrators banished cars from the village and, in

Figure 39. Lincoln Boyhood National Memorial, Lincoln City, Indiana. Added in 1968, the Living History Farm was intended to help visitors understand how Lincoln lived as a boy. (Photograph by the author, 2012)

an effort to make the village more authentic and life-like, introduced guides in period clothing operating spinning wheels and looms and working in blacksmith and cooper shops.[49] Today the state historic site exhibits two dozen buildings, all but one of them log, in this reconstructed village. The site depicts a turning point in Lincoln's life, when he sampled several careers and ended up a lawyer, in the setting of a pioneer village.

The role of the log cabin in understanding Lincoln is a curious one. Over more than a century the interpretation has shifted from curiosity to hagiography to biography. The log cabin association imparted character traits that benefited Lincoln's memory in the public mind: humble beginnings, hardscrabble childhood, common touch. The log cabin also served as a tangible representation of the man, particularly of his early years, before photographs and documents could serve the purpose.

The sudden rise of Lincoln's popularity in the early twentieth century can be attributed to greater shifts in the nation. With the development of an urban industrial economy, the democratic ideals associated with Lincoln were invoked to guide the Americanization of an influx of immigrants. The popularity of his log cabins related to the commemoration of Lincoln as a self-made man and as a man of the people. The log cabin trope—that most presidents had plebeian origins—exaggerated the poverty of Lincoln's childhood. His father owned land, and while he might not have had much cash, he was not poor. Nor was Lincoln, who had a profitable career in law before becoming president.[50] But hardscrabble childhood to revered president was an appealing story line to early twentieth-century Americans, and it still resonates. It demonstrates the egalitarianism implicit in U.S. democracy, that anyone can be president.

The simplicity of the pioneer life also appealed to a modernizing nation looking nostalgically at earlier times. In general, increased urbanization provoked a sentimental longing for rural life. Given these broad sentiments, it is perhaps not surprising that the details of log cabins were not important, nor that authenticity was hardly the goal. The growing use of the automobile encouraged destination tourism, where the tourists traveled to hallowed sites. There, new buildings with architectural associations to the old—such as being built of logs—served visitors as inns, taverns, and motel rooms. Even with the historic buildings, the association, vague as it might be, with the great man was what was important.

In the latter half of the twentieth century, the self-made man narrative of Lincoln's life became less important to Americans. Lincoln became revered for being the Great Emancipator, and secondarily as the Savior of the Union, with comparatively little interest in his character or life story. As the nation grows farther away from thinking of Lincoln as a person—generations away from anyone who knew him—Americans apparently need more literal representations of where he came from.[51] No longer are ideas of log cabins, with greater or lesser connection to Lincoln, enough to help the public appreciate the man; they need to be shown how he might have lived in them, so living-history farms and furnished interiors provide the context for Lincoln's iconic log cabin.

The association of the log cabin with Lincoln continues to resonate, both in name and in artifacts that had only a remote connection to Lincoln. Lincoln Logs, a toy construction system still in production today, is one of these (plate 4). Small wooden cylinders, 11⁄16 of an inch in diameter and ranging in length from 1½ to 7½ inches, interlock to form the walls of small "log" buildings. The notching system, flattened rather than curved, and with a pronounced overhang, is similar to the double notching introduced by Scandinavians in the northern Midwest in the early twentieth century. The inventor of Lincoln Logs, though, claimed a different source. John Lloyd Wright, son of the famous architect Frank Lloyd Wright, was working with his father in Tokyo on the design of the Imperial Hotel in 1917. For the earthquake-resistant foundation, the elder Wright designed a system of interlocking pieces that allegedly gave his son the idea for this toy.[52]

John Lloyd Wright had a troubled relationship with his father and never trained formally as an architect. After his father fired him at the conclusion of the Imperial Hotel commission, young Wright returned to Chicago. As a child, Frank Lloyd Wright had played with Froebel blocks, geometric forms designed by an educator to spur creativity, and he similarly exposed his children to building blocks. Beginning in 1918, John Lloyd Wright developed wooden toys produced under the Red Square label. Lincoln Logs went on the market that year, and Wright received the patent in 1920. Unlike standard building blocks, Lincoln Logs interlocked, so children's creations stood up to rough play. For its name Wright claimed inspiration from Abraham Lincoln, the most famous log cabin occupant, but it was more likely that the resemblance of "Lincoln" to "linkin'" provided a smart marketing ploy. While an early box showed only a picture of an assembled log cabin, by 1923 the box carried pictures of a completed log cabin and Abraham Lincoln, along with the wording "Lincoln Logs: Interesting Play Things Typifying 'The Spirit of America.'"[53]

Sales were modest, so Wright sold Lincoln Logs to Playskool for $800 in 1943. In the next couple of decades, the popularity of television westerns resulted in increased sales for Lincoln Logs. In 1953 Playskool promoted Lincoln Logs on *Pioneer Playhouse,* making it one of the first toys to be marketed on television. By the mid-1990s Americans were buying as many as a million sets per year.[54]

Lincoln Logs have a tangential relationship to Lincoln—a marketing strategy, at best—but they show the strength of the identification of Lincoln with log cabins.[55] The meaning of that association has changed over time, providing him with character traits desirable in a president, or furnishing a tangible representation of a long-departed hero. The association also ennobled the log cabin, not only making a modest building capable of sheltering ability and ambition, but also equating it with one of the greatest presidents.

3

HOVELS AND COTTAGES

The Log Cabin as a Symbol of Poverty

While the log cabin could symbolize suitability for higher office, in different contexts it could also symbolize abject poverty. Two populations with considerably less standing in society than presidential contenders were particularly associated with the log cabin: enslaved African Americans and white people in Appalachia. The association of enslaved people with log cabins was entirely a negative one—the poorest kind of housing for a degraded people. Observers looked at the Scotch-Irish in Appalachia, though, and understood their log cabins as a reflection of an independent spirit and other positive qualities. In both cases, the same minimal log cabin—one room, without floor or windows—was the building type most often evoked, but it assumed different meanings depending on whom it sheltered. It also assumed different names: "hovel" referred to the most rudimentary shelter, while "cottage" described a building form associated with middle-class domesticity. Depending on their perceptions, outsiders referred to both enslaved and Appalachian peoples' log cabins as hovels and cottages.

Outsiders—abolitionists, pro-slavery advocates, and reformers—influenced Americans' understanding of the log cabins of both enslaved and Appalachian people. The nature of their housing became part of the argument for intervention, or not, into the situations of both groups. The log cabin, already functioning as image and reality, or icon and simple shelter, fit easily into the discourse, with the reality of hovel playing off the image of the cottage. That the same building that fostered political careers could also symbolize abject poverty, as well as possible redemption of that desperate state, suggests the malleability of the log cabin image.

SLAVE QUARTERS

The title of one of the most influential books in American history, *Uncle Tom's Cabin,* published in 1852, indelibly printed slave housing on the American consciousness (fig. 40). Harriet Beecher Stowe's searing portrait of slavery was not about the cabin of the title in a literal sense. She initially gives it short shrift, describing it only as "a small log building close adjoining to 'the house.'" Recognition of the inadequacy of the one-room dwelling falls to George Shelby, Tom's master's son, who promises to build him a better house: "I'll build your house all over, and you shall have a room for a parlor with a carpet on it, when I'm a man." But Shelby's father sells Tom, who was never to see his wife and children again. The meaning of the cabin is revealed at the end of the book, after a cruel owner has beaten Tom to death and George, now an adult, frees his remaining slaves and says to them: "Think of your freedom every time you see UNCLE TOM'S CABIN; and let it be a memorial to put you all in mind to follow in his steps, and be as honest and faithful and Christian as he was."[1] The cabin stands as a memorial for the man.

Stowe's choice of a dwelling as Tom's representation accords with her characterization of him, which is essentially domestic: pious, obedient, humble, and family oriented. Rather than put forth an abolitionist argument of liberty, justice, or economics, Stowe chooses to expose slavery as a violation of the family. Stowe's antislavery opus evokes domesticity to remind readers of the toll on the family that slavery exerts when families are destroyed in the interest of the marketplace. In the middle third of the nineteenth century, the appreciation of feminine virtues such as the sanctity of the home clashed with the abrogation of those values by slavery, as Stowe reminds her readers. Tom's cabin thus represents an idealized home, although Stowe recognizes that it could be improved, as when George promises Tom a better house. She also refers to it as a flower-bedecked "cottage," a romanticized version of home.[2]

Observers' views of slave quarters depended on their political persuasion. John Pendleton Kennedy's *Swallow Barn, or A Sojourn in the Old Dominion* defends slavery, adopting the strategy that African Americans are ignorant and defenseless

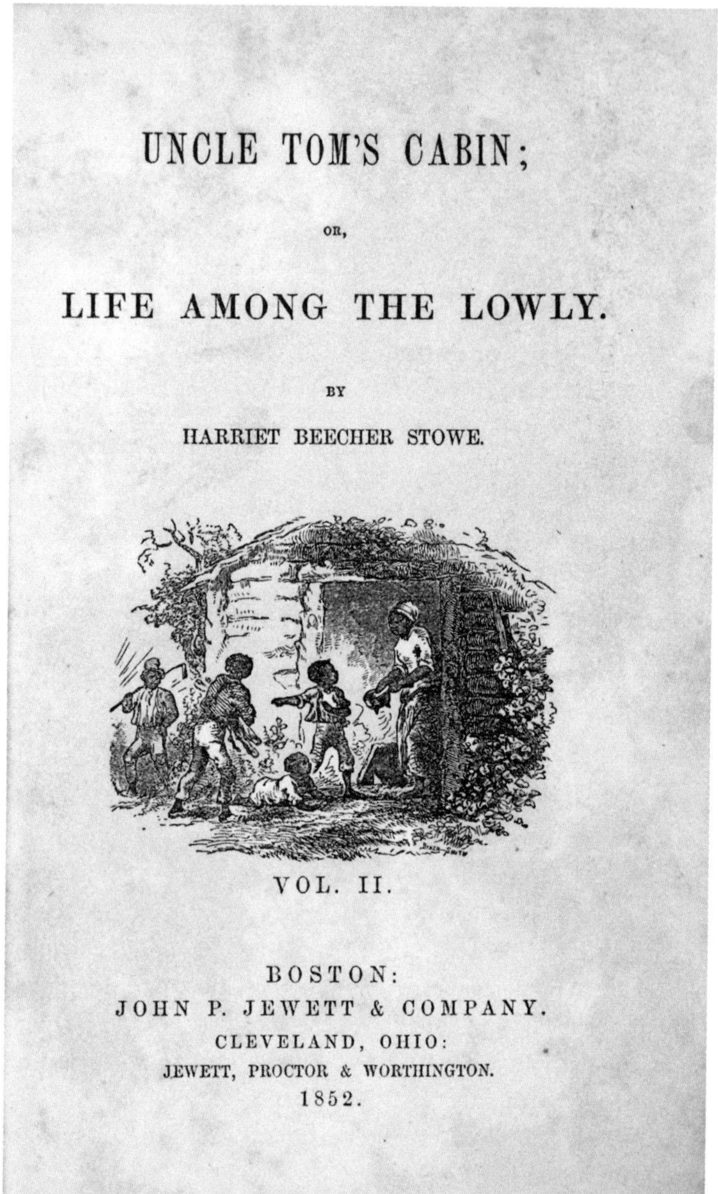
UNCLE TOM'S CABIN;

OR,

LIFE AMONG THE LOWLY.

BY

HARRIET BEECHER STOWE.

VOL. II.

BOSTON:
JOHN P. JEWETT & COMPANY.
CLEVELAND, OHIO:
JEWETT, PROCTOR & WORTHINGTON.
1852.

Figure 40. Title page of Harriet Beecher Stowe's *Uncle Tom's Cabin*, 1852. Stowe used the domestic image of the cabin to highlight slavery's impact on families.

and need a wise patriarch to guide them. Published in a small edition in 1832, then reissued in 1851, just as *Uncle Tom's Cabin* was garnering attention, *Swallow Barn* reveals the author's familiarity with slave quarters, as opposed to Stowe's vague understanding. In the novel, a northerner visiting his cousin in Virginia explores the slave quarters, which he depicts almost as romantic ruins: "These hovels, with their appurtenances, formed an exceedingly picturesque landscape. They were scattered, without order, over the slope of a gentle hill; and many of them were embowered under old and majestic trees. The rudeness of their construction rather enhanced the attractiveness of the scene. Some few were built after the fashion of the better sort of cottages; but age had stamped its heavy traces upon their exterior: the green moss had gathered upon the roofs, and the course weatherboarding had broken, here and there, into chinks." He goes on to describe the most minimal dwellings:

> But the more lowly of these structures, and the most numerous, were nothing more than plain log-cabins, compacted pretty much on the model by which boys build partridge-traps; being composed of the trunks of trees, still clothed with their bark, and knit together at the corners with so little regard to neatness that the timbers, being of unequal lengths, jutted beyond each other, sometimes to the length of a foot. Perhaps, none of these latter sort were more than twelve feet square, and not above seven in height. A door swung upon wooden hinges, and a small window of two narrow panes of glass were, in general, the only openings in the front. The intervals between the logs were filled with clay; and the roof, which was constructed of smaller timbers, laid lengthwise along it and projecting two or three feet beyond the side or gable walls, heightened, in a very marked degree, the rustic effect.

The chimneys particularly amuse the narrator:

> The chimneys communicated even a droll expression to these habitations. They were, oddly enough, built of billets of wood, having a broad foundation of stone, and growing narrower as they rose, each receding gradually from the house to which it was attached, until it reached the height of the roof. These combustible materials were saved from the access of the fire by a thick coating of mud; and the whole structure, from its tapering form, might be said

to bear some resemblance to the spout of a tea kettle; indeed, this domestic implement would furnish no unapt type of the complete cabin.

The narrator, a visiting northerner, finally inserts some criticism: "From this description, which may serve to illustrate a whole species of habitations very common in Virginia, it will be seen, that on the score of accommodation, the inmates of these dwellings were furnished according to a very primitive notion of comfort."[3] For a defense of slavery, which this novel was, this description does not depict the dwellings in a very favorable light; only Kennedy's underlying belief that an inferior race needed nothing better can explain his cavalier disregard for comfort, in favor of picturesque dilapidation.

Despite their overblown prose and romantic views, Stowe's and Kennedy's depictions of slave quarters captured some essential qualities (fig. 41). First, they were log. Overwhelmingly, log cabins housed slaves on farms and plantations, both near the house and in distant field quarters.[4] By the end of the eighteenth century and until emancipation, the typical slave dwelling was the most basic kind of housing: log walls, one room, dirt floor, no windows, mud-and-stick chimney—the quintessential log cabin. A visitor to southeast Virginia in 1793 described one plantation: "Adjoining the house of the master was a hut for his blacks, formed of small pine trees, laid one upon the other and fastened at the end with a notch; but they were not plaistered either on the inside or outside." Frederick Law Olmsted, who journeyed through the slave states in the 1850s to study the economic viability of slavery, also wrote of quarters in Virginia: "The houses of the slaves are usually log-cabins, of various degrees of comfort and commodiousness. At one end there is a great open fire-place, which is exterior to the wall of the house, being made of clay in an inclosure, about eight feet square and high, of logs. . . Several cabins are placed near together, and they are called 'the quarters.' On a plantation of moderate size there will be but one 'quarters.'"[5]

Whether on a large plantation or small, the size and soundness of slave quarters varied with the wealth and inclination of the owner. The large plantation that accords with a romantic view of the antebellum South was not representative; in 1850, only about 10 percent of slave owners owned more than twenty slaves, and only about 1 percent owned more than a hundred. George Washington, as an example of a large plantation owner, owned about three hundred slaves in the 1790s and housed some of them in a large masonry building near the main house, others

Figure 41. Slave quarters, Will Crenshaw Plantation, Greenville, Alabama. The round logs and lack of windows were typical features of slave quarters. (W. N. Manning, photographer, 1935, Historic American Buildings Survey, Library of Congress)

in dual-purpose outbuildings, and still others in log cabins on the outlying farms. A visitor in 1788 noted that "three hundred Negroes live in a number of log houses in different parts" of the plantation. While Washington, in a 1796 advertisement, claimed his slaves were "warmly lodged," a visiting Frenchman said they were "housed in wretched wooden cabins," and a Polish traveler wrote, "We entered one of the huts of the Blacks, for one can not call them by the name of houses. They are more miserable than the most miserable of the cottages for our peasants."[6]

More modest plantations had log cabins for owners, slaves, and other employees, as illustrated by a series of maps. In the District of Columbia in 1796, surveyors drew plats of seventeen plantations that fell within the borders of the new City of Washington, showing the layouts of buildings and often noting dimensions and building materials. Overwhelmingly, the outbuildings were of log, such as those at Widow Young's lot: "They are all log-houses, mansion house and kitchen excepted." The four log buildings, ranging in size from 8 by 10 to 12 by 18 feet, formed a rough semicircle. The adjacent tract of Abraham Young, her brother-in-law, boasted a 22 by 22–foot mansion house, a frame barn, and five buildings, each of the latter labeled "log-house," ranging from 10 by 12 to 17 by 30 feet. When Abraham Young died in 1797, his estate included seventeen slaves. George Walker, besides his mansion house and kitchen, had two log houses, both double; he was not among the slaveholders listed in 1798 (fig. 42). Robert Peter had a log mansion house, 22 by 36 feet, six other log buildings, and one frame building. The largest slave owner in the District was Notley Young, with sixty-one slaves in 1798. His extensive estate along the Potomac included twelve buildings identified as "Houses occupied by Negro's," of which nine were definitively labeled log; two were frame buildings, one quite large at 12 by 34 feet, the other, whose dimensions were not given, was adjacent to the "overseers garden"; and one building's material was not identified (plate 5).[7] These maps illustrate that all of the properties, large estates and small, slave owners and not, had log buildings.

Across the South, slave cabins differed in size but seem to have averaged about 200 square feet, or about 12 by 16. Usually five or six enslaved people, including children, shared a cabin. While the single-pen cabin predominated, double cabins were also common. In these, two unconnected units would be joined, either with the common chimney on the shared wall, or with chimneys at either end (see fig. 16).[8] Slave housing also could have more than two units in a building, but this was less practical for log construction.

As with the amount of space, the quality of construction affected living conditions. Contemporary commentaries on slave quarters appear in advice that slave owners gave to each other in southern agricultural journals of the 1820s through 1850s. These articles describe the state of housing and, because slave owners assumed they were writing to each other, their statements are less polemical than in other settings. Overwhelmingly, the slave owners recommend log construction for slave quarters; of ten articles that mention building materials, eight advise log, one suggests brick, and one plank.[9]

The slave-owners' greatest concern was sanitation, whether due to paternalistic interest in the well-being of dependents or to a desire to protect their investment. As one slave owner summarized, "Planters do not always reflect that there is more sickness, and consequently greater loss of life, from the decaying logs of negro houses, open floors, leaky roofs, and crowded rooms, than all other causes combined; and if humanity will not point out the proper remedy, let self-interest for once act as a virtue, and prompt him to save the health and lives of his negroes,

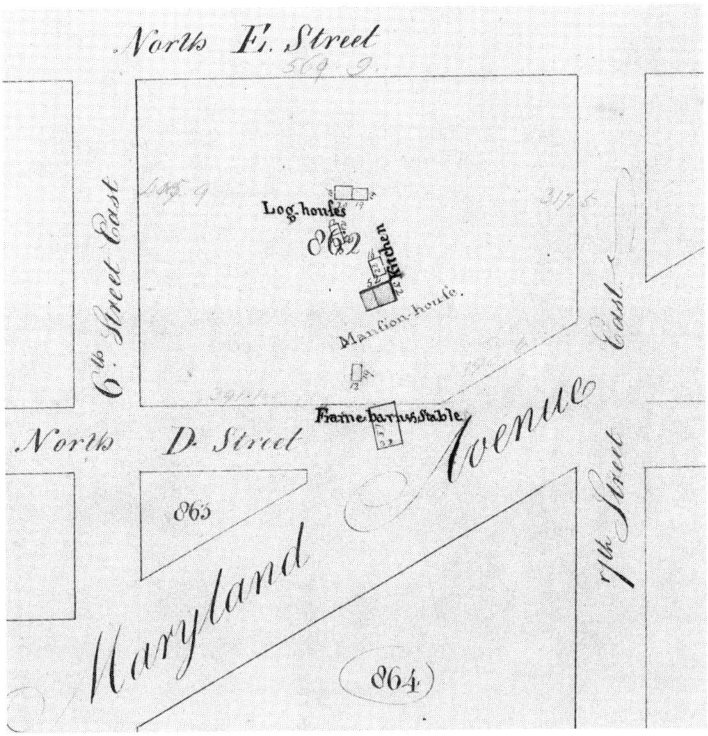

Figure 42. George Walker property, District of Columbia. Although Walker was not a slave owner, he nonetheless had several log houses behind his mansion house. The street plan of the new City of Washington has been overlaid onto his property. (Nicholas King, delineator, 1796, Library of Congress)

by at once providing comfortable quarters for them." Dampness in log cabins constituted a particular hazard; one writer mentioned "the noxious exhalations emanating from the half-buried and decaying timbers." Elevating the sill logs provided an obvious solution, but one that usually required plank floors. Dirt floors, if used, "should be raised a foot higher than the surrounding surface of the earth, and well rammed, to keep them dry." Dirt floors, remembered as being very hard, were common. Bluesman W. C. Handy, the son of a former slave, recalled in his autobiography that he had been born in a hewn-log cabin in Alabama built by his grandfather. He noted, "Our first kitchen had a dirt floor which my father had beat down so that it looked like asphalt."[10]

Another concern for slave owners was the weathertightness of the dwelling. Most recommended a framed roof; "the old fashioned cabins, with log roofs, and slabs not nailed, but entirely confined by logs, almost invariably leak, and keep the cabin floor always wet." Most slave owners advised chinking the logs or covering

Figure 43. Unidentified log cabin. Whitewashing the exterior of a log building created a more finished look. In this example, much of the whitewash has fallen off. (1900 photograph, Library of Congress)

the gaps with weatherboards, but they also viewed some ventilation as beneficial. Some slave owners felt that chinking left the houses too warm in the summer and unhealthily stuffy in winter, while others conceded that it was "wholly unnecessary" to provide for methods "of admitting fresh air," because the cabins were so poorly sealed. Slaves often removed chinking during the summer to increase ventilation. Few slave owners advocated glass windows; any opening other than a doorway would be furnished with a shutter. While the advice givers recommended brick chimneys, it appears that few cabins had them; the wooden chimney, heavily daubed and lined with mud, remained standard. The advisers preferred hewn logs over round ones and recommended whitewashing, inside and out (fig. 43). They did not mention partitioning the cabin into rooms or any other provision for privacy. They discouraged lofts, which would provide space for unsanitary clutter.[11]

To the slaves who inhabited the log cabins, this inadequate form of housing was one of many injustices perpetrated by the slavery system. Slaves' autobiographies usually described their crude housing in highly critical terms. Josiah Henson provides one example:

> Our lodging was in log huts, of a single small room, with no other floor than the trodden earth, in which ten or a dozen persons—men, women, and children—might sleep, but which could not protect them from dampness and cold, nor permit the existence of the common decencies of life. There were neither beds, nor furniture of any description—a blanket being the only addition to the dress of the day for protection from the chillness of the air or the earth. In these hovels were we penned at night, and fed by day; here were the children born, and the sick—neglected. Such were the provisions for the daily toil of the slave.

Henson, who was born in Montgomery County, Maryland, escaped to Canada in 1830 and published his autobiography in 1849. Harriet Beecher Stowe cited his account as evidence for the veracity of *Uncle Tom's Cabin.*[12]

Aside from contemporary documents, surviving slave cabins also offer a sense of the building type, although they typically exemplify the more substantial modes of construction. At Sotterley, a plantation in southern Maryland, situated near where the Patuxent River flows into the Chesapeake Bay, the one remaining slave cabin, dating from the 1830s, is typical in its size, measuring about 16 by 18 feet, with a large fireplace, and atypical in its quality of construction: the logs are planks, hewn and sawn to a thickness of 4½ or 5 inches, square-notched at the corners (fig. 44). To provide stability, earthfast log posts were placed at intervals outside the walls and pegged into the logs. The exterior brick chimney, which appears to be original, would have been better than most. A loft space was originally reached by a ladder in the corner near the fireplace.[13]

The building also reveals changes over time. In about 1910, when new owners acquired the plantation, the cabin received some improvements and continued to serve as housing. Workers installed windows on three sides, covered the logs with board-and-batten siding, and laid a wooden floor. In the 1950s, when the cabin was no longer inhabited, a new owner restored some of the old features, removing the siding from three sides, removing the wood floor, and bringing in dirt to raise the height of the floor. Today board-and-batten siding clads two exterior walls, and

Figure 44. Slave quarters, Sotterley, Hollywood, Maryland. In these log slave quarters, the logs were square notched, then held in place by vertical posts on the exterior. (Douglas Barber, photographer, 1972, Historic American Buildings Survey, Library of Congress)

whitewash covers the building inside and out. The necessary additions of windows to provide light, siding to provide additional insulation, and a wooden floor to provide warmth and cleanliness indicate how uncomfortable the original cabin would have been.

A remaining saddlebag log cabin at Hampton plantation, north of Baltimore, likewise has hewn-log construction (fig. 45). The cabin with half-dovetailed notching dates from about 1850.[14] Its stone foundation, which helps account for its survival, encloses a basement room with a dirt floor and a fireplace. A log cross wall divides the first floor into two rooms, each with a door to the exterior; the central chimney serves fireplaces in each room, as well as those in the basement. Whitewash in the lofts indicates they were probably occupied as well.

The cabin stands among others clustered around the overseer's house. Two other buildings that may have been slave quarters are far grander, however: stone buildings in saddlebag plans. Scalloping at the eaves indicates a desire for these outbuildings to be picturesque adornments to the landscape, not mere service buildings. From the perspective of the main house, the stone buildings are visible, but

Figure 45. Slave quarters, Hampton, Towson, Maryland. This double-pen log building contrasts with the more substantial stone one in the background. (Photograph by the author, 2013)

the overseer's house obscures the log cabin. The cabin's more humble appearance would not be one that accorded with a decorative farm landscape.

The third example derives from a president's house, which offers an intriguing if anomalous perspective on log slave quarters. At President Andrew Jackson's house near Nashville, Tennessee, Jackson and his wife, Rachel, lived in a log building from 1804, when they acquired the property, until 1821, when they built a grand mansion, the Hermitage, nearby. Soon after, they had their log dwelling converted to slave quarters. That the same log building would serve to house both a future president and his slaves illustrates two common characteristics of the log cabin: it was ubiquitous, and it took its meaning from its occupants.

In 1804 the Jacksons moved into an existing two-story hewn-log house, 26 by 24 feet, with half-dovetail notching. The first floor was one room, with beaded joists and an enclosed corner stair. Board walls partitioned the second floor into

Figure 46. Slave quarters (left) and kitchen (right), the Hermitage, Tennessee. Andrew Jackson and his wife inhabited the building on the left, when it was two stories tall and much grander; it was reduced in size and converted to slave quarters when the Jacksons moved to a brick mansion. (Photograph by the author, 2013)

three rooms. The Jacksons immediately improved the log house with wallpaper and painted trim. After they moved to a grand columned brick mansion, workers reduced the cabin in height by removing the first story, and the resulting one-story building housed slaves (fig. 46).[15] To effect the change in use and indicate its now-reduced state, workers removed the signs of gentility: window glass, doors, interior stair, wallpaper, and trim. Subsequent occupants, who were enslaved people, added root cellars and exterior shelving.

Although Jackson never advertised his log cabin residency—and he may have been born in one as well, but the place of his birth is uncertain—historians credit him with making the presidency accessible to the common man. Unlike previous presidents, Jackson came from humble birth and epitomized the self-made man. His populist message paved the way for the positive connotations that being born in a log cabin held for future presidential contenders. Today, Jackson has a mixed legacy: he was responsible for the egregious deportation of Native Americans from the southern states, and he was an unflinching supporter of slavery. When Jackson moved to his property in 1804 he owned nine slaves, but by the time he assumed the presidency in 1829, he had more than a hundred.

The Jacksons' first house was not the only log building on their property. A log kitchen in a double-pen plan, with exterior end chimneys, sat behind their log house. The kitchen building probably also housed slaves, most likely the cook, Betty, among them. Nearby a log building in a saddlebag plan also probably served as slave housing (see fig. 16). Dated to about 1840, this 20 by 40–foot house has hewn logs with half-dovetail notching. A large stone fireplace in the center opens to both rooms. This slave quarter was one of a number of buildings, both log and brick, gathered around the original house, the later mansion, and the fields.[16]

The absence of surviving slave quarters has moved some historic sites to reconstruct long-gone slave quarters in order to present a more accurate historical interpretation. With African Americans forming half of the population of Williamsburg, Virginia, in the eighteenth century, historians at Colonial Williamsburg felt that it was essential that slaves' lives be depicted in a tangible way. The lack of surviving slave quarters led them to reconstruct a small group of cabins at Carter's Grove, a plantation located about eight miles from Williamsburg, in 1987–90 (plate 6). The meticulously researched slave quarter consisted of three cabins, two of them log, on the original site of an eighteenth-century slave quarter, close by the main house. African American staff members interpreted the site to visitors, stressing the slaves' material lives and community. Unfortunately, with falling revenues and a change in direction, Colonial Williamsburg sold Carter's Grove to a private individual in 2003.[17]

A similar lacuna led to another reconstruction. Booker T. Washington, one of the most prominent African American educators in the late nineteenth and early twentieth centuries, was born in southwestern Virginia, about twenty miles southeast of Roanoke. His personal narrative, crystallized in the title of his autobiography, *Up from Slavery,* lent credence to his message of self-empowerment, so his birthplace, as a symbol of the degradation that he had overcome, held significance.

Washington was born in 1856 on the Burroughs farm, a middle-range tobacco farm with ten slaves. His mother, a cook, soon moved from his birthplace cabin to the log cabin that served as the kitchen, and it is this 14 by 16–foot cabin that Washington described in his autobiography:

> The cabin was not only our living-place, but was also used as the kitchen for the plantation. My mother was the plantation cook. The cabin was without glass windows; it had only openings in the side which let in the light, and also the cold, chilly air of winter. There was a door to the cabin—that is, something that was called a door—but the uncertain hinges by which it was hung, and the large cracks in it, to say nothing of the fact that it was too small, made the room a very uncomfortable one. In addition to these openings there was, in the lower right-hand corner of the room, the 'cat-hole'—a contrivance which almost every mansion or cabin in Virginia possessed during the ante-bellum period. The 'cat-hole' was a square opening, about seven by eight inches, provided for the purpose of letting the cat pass in and out of the house at will during the night. In the case of our particular cabin I could never understand the necessity for this convenience, since there were at least a half-dozen other places in the cabin that would have accommodated the cats. There was no wooden floor in our cabin, the naked earth being used as a floor. In the centre of the earthen floor there was a large, deep opening covered with boards, which was used as a place in which to store sweet potatoes during the winter. . . . While the poorly built cabin caused us to suffer with cold in the winter, the heat from the open fireplace in summer was equally trying. . . . [He and his brother and sister] slept in and on a bundle of filthy rags laid upon the floor.

From his vantage point in 1908, Washington positioned this cabin as typical, something easily recognized by other former slaves. He wrote, "Probably there is no single object that so accurately represents and typifies the mental and moral condition of the larger proportion of the members of my race fifty years ago as this same little slave cabin."[18]

Neither of the log cabins survived until the mid-twentieth century, when Sidney J. Phillips began kindling interest in some sort of commemoration at the site. Phillips was a former professor at the Tuskegee Institute, the Alabama college that

Figure 47. Kitchen, Booker T. Washington National Monument, Franklin County, Virginia. The National Park Service built this replica in 1960, basing it on the vivid description in Washington's autobiography. (Photograph by the author, 2013)

Washington had developed. After establishing the Booker T. Washington Birthplace Memorial in 1946, Phillips reconstructed the birthplace cabin with very little evidence. After Phillips's organization went bankrupt in 1955, the National Park Service acquired the site, somewhat reluctantly. The Park Service was highly critical of Phillips's interpretation of the site, which featured a nonhistoric driveway, a popular wishing well, and a romanticized version of the birthplace cabin, as well as other new construction.[19] The Park Service demolished the replica cabin, which had deteriorated, and built its own version of a cabin on the site of the kitchen (fig. 47).

The Park Service's first interpretative approach was to treat the property as representative of a typical middle-class farm of the 1850s. In the early 1970s the Park Service built a smokehouse, corn crib, privy, horse barn, and chicken house and interpreted the site as a living-history farm—a popular National Park Service approach at the time.[20] Not until the mid-1990s did interpretation shift back to Booker T. Washington and his experience as a slave there. Today stones mark the footprints of the big house and birthplace cabin site. Nearby stand two replica buildings, both of log: the kitchen and smokehouse. The one-room kitchen has hewn logs with diamond notching and a stone chimney on the gable end. Inside, the dirt floor is well replicated by concrete; the root cellar remembered by Washington is also present, covered by boards. The windows have wooden shutters and no glass. An exterior ladder gives access to a loft area.

The log slave cabins at Sotterley, Hampton, the Hermitage, and Booker T. Washington National Monument are all hewn log, not round, making them better quality than average, while the ones at Carter's Grove were left in the round. At the first three sites the cabins have necessarily undergone changes in order to survive for more than 150 years. But even accounting for these qualifications, these surviving cabins as well as the reconstructions manage to convey the general characteristics of slave quarters: one room, unfinished log interiors, dirt floors, glass-less windows, open fireplaces. Slave cabins resemble the quintessential log cabin associated with the frontier, but they are rarely admired as the building type assumed to breed a hardy individualism, presidential grit, or a pioneer can-do spirit. Contemporary observers compared slave quarters to the housing of European peasants as well as poor whites in the South and found them no worse.[21] The one-room log cabin without windows or flooring was the common building type throughout the South and backcountry and accommodated both free whites and enslaved blacks.

The perception of this cabin is what differed, with contemporary observers describing it both as a "hovel" and as a "cottage." Abolitionist New Englanders would have identified a basic log cabin with a hovel; log cabins were rare in New England by the mid-nineteenth century, and they seemed crude and rudimentary.[22] To rural southerners, however, the log cabin was the standard building type; while the quality could range from shoddy to highly finished, the form was acceptable. These views are complicated by the terms employed by novelists. Pro-slavery advocate John Pendleton Kennedy called the quarters "hovels" but found them picturesque and inoffensive. Abolitionist Harriet Beecher Stowe, on the other hand, referred to Uncle Tom's cabin as a "cottage," seeing it as a place of aspirational domesticity. The terms were as charged as the views on slavery.

After emancipation the former slaves moved off plantations but built minimal dwellings, similar to those they had been living in—log cabins. By the turn of the century reformers were pleased to witness the disappearance of the log cabin. As Booker T. Washington wrote in 1908, "There has been a marked improvement in the character of the Negro farmer's home. The old, one-roomed log-cabins are slowly but steadily disappearing. Year by year the number of neat and comfortable farmers' cottages has increased." W. E. B. Du Bois undertook more scientific studies beginning in the last years of the nineteenth century and concluded, "The dirt-floor has practically disappeared, and fully half the log-cabins have been replaced by frame buildings, and glass windows have appeared here and there." But Du Bois also found that while these log cabins might have been replaced by frame, they had not grown much in size, with the addition of only one room, maybe two.[23]

Both Washington and Du Bois welcomed the movement of African Americans into frame cottages. Washington described small urban settlements: "Most of the houses in these settlements are still modest cottages, but they are clean and neat. There are curtains in the windows, flowers in the gardens, and doorways are swept, there is a little vine growing over the porch, and altogether they have a wholesome air of comfort and thrift." Even better, however, was when blacks owned middle-class houses indistinguishable from those of whites; Washington heralded these achievements by publishing photographs and citing these success stories. The *Crisis,* the publication of the National Association for the Advancement of Colored People edited by Du Bois, also featured photographs of the houses of the black elite as well as bungalows and other middle-class houses as symbols of black achievement. Du Bois also recognized the potential drawback of such a tangible statement of success, however; such houses were occasionally the targets of racial violence. Blacks had been identified so long with log cabins that their move into decent housing sometimes provoked whites to violence.[24] Housing was a powerful symbol.

Log cabins continued to house African Americans in rural areas well into the twentieth century. One isolated community, Gee's Bend, Alabama, attracted the attention of the Resettlement Administration in the late 1930s. This former plantation had become a community of about seven hundred blacks, many of whom lived in log cabins they had built over the years since emancipation. Arthur Rothstein of the Farm Security Administration photographed the community in 1937, emphasizing the log cabins, unglazed windows, stick chimneys, and other signs of poverty (fig. 48). His picturesque photographs accompanied an article in the *New York Times Magazine* that included this description: "The cabins are shabby and poor as they lift their tattered tops above the cotton rows, but the logs that wall them are hand-hewn; the hand-split shingles that roof them are weathered to a gray so silvery and soft that Eastern architects would sell themselves down the river for the sight of them; the bare yards are clean and sandy-white, and the picket

Figure 48. Cabin, former Pettway Plantation, Gees Bend, Alabama. The round saddle-notched logs and wood-and-clay chimney are visible in this view of a log cabin. (Arthur Rothstein, photographer, 1937, Farm Security Administration, Library of Congress)

fences are all in place."[25] Even log cabins exemplifying poverty could be portrayed as cottages.

APPALACHIA

In the southern Appalachian Mountains, the log cabin proved to be a symbol not only of poverty and backwardness, but also of a redeeming domesticity. Through their writings, outside observers interpreted the log cabin as the characteristic housing and welcomed its rustic charm. Reformers and missionaries similarly embraced the log cabin, advocating for its improvement rather than wholesale replacement, emphasizing its "cottage" aspect. The log cabin played a critical role in defining these outsiders' understanding of Appalachia, which in turn influenced Americans' attitudes toward the region until the mid-twentieth century.

The Appalachian Mountains stretch from Alabama into Canada, but the southern sections—including all of West Virginia and portions of Virginia, North Carolina, Georgia, Alabama, Kentucky, and Tennessee—are most commonly identified as Appalachia. Also called the Southern Highlands, Appalachia received attention in the mid-nineteenth century when writers for newly popular journals provided travel pieces that highlighted different areas of the country. Outsiders' first interpretation of Appalachia emphasized its difference. One of the first such articles to explore Appalachia was a four-part piece published in *Harper's New Monthly Magazine* in 1857. In the part titled "A Winter in the South," David Hunter Strother, writing under the pseudonym "Porte Crayon," traveled around North Carolina and Tennessee, telling stories about the mishaps he and his travel companion endured, while depicting the local population sympathetically and even somewhat admiringly. He illustrated the articles lavishly with drawings of attractive local people and picturesque log cabins. After the war, Will Wallace Harney's article in *Lippincott's Magazine of Popular Literature and Science,* titled "A Strange Land and a Peculiar People," set the tone for future examinations: these people were different. Harney mentioned the mountaineers' "quaint speech and patient poverty" as well as "marked peculiarities of the anatomical frame."[26] He attributed their feuding—a theme that would also recur in descriptions of these people—to divisions exacerbated by the Civil War.

Novelists of the related local color movement, such as Sarah Orne Jewett in New England and Bret Harte in the West, developed the popular identity of regions. A chief popularizer of Appalachia was Mary Noailles Murfree, writing under the pseudonym Charles Egbert Craddock. Murfree's *In the Tennessee Mountains,* a collection of eight stories she had written for the *Atlantic Monthly* between 1878 and 1884, went through seventeen editions in the first two years after publication in 1884. Her characterizations relied heavily on dialect and were heralded for their accuracy, although her experience of the people and places she was writing about was indirect. She emphasized the picturesque: "A little log house surmounted the slope. It was quaintly awry, like most of the mountaineers' cabins, and the ridgepole, with its irregularly projecting clapboards serrating the sky behind it, described a negligently oblique line. Its clay chimney had a leaning tendency, and was propped to its duty by a long pole." Each of her stories included mention of a log cabin, emphasizing the domestic life of the mountaineers.[27]

As other writers took up Appalachia as their subject, certain themes emerged:

Figure 49. "Education—from such homes come the students who attend Lincoln Memorial University," Harrogate, Tennessee. This small, window-less log cabin is the type that reformers aimed to improve. (Ca. 1906 photograph, Library of Congress)

the region was isolated yet beautiful, the people were ignorant yet resilient, their customs included hospitality yet also feuding. The "strange land" and "peculiar people" trope endured and encouraged the identification of "unstable, thriftless, improvident and ignorant" people, living in windowless log cabins and in need of Christian enlightenment. Missionaries and reformers responded to the call (fig. 49).[28]

When Ellen Churchill Semple, a geographer, published "The Anglo-Saxons of the Kentucky Mountains: A Study in Anthropogeography" in 1901, she depicted an isolated region rooted in the eighteenth century, where people spoke a Shakespearean English, traded in barter rather than in cash, and had no familiarity with steamboats and railroads. While describing hard, impoverished lives, Semple also credited the people with self-reliant and independent spirits. Their houses reflected the poverty: "The home of the mountaineer is primitive in the extreme, a survival of pioneer architecture, and the only type distinctly American. It is the blind or windowless one-room log cabin." She also described a dog-trot: "two cabins side by side, with a roofed space between, which serves as a dining-room during the warmer months of the year." She conceded that two-story frame dwellings appeared on the edges of the mountain district and near sawmills, but held that the "usual home of the mountaineer is the one-room cabin." For Semple, the most important aspect of the people was that the mountaineers were of pioneer stock, "the purest Anglo-Saxon stock in all the United States," untainted by "the tide of foreign immigrants which has been pouring in recent years into the States."[29]

William G. Frost, president of Berea College in Kentucky from 1892 to 1920, who coined the term "Appalachian America" to apply to the southern Appalachian Mountains, pushed the analogy further. In an 1899 article, Frost asserted that the highlanders not only came from Anglo-Saxon stock, but they were just like the pioneers—in his words, "our contemporary ancestors." They were living "in the conditions of the colonial times" in the building most associated with "the first type of American architecture," the log cabin. While Frost also depicted Appalachians as in need of enlightenment—he was raising funds for a school, after all—he urged that "they should be encouraged to retain all that is characteristic and wholesome in their present life," and he asserted, "Let them not be taught to despise the log cabin, but to adorn it."[30] That essentially became the policy for the reformers.

Faced with the association of mountaineers with a pioneer form of architecture, the reformers celebrated log construction. They saw it as an emblem of local pride and, perhaps, hoped that their tolerance of the log cabin would be perceived as a symbol of their own willingness to accommodate local tradition. Settlement workers, who were intent on helping the poor, educating children, and training women in the domestic arts, tended to be middle-class, college-educated women. Appalachia seemed ripe for their attentions: pioneer-stock Americans who had been bypassed by the problems as well as the riches of industrializing America. While both missionaries and settlement workers provided teachers and schools for underserved children, missionaries concerned themselves with religious matters while settlement workers generally focused on improving domestic situations. The settlement workers offered an improved version of the houses that characterized the mountaineers.

Susan Chester Lyman founded one of the first settlements in about 1894 near Asheville, North Carolina, and called it the Log Cabin Settlement. The Vassar College graduate aided the activities of both church and school, provided a library, and hosted clubs and classes for children and adults. Lyman also wanted to "reach the homes of the mountaineers as can be done only by living among the people." To this end she built a large log house, which survives in a damaged photograph; it owes more to the burgeoning Arts and Crafts movement than to local tradition (fig. 50). As an article described it, "The home of the settlement is a log cabin of somewhat larger proportions and better construction than the one-roomed windowless cabins of the mountaineers in the vicinity." She intended to live in that house along with her coworkers, modeling domesticity, as the article explained: "Especial attention will also be given to the home life in order that it may be an example to other homes in the neighborhood, showing the people how their homes may be improved and made more beautiful." Improvement of domestic environments was a common goal of settlement houses in immigrant neighborhoods in urban areas, and modeling them through furnishings and decor was an accepted strategy.[31] Lyman's "Log Cabin Settlement" set out to do the same in Appalachia, as did many settlements that followed.

May Stone and Katherine Pettit, both from Kentucky, received funding from the Women's Christian Temperance Union to establish their settlement in Knott County, Kentucky, in 1902. After testing the waters with camps for three summers, Pettit and Stone founded the Hindman School, which still exists today. Beginning with a schoolhouse and a six-room cottage, the facility was initially called the Log Cabin School. In 1905 construction began on a twenty-eight-room log school building. The enormous undertaking required five hundred locally cut logs and thirty-six thousand shingles, as well as flooring and other dressed lumber, doors, and windows brought in over the mountains. For such a large building, it is usually more efficient to set up a sawmill and construct a wood frame, but obviously the identification with logs, as well as traditional construction methods, were important.

In a fictional account of this construction, a group of men assembled for a "working" hewed the logs by hand and moved them into place with a skid:

> In the school bottom, herculean labors were in progress. The huge log-pen, forty by fifty-five feet, was already breast-high. A log would be dragged by ox-

Figure 50. Log Cabin Settlement, near Asheville, North Carolina. This damaged photograph shows the school and residence that Susan Chester Lyman built in order to model domesticity to the mountain people she was trying to help. (David E. Whisnant Papers, #4326, Southern Historical Collection, Louis Round Wilson Special Collections Library, University of North Carolina at Chapel Hill)

> teams to the bottom of the skid-poles, then a score of powerful men would push and shoulder it up, while a dozen more pulled with ropes from the top of the wall. On arrival, it would be quickly and skillfully notched by the men at the corners—Uncle Ephraim and Uncle Lot, or two other equally famous notchers—and dropped into its place. Other men, not needed for the main job, worked about it in groups, finishing the hewing of joists, beams, and rafters, or with froes riving boards for the roof or palings for the fence.[32]

The real log school burned down within two months of its completion, but it was rebuilt the following summer (fig. 51).

The fictional account described reconstruction the next summer, this time with a sawmill and derrick. Tradition had now given way to expediency: "After incred-

Figure 51. Log school building, Hindman School, Hindman, Kentucky. Its log construction material linked this large school building, erected in 1906, to local traditions. (Harvard Art Museums/Fogg Museum, Transfer from the Carpenter Center for the Visual Arts, Social Museum Collection, 3.2002.100.1; Photo: Imaging Department © President and Fellows of Harvard College)

ible difficulties in hauling, the sawmill was brought in and set up in the school bottom, and thereafter its whine and buzz became a regular accompaniment of the day. . . . Quite a force was needed to handle the big logs, which had to be run through the sawmill and squared—a great improvement in point of time on the hand-hewing of the summer before . . . the big derrick our builder has constructed pick[s] up a great log as if it were a straw, and swing[s] it to its place on the wall (you recall how, last year, all this had to be done by muscle-power)." The real log building had electricity, steam heat, and running water—a thoroughly modern building, yet it was an evocation of the past in its log construction.[33]

Simple log construction was not enough, however. As Frost had urged, the proper adornment of the log cabin had to be taught. The reformers modeled progressive, modern households, so the teachers' quarters and their decorations were critical. Geographer Ellen Semple described a tent erected during the three summer camp years of Hindman: "It was made as clean and attractive as possible, decorated with flags, Japanese lanterns, and photographs of the best pictures. . . . Outside were hammocks, steamer chairs, and a table with flowers and books. . . .

One who has seen the dirt, poverty, and desolate lack of beauty in the interior of a mountain cabin, can realize what a revelation this camp was to the people who visited it."[34] Essential to their success was attracting students, both adults and children, so the reformers walked a fine line between respecting local traditions and trying to improve them. While they disparaged the ignorance, immorality, and lack of cleanliness of those they tried to help, they also found much to admire, particularly their handcrafts and music. "Fireside Industries," first promoted by Frost at Berea College, was also the term applied by Pettit and Stone at Hindman to a program in which local women sold their cloths, quilts, and other handcrafts.

The attraction of settlement workers to handcrafts was natural: products of the Progressive Era, the reformers were also influenced by the Arts and Crafts movement that emphasized handcraft in an age of industrial production. The Colonial Revival style likewise popularized preindustrial architecture and artifacts. What better than pioneer-stock American women who had always woven and quilted in distinctive, original patterns? Similarly, descendants of British immigrants built log cabins, which in the early twentieth century were associated with English settlers of the East Coast. The log cabin became the embodiment of this handcrafted, self-reliant society. Just as women made their own cloth, their husbands made their own houses without manufactured parts. The settlement workers borrowed this housing form, building their own log buildings, both out of respect for the local ways and also as an embodiment of their own ideals.

Yet there was a problem with log cabins—they also represented everything that the reformers were trying to change: families living in one room in filthy, overcrowded conditions. Stone and Pettit, reporting on their first summer in the mountains, described one cabin they visited: "It was made of rough, round logs with the bark on them and not very well chinked. There was one long, narrow room with no sign of a window and only a low, narrow door. Inside I could hardly see anything, though it was a bright, sunny, summer morning and the door open. After a few minutes, I could dimly make out a large, empty fireplace, two or three beds and some broken chairs. In this house live the father, mother and five or six children, the youngest a boy of four, blind from his birth."[35] There was not much that reformers could do about families living together in one room; instead they seized on the darkness of these cabins as a cover for filth and directed their energies toward advocating cleanliness.

An interesting distinction emerged in reformers' architectural assessments: the difference between hovel and cottage, although they did not use those terms. Instead, the contrast was cast as one between a cabin with windows and one without. Lucy Furman, a Hindman worker, wrote a series of popular books about the settlement. Her second book, published in 1925 but set in the first decade of the century, was titled *The Glass Window: A Story of the Quare Women,* "quare" being the term applied to the reformers.[36] The novel revolves around the attempt of one resident to install a glass window in her log cabin over her husband's objections. Other characters get glass windows, romantic involvements are described, a twenty-four-room log building is constructed, and, finally, Ailsie Pridemore gets her glass window. But the contrast is clear: a windowless, dark cabin versus a well-lit, bright, clean space. By advocating glass windows, the reformers could encourage the local residents to maintain their pioneer-associated architecture, yet modernize as well.

The administrators of the Hindman School also saw log cabins as an important part of the school's past. The cabin of its progenitor, "Uncle" Solomon Everidge, who encouraged Stone and Pettit to build their school in Hindman, was moved to the heart of the campus after Everidge's death in 1903. The hewn-log structure with dovetailed corners served not only as a memorial but also as an acknowledgment of a respected tradition of log cabin building.[37]

All the emphasis on log cabins obscured the fact that they were no longer the most common new building form in Appalachia by the early twentieth century. Despite the popular emphasis on isolation, Appalachia was undergoing a profound engagement with the world. Commercial lumber companies began buying up forests in the 1870s, and coal companies undertook large-scale mining beginning in the 1890s. Rather than an isolated, preindustrial haven, parts of Appalachia experienced intensive resource exploitation. With the coal and lumber companies, a new form of housing reached Appalachia: the company town made of cheaply built, identical wood-frame or boxed houses. Requiring sawn lumber, boxed-house walls were vertical planks, erected with only a minimal frame, constituting single-wall construction. In the mountains, residents now had money with which to purchase sawn lumber. The cash economy also made boxed houses more efficient, because steady jobs meant less time to spend on construction, and boxed houses were much faster to build, as opposed to the time devoted to workings that log buildings required. Log cabins continued to be built, usually with the aid of neighbors at a working and needing considerably less cash. And people still chose to build log cabins for reasons that had nothing to do with available cash. Most new construction, however, was the boxed house.[38]

Despite the increasing popularity of boxed houses, reformers found it worthwhile to promote log cabins, which both sounded more romantic and also reinforced the image of a backward people who needed saving. Whether the local residents appreciated the attachment to log construction is another matter. Witherspoon College, a Presbyterian mission school in Perry County, Kentucky, built log structures that drew this comment from a local woman: "When they first put those buildings up, we wondered why they didn't use lumber, like other wooden buildings in the town, but now we like these best."[39]

After World War I, though, settlement workers no longer maintained that the people they were helping all lived in shabby log cabins; they recognized that contemporary mountain architecture was increasingly sawn wood. Reformers continued to use log construction for their buildings, but more as a self-conscious acknowledgment of traditional architecture than as an attempt to replicate contemporary forms. In 1925 in Brasstown, North Carolina, Olive Campbell founded the John C. Campbell Folk School, named after her late husband. The school offered a model farm as well as an emphasis on handcrafts. In 1926 Campbell acquired logs from two old cabins in order to build a dogtrot cabin, in response to the community's desire that the Folk School preserve something of its past. Local craftsmen hewed and notched the logs, built one chimney of logs and sticks and the other of stone, laid puncheon floors, and rived shingles (fig. 52). As Allen Eaton, an investigator for the Russell Sage Foundation, noted, "This work brought out many of the skills of the community and aroused great enthusiasm among the old people who recalled their own, their parents', and grandparents' unforgettable experiences here and in other parts of the Highlands in home building and pioneer living." The cabin served as a museum of local crafts, with beneficial effect, as described by Eaton: "Building a museum for the sole purpose of preserving the old things of the community brought about a marked change, especially among the younger people. Those who had been anxious to replace their hand-made native walnut bedsteads with factory-made iron ones, and their comfortable light-weight wooden chairs of mountain make for upholstered chairs from the store, now came to place a new value on the old furniture." Despite the construction of this log cabin, though, Olive Campbell was well aware that it was no longer the only hous-

Figure 52. Log cabin, John C. Campbell Folk School, Brasstown, North Carolina. Local craftsmen used logs salvaged from preexisting cabins to make this new cabin with a dogtrot plan in 1926. (Photograph by the author, 2013)

ing form in Appalachia. In a thorough study by her husband, published posthumously and probably written by her from his notes, Campbell observed that the log cabin was disappearing and, at any rate, housed only the poorer class of Appalachians.[40]

Lucy Morgan founded Penland about thirty miles northeast of Asheville, North Carolina, as a center for weaving in 1923. Morgan's goals were to revive the craft of hand-weaving and to provide local women with a source of income. The school's first building was the Weaving Cabin, constructed in 1926. Local weavers and their families built the cabin, which measured 30 by 18 feet, of logs they had donated (fig. 53). As Allen Eaton, the Russell Sage Foundation investigator, described it: "Tacked to a log in an obscure place on the wall behind one of the looms was a sheet of paper on which was written in that brevity of expression characteristic of mountain people the legend of the cabin. A part of it ran about like this:

Figure 53. Weaving Cabin, Penland School of Crafts, Penland, North Carolina. Local weavers and their families built this well-lit cabin in 1926 as the first building of a school intended to promote handcrafts. (Photograph by the author, 2013)

3 logs by Henry Willis
1 log by Doc Hoppas
2 days work by Dave Hoyle
2 loads of stone for fireplace by John Maughn
4 logs by Sally Sparks[41]

Along with reviving hand crafts, Penland also recovered the traditional working to construct its building.

Both Campbell and Morgan were instrumental in the founding of the Southern Highland Handicraft Guild, which held its first meeting in the Weaving Cabin in 1928. The guild, a cooperative venture of eleven handicraft centers, aimed to improve quality and find markets for the items produced by the Appalachian men

Figure 54. "Travelog." Lucy Morgan devised this mobile log cabin to market handcrafts at the Century of Progress Exposition in Chicago in 1933. (Postcard in author's collection)

and women. With declining sales during the Depression, Morgan devised a small log cabin to travel on the back of a truck to advertise Penland's products (fig. 54). The "Carolina Cabin" or "Travelog" went to the Century of Progress Exposition in Chicago in 1933.[42]

The disparity between contemporary and traditional in Appalachia became crystallized with the arrival of the National Park Service in the 1930s. Great Smoky Mountains National Park encompassed more than half a million acres in North Carolina and Tennessee, Shenandoah National Park took 200,000 acres in the Blue Ridge Mountains in Virginia, and the Blue Ridge Parkway extended 469 miles from one park to the other. Both parks and the parkway were under development in the 1930s, part of extensive federal spending in Appalachia during the Great Depression.

Besides their natural beauty, the parks contained both residents and a long-standing cultural history. State agencies acquired the land for the parks, evicting the residents—more than 1,500 families—so that park administrators could create carefully crafted historic sites and vistas. Park officials decided which farmsteads remained as exhibits and which were destroyed to reinforce the sylvan beauty of the parks. Not surprisingly, given the previous half-century of promotion of the log cabin heritage of southern Appalachia, they favored log cabins at the expense of more modern boxed houses and wood-frame dwellings.[43]

One of the more extreme examples occurred at Mabry Mill, southeast of Roanoke on the Blue Ridge Parkway. There the two-story frame farmhouse that Ed Mabry had built in 1914 was demolished and replaced by a ca. 1865 log cabin brought in from an adjacent county. The grist mill powered by a kerosene engine was removed in favor of the overshot waterwheel that the Mabrys had stopped using. Park employees then built a photogenic lake in front of the waterwheel.[44] The Park Service's intention was clearly to provide an image of preindustrial charm and simplicity. The small log cabin reinforced the image of Appalachia as a place isolated from the modern world.

National Park Service officials were capable of changing their minds, though, as illustrated by the Johnson Farm, also in the Blue Ridge Parkway at the Peaks of Otter, near Bedford, Virginia. The farmhouse was built in the mid-nineteenth century as a log dwelling. Later, its single pen received an addition, transforming it into a saddlebag (fig. 55). During nearly a century of occupation by the Johnson family, the log cabin also gained weatherboard siding, enclosed porches, a metal roof, and larger windows. Also on site were seven outbuildings. In 1968 the Park Service restored the log house to an earlier appearance: workers removed the siding and porches and replaced the metal roof with one of shakes.[45] Only three log outbuildings remained, and the Park Service restored these as well. Live-in interpreters, whose interest in the site led to the first extensive research on it, inhabited the farm.

Soon, Park Service professionals concluded that the site would be better served by an interpretation that considered its full history. Accordingly, workers replaced the house's additions and siding in 1974 in order to interpret it as a 1930s farmstead (fig. 56). The new plan called the Johnson Farm "a rare opportunity to interpret a mountain home from its beginning as a rather rude, one-story cabin that grew and became somewhat refined as the economic lot of its owners improved. Thus, we

Figure 55. Johnson Farm, Blue Ridge Parkway, Virginia. National Park Service officials removed siding, a porch, and additions to restore this house in 1968. (Andy Ketterson, photographer, 1973, courtesy of National Park Service, Blue Ridge Parkway)

take the cabin from its one-room stage, to a two-room saddlebag log cabin with upstairs rooms on both sides, then a dining room and kitchen are added as the economic fortune of the family continues to improve, and finally, the log cabin is weatherboarded and a metal roof put on." Only ten years earlier, the 1964 plan had noted, "These buildings have been kept for the purpose of perpetuating the rapidly disappearing story of the pioneer mountain farms in the Southern Appalachians." The contrast could not be clearer.[46] One viewed the building as a static symbol of a bygone, romantic past, while the more recent plan saw it as an evolving illustration of changing fortunes.

Great Smoky Mountains National Park claims the largest collection of log buildings in the United States. Although they are located throughout the park, two major concentrations are found at the Mountain Farm Museum near the Oconaluftee Visitor Center in North Carolina and at Cades Cove, Tennessee. At the former, park employees assembled a farm house and various outbuildings from scattered sites throughout the park to create an open-air museum, which opened in 1953 (fig. 57). Moved to the site to replace a frame house, the one-and-a-half-story log house, built about 1899 by John E. Davis, utilizes wide chestnut logs, hewn flat and split in half, placed in matching positions on opposite walls. The corners are half-dovetailed. Initially, park officials asked Lucy Morgan of the Penland School to arrange exhibits in the Pioneer Handicrafts Room and provide live demonstrations of carding, spinning, and weaving. Morgan saw Mountain Farm

Figure 56. Johnson Farm, Blue Ridge Parkway, Virginia. A few years later, National Park Service officials rethought their interpretive approach and restored the siding, porch, and addition. (David Haas, photographer, 1996–97, Historic American Engineering Record, Library of Congress)

as "the beginning of an outdoor museum comparable to so many interesting ones that have been established in the countries of northern Europe."[47]

Cades Cove, once the largest community within park boundaries, occupies a wide valley three miles long. Today a loop road winds eleven miles through the valley, connecting five log cabins, one frame house, three frame churches, and one mill. These few buildings only hint at the life that once occupied the valley; the population reached 671 in 1850, when Cades Cove had two sawmills and an iron forge and was well connected to the outside world. Population declined for several decades but then rose to a peak of 708 in 1900.[48] These two surges in population produced a number of frame and boxed houses, only one of which remains today.

With the arrival of the National Park Service, Cades Cove was vacated of people and boxed and frame houses. The Tennessee Park Commission, established

Figure 57. Mountain Farm Museum, Great Smoky Mountains National Park, North Carolina. Near one entrance to the park, National Park Service officials assembled a collection of buildings to form a farm, which opened in 1953. (David Haas, photographer, 1996, Historic American Engineering Record, Library of Congress)

in 1927 to acquire land for the National Park Service, used eminent domain to force residents—then about 110 families—to sell. The Park Service interprets the remaining five log cabins in isolation, lacking a sense of both community and change over time. They do, however, offer interesting examples of architecture, such as the dogtrot built by Elijah Oliver in 1866, and the boards that cover the spaces between the logs in the Carter Shields Cabin. The Henry Whitehead Place has two adjacent cabins: one of hewn logs, saddle-notched at the corners; the other of sawn logs neatly dovetailed. The Cades Cove cabins have porches and stone chimneys, emphasizing the picturesque qualities, but there are few if any outbuildings (fig. 58). Rather than depict a community that expanded and contracted, just

Figure 58. John Oliver House, Cades Cove, Great Smoky Mountains National Park, Tennessee. National Park Service officials preserved log houses, such as this 1820s cabin, and removed twentieth-century ones. (Jack Boucher, photographer, 1960, Historic American Buildings Survey, Library of Congress)

as its farmsteads grew and changed, the National Park Service elected to preserve a poorly researched pioneer culture. The secretary of the interior's 1939 annual report mentioned "the unique opportunity presented in the Great Smoky Mountains National Park to preserve frontier conditions of a century ago, which have vanished elsewhere" (fig. 59).[49] The log cabin mindset did not encourage the preservation of boxed houses or wood-frame dwellings.

By the mid-twentieth century, Appalachia was seen more as a place of deep poverty than as an exotic "other." Books such as Henry Caudill's 1962 *Night Comes to the Cumberlands* depicted the economic devastation that resulted once the lumber and coal companies had pulled out. With the decline in agriculture and increasing dependence on extractive industries through the twentieth century, the region suffered particularly with the decline in coal production in the 1950s. John F. Kennedy was apparently shocked by the poverty he witnessed in West Virginia when he made a campaign stop there in 1960. A few years later, Lyndon Johnson used a visit to eastern Kentucky to help launch the War on Poverty. It was a calculated move: Appalachian people had a certain acceptability as recipients of concern about poverty, being sympathetic, pioneer-stock whites, as opposed

Figure 59. Walker Farm, Great Smoky Mountains National Park, Tennessee. Louisa and Margaret Walker were able to live out their lives in their family home after the formation of the park. (Jack Boucher, photographer, 1962, Historic American Buildings Survey, Library of Congress)

to blacks or recent immigrants. But their houses were no longer described as log cabins; instead, they were identified as tarpaper-covered shacks.[50] Log cabins had receded into the romantic past.

The log cabin served as housing for both slaves and Appalachian whites, as it did for many other Americans. For most people, there was an element of choice about their house, whereas slaves were provided what their owners saw fit, while poverty and isolation in nineteenth-century Appalachia made the log cabin a necessity for many whites. Whether these cabins were seen as hovels or cottages depended on who was describing them, but the appropriation of the log cabin by the reformers for their own housing illustrates the malleability of this architectural form. Later in the twentieth century, the log cabin became a picturesque element of a romanticized Appalachian landscape.

4

ROMANCING THE WILDERNESS

The Log Cabin as a Symbol of the Pioneer

The log cabin enhanced the image of the pioneer in the West. Beginning in the 1840s and lasting for a century or more, when white Easterners headed west, they found that log cabins often suited their purpose as expedient dwellings and also suited their image as pioneers, as they ventured beyond the limits of civilization and sawmills. Not all of the American West was as generously endowed with trees as the eastern third of the continent, but where there were trees there were soon log cabins. In the late nineteenth century, sawn lumber was far more readily available, being shipped by rail once the railroads penetrated the continent, but in remote forested regions the log cabin continued to serve. People attracted to mining, ranching, and even just remoteness all built log cabins.

Although explorers and frontiersmen were too mobile to leave many buildings behind, pioneers and settlers often built log cabins, which underwent a shift in the public mind from a degraded form of dwelling to a noble one. Just as Americans initially saw the wilderness as something to subdue, not celebrate, they first viewed the log cabin as an inadequate, temporary solution. But as the wilderness began to garner admiration and respect in the mid-nineteenth century, so did the pioneers and their log cabins. One of the main proponents of this new attitude toward the wilderness was Massachusetts resident Henry David Thoreau, who extolled the wilderness in a lecture he gave in 1851.[1] At the same time that the concept of wilderness was being reexamined by eastern literati, settlers were moving west where they faced expansive open spaces and forbidding mountain ranges. The settlers relied, where possible, on log cabins to give them their foothold in the wilderness. The log cabin carried associations of hardy individualism, resourcefulness, diligence, and egalitarianism.

This chapter examines the cabins and experiences of four individuals who wrote about log cabins: Caroline Kirkland, Laura Ingalls Wilder, Theodore Roosevelt, and Richard Proenneke. Each of them shaped contemporary understandings about their wilderness experiences, which they cast as adventurous, character building, and enviable. All of them valued the surrounding landscape, highlighting not only the remoteness but also the strange beauty. Although "wilderness" might be a disputable term—as soon as someone builds a cabin in it, is it wilderness any more?—all of these authors viewed their settings as wilderness, mentioning the remoteness, isolation, and risks inherent in their surroundings. Similarly, the West was as they perceived it, usually meaning west of where they had been. Caroline Kirkland, settling in southeast Michigan around 1840, described her location as the West, just as Theodore Roosevelt in western North Dakota in the 1880s did. (Richard Proenneke, living in Alaska, did not call it the West, but Alaska is in its own category, claiming the moniker of the Last Frontier.)

In the very act of writing about these experiences, the authors romanticized them. None of their books contained litanies of complaints and hardship. Each carried the message that the writer had overcome adversity and triumphed in a challenging land and, implicitly, that he or she was a better person for it. Each of them wrote about their own experiences with varying degrees of verisimilitude, and critics have taken delight in pointing out where their writings departed from fact. In fiction, memoir, or even daily journal entries such as Proenneke's, the writers adjusted, or selected, the facts that accorded with their own views of the world.

These four writers sought out the wilderness and lived in log cabins for different reasons, and consequently they thought about their experiences differently. One decided division is along gender lines. Roosevelt's experience was in an all-male world, reveling in masculinity, and Proenneke lived, contentedly, alone. But the image of noble pioneers living in remote log cabins affected women very differently. The very act of building a cabin was often a prelude to settling down and having a family. Men might have physically built the cabin, but women made it a home, and their views on log cabin life revealed a different side of the hardy individualism so easily invoked. Instead, behind the romantic gloss of their accounts was a grim acceptance of homemaking made more difficult by rough living conditions.

Recording their log cabin experiences over more than a century, these four authors reflect their time, gender, and station in life. Caroline Kirkland, settling in Michigan in 1837, described miserable living conditions in log cabins and how genteel touches might improve them. Of the four writers, she was the least enamored of her situation, reflecting the early nineteenth-century distaste of log cabins and wilderness. Laura Ingalls Wilder, writing in the 1930s about her childhood in the 1870s, cast her family's experiences of bare survival in a matter-of-fact tone of child-like acceptance. She expressed amazement at everything her family endured, but she evidently thought that these offered good lessons for children. The two male writers offer more romantic views of western living. Theodore Roosevelt is another president with log cabin connections (he was even profiled in the *From Log Cabin to White House* series in 1906), but his log cabin experience and his political actions connect more directly than those of Harrison or Lincoln.[2] For Roosevelt, the log cabin offered far more than a campaign opportunity; it was also a tangible connection to a glorified past that presaged an imperialist foreign policy. Finally, Richard Proenneke, who built a well-documented log cabin in Alaska in 1968, explained the process so adeptly that he garnered a large following. Not many of his adherents built their own log cabins, but the number of armchair enthusiasts he inspired suggests a deep and ongoing desire to do so. Although the attitudes and experiences of these four authors differ, they all associated their log cabins with the romance of the wilderness.

A NEW HOME

Conquering the wilderness is an aspiration most commonly ascribed to men. Certainly, women, too, have ventured alone into remote areas, but more commonly they venture with their families. Their test becomes one of making a home rather than merely surviving. Caroline Kirkland described her adventures in the wilds of Michigan in the late 1830s and early 1840s in two books and several articles, depicting her struggle to establish a genteel household in the midst of rough surroundings and uncouth neighbors (fig. 60). A particular struggle was with the log cabin in which she briefly lived.

Figure 60. Caroline Kirkland in 1852. She published her acute perceptions about life in a log cabin in a frontier Michigan town beginning in 1839. (Library of Congress)

Caroline and her husband, William, were both schoolteachers. Born in New York City in 1801, Caroline moved to Clinton, New York, to join William, who was teaching at Hamilton College. They married in 1828. Caroline was exceptionally well educated, versed in Latin, French, and Italian, and with a passing knowledge of German. New land in the West tempted William Kirkland, and he acquired eight hundred acres in Livingston County, Michigan, about sixty miles northwest of Detroit. There he laid out a new town, christened Pinckney (called Montacute in Caroline's book), and in 1837 William and Caroline moved there with their four children.[3]

Caroline found a town that was more imagined than real, with mud holes for streets and rambling log cabins instead of the frame houses with which she was familiar. Her first book, *A New Home: Who'll Follow? or, Glimpses of Western Life,* was published in 1839 and became an instant success, going through thirteen printings in eleven years. In a series of related sketches, she described her interactions with the country and her neighbors in sharp, critical portrayals that made for lively reading but did not win her any friends. Although she published under the pseudonym of Mrs. Mary Clavers and did not expect that her book would find its way back to her wilderness community, it did, and her neighbors resented their characterizations. In her next book, *Forest Life,* published in 1842, she was more circumspect, but her unpopularity, along with her husband's lack of financial success, forced them to leave Pinckney the next year. The Kirklands returned to New York City, where she opened a school for girls, edited a new literary periodical, *The Union Magazine of Literature and Art,* and wrote short pieces for other publications.[4]

Critics today regard Caroline Kirkland's books as pioneers of realism; she rejected the romantic literature that was then dominating the literary scene. She insisted that her work was true to life—"I claim for these straggling and cloudy crayon-sketches of life and manners in the remoter parts of Michigan, the merit of general truth of outline"—while at the same time acknowledging some embellishments—"there be glosses, and colourings, and lights, if not shadows." Although *A New Home* was not strictly autobiographical—she omitted many aspects of her life—she oriented her tales around her confrontation with a strange place. As critical as she was of the people she met, she was also critical of her own naïveté and lack of preparation. At one point, as she sank into a mud-hole after getting out of a wagon, she chided herself: "Silly thin shoes again. Nobody should ever go one mile from home in thin shoes in this country, but old Broadway habits are *so* hard to forget." She aimed her book at an audience of similarly genteel readers who might be considering a similar venture into the wilderness—as she called it, "a sort of 'Emigrant's Guide.'"[5] She employed explicit directives as well as indirect morality tales to convey her advice.

One aspect of her books that she kept in the background was the fact that she had a financial interest in encouraging other settlers. Although she strongly resented booster literature and claimed to be accurately representing life in the wilderness, her welfare depended on the financial success of her husband's real estate dealings. The combination of the financial depression of 1837, poorly regulated "Wild Cat" banks, opportunistic businessmen (one of whom swindled her husband), and speculation made the financial aspects of living in a new town precarious. The very nature of speculation was the opposite of creating a home: "The habit of selling out so frequently makes that *home*-feeling, which is so large an ingredient in happiness elsewhere, almost a nonentity in Michigan." She saw this as a hardship on women in particular: restless men "purchase a lot or two of 'government land;' build a log-house, fence a dozen acres or so, plough half of them, girdle the trees, and then sell out to a new comer; one whose less resolute spirit has perhaps quailed a little before the difficulties of the untouched forest. The pioneer is then ready for a new purchase, a new clearing, and a new sale. How his wife and children enjoy themselves meanwhile is matter of small doubt, but this is a trifle for the present. The future—the bright far-ahead, vague Western future—is to make up for all."[6]

Her husband was one of these men who hoped to profit from real estate, the value of which would increase only if he could convince others to settle in his wilderness town. As a result, Caroline Kirkland encouraged her readers to follow in her footsteps. When she described her hardships, she employed a tone of bemusement, not despair. She implied that setbacks could be overcome if one only had the proper attitude of resolve and flexibility. She also welcomed signs of settlement; at the end of her book, she cited, among other signs of progress: "Loggeries are becoming scarce within our limits, and many of our ladies wear silk dresses on Sunday."[7]

Her discussions of log cabins describe not only a genteel woman's encounter with one, but also what the cabin meant to her. The Kirklands rented a log cabin for several months while their frame house was being built. The cabin measured 24 by 18 feet, which, as she pointed out, would have been adequate for a kitchen and dining room, but a bedchamber and nursery also had to occupy the space. She strung heavy curtains to create two bedrooms "about as large as a steamboat stateroom." She found life in the log cabin difficult:

> The circumstance of living all summer, in the same apartment with a cooking fire, I had never happened to see alluded to in any of the elegant sketches of western life which had fallen under my notice. It was not until I actually became the inmate of a log dwelling in the wilds, that I realized fully what 'living all in one room' meant. The sleeping apparatus for the children and the sociable Angeline [her servant], were in the loft; but my own bed, with its cunning fence of curtains; my bureau, with its 'Alps on Alps' of boxes and books; my entire cooking array; my centre-table, which bore, sad change! the remains of to-day's dinner, and the preparations for to-morrow, all covered mysteriously under a large cloth, the only refuge from the mice: these and ten thousand other things, which a summer's day would not suffice me to enu-

> merate, cumbered this one single apartment; and to crown the whole was the inextinguishable fire, which I had entirely forgotten when I magnanimously preferred living in a log-house, to remaining in Detroit till a house could be erected.[8]

In a later article, Kirkland described the log cabin in more detail. Sticks and mud formed the exterior chimney: "after the fashion of what the children call a jackstraw house, i.e., with sticks laid in a square, crossing at the corners. . . . The clay with which the stick chimney was lined, fell off, day by day, so that its catching fire in spots was almost a daily occurrence, and continual watchfulness was required." The stone hearth was laid unevenly, and a wooden crane "swung far enough above the fire not to catch, unless the blaze was more aspiring than ordinary." The floors, made of "heavy oak plank, laid down without nails or fastening of any kind, somewhat warped, and not very closely packed" caused tripping and lost toys "which slid through the cracks to regions unexplored." The walls were unhewn logs, chinked with strips of wood, "then plastered with wet clay, which falls off continually, and requires partial renewing every autumn. This clay, in its dry state, gives off incessantly an impalpable dust, which covers and pervades everything." The unplastered beams were worm-ridden. Despite all of these drawbacks, as well as a snake that lived under the house and a toad that resided within, Kirkland maintained her attitude of wry detachment.[9]

Some log cabins were better than others, and Kirkland often equated a building's presentability with the character of the people who resided within. Well-kept cabins with ornamental plantings and imported furnishings reflected well on their middle-class, hard-working residents, while deteriorating, poorly equipped cabins housed lower-class people of low morals and little ambition. William Kirkland stayed overnight with one family in a log cabin "like many others which have served for the first homes of settlers in Michigan": "It was logs and nothing else, the fire made on the ground, or on a few loose stones, and a hole in the roof for the escape of the smoke. . . . After the conclusion of the meal, the blankets were spread on the ground, and happy he who could get a bag for a pillow."[10]

In contrast to uncivilized log cabins, frame houses were the true sign of a permanent settlement. When Kirkland moved into a frame house after several months in the log cabin, she described her new home as "a palace of some twenty by thirty feet, flanked by a shanty kitchen, and thatched with oak shingles." The move was literally one from darkness into light: "After many trials (of patience) and many hardships (in a small way) we emerged from the dark precincts of the loggery into the bright atmosphere of the 'framed house'—exchanged worm-eaten beams for a plastered ceiling—and miniature Rocky Mountains for a tiled hearth—and succeeded in excluding the pigs, and discovered some amiable traits in the neighbors." For Kirkland, the dichotomies were clear: log vs. frame, uncivilized vs. genteel, West vs. East, low-class vs. middle.[11]

Kirkland brought a distinctly feminine perspective to the story of settling on the wilderness. Women civilized not by conquering savages, but rather by introducing refinement to a rough settlement. As she noted, men did not care as much about their surroundings; it was the women who had to insist on wood-frame houses and the comforts of life.

> Woman's little world is overclouded for lack of the old familiar means and appliances. . . . She has found a thousand deficiencies which her rougher mate can scarce be taught to see as evils. What cares he if the time-honoured cupboard is meagerly represented by a few oak-boards lying on pegs and called shelves? His tea-equipage shines as it was wont—the biscuits can hardly stay on the brightly glistening plates. Will he find fault with the clay-built oven, or even the tin "reflector?" His bread never was better baked. What does he want with the great old cushioned rocking-chair? When he is tired he goes to bed, for he is never tired till bed-time.[12]

Kirkland dwelt extensively on furniture and other possessions. In several cases, she poked fun at her own belongings (fig. 61). When she moved her "nest of delicate japanned tables" into her crowded log cabin, her neighbor Mrs. Jennings eyed them doubtfully and said, "I guess they'll do better for kindlin's than any thing else, here." Kirkland realized she was right: "And I began to cast a disrespectful glance upon them myself, and forthwith ordered them up stairs, wondering in my own mind how I could have thought a log house would afford space for such superfluities." But she also disapproved of her neighbors' predilection for multipurpose items. After spending the night in a log "hotel," she descended from the loft and looked around inquiringly. Her hostess said, "'Oh! you'm lookin' for a wash-dish, a' n't ye!' and forthwith put some water into a little iron skillet, and carried it out to a bench which stood under the eaves, where I performed my very limited ablutions

Figure 61. Unpacking. This interior view depicts the unpacking process, in which Kirkland supervises two workers. (F. O. C. Darley, delineator, in 1850 edition of *A New Home: Who'll Follow?*, opposite p. 69)

al fresco, not at all pleased with this part of country habits."[13] Having a skillet do double duty as a washbowl, or a handkerchief as a towel, offended her sensibilities. The genteel life required differentiated items, just as the genteel house required separate rooms for separate functions.

Kirkland drew several conclusions from her experience in a log cabin. For herself and her family, she thought that it enabled them to appreciate their new frame house, as modest as it was: "the sojourn in the log-house, though 'ugly and venomous' enough while it lasted, fulfilled yet the sweet uses of such things, by giving to very humble arrangements a charm which they would have lacked if we had come into possession of the new abode directly from the city."[14] She did not abandon her desire for the comforts and customs of her class but merely appreciated them more. As a volume of advice for others, she recommended that her middle-class friends sacrifice—but only temporarily—their insistence on decorum, culture, and leisure. The triumph of a pioneer, in her view, was not just to conquer the wilderness physically, but to create a home that valued the culture and lifestyle of eastern gentility. Although she clearly preferred life in a frame house, her sojourn in a log cabin was part of the romance of her story; it allowed her opportunities to overcome adversity, face inconvenience with bemusement, and understand how basic a household could be.

LITTLE HOUSE

The *Little House* books penned by Laura Ingalls Wilder also describe efforts at homemaking in log cabins, but from the viewpoint of a child. In 1932 Wilder published the first book in the series that has helped frame Americans' understanding of log cabin life on the frontier. Geared toward a young audience, the books made a great impression, being part of many readers' growing up as well as learning to read. Like Kirkland, Wilder wrote not only accessibly, but also vividly. The theme of how to live in the woods or on a prairie, with descriptions from building log cabins to preserving venison, is enlivened with scenes of real danger from bears, panthers, prairie fires, and more. She set the books in the distant past of the 1870s and 1880s.

Laura Ingalls was born in a log cabin near Pepin, Wisconsin, in 1867. Her family's frequent moves around the Midwest, Great Plains, and Ozarks formed the core of the experiences she recounted in her novels. She married Almanzo Wilder in 1885 and continued her peripatetic life until they settled in Missouri in 1894. In 1932, at the age of sixty-five, she published her first novel, *Little House in the Big Woods,* describing life in the Wisconsin cabin. Her next novel, *Farmer Boy* (1933), depicted her husband's youth in New York State. With the 1935 publication of *Little House on the Prairie,* set in Kansas, she began to envision the books as a series about herself and her experiences. *On the Banks of Plum Creek* (1937) was set near Walnut Grove, Minnesota, and the next four in South Dakota.[15] Wilder died in Missouri in 1957. Her books have remained in print, have won accolades from various sources, and have sold 60 million copies in thirty-three languages. Much of Wilder's popularity is due to a TV show, *Little House on the Prairie,* which aired on NBC from 1974 to 1982. The show, situated in Walnut Grove, had only passing resemblance to the books but gave Wilder wide exposure.[16]

Wilder tells her story in the third person but focuses on Laura, the second-oldest daughter. The reader sees the world through Laura's eyes, almost from the inside out. The interior of the cabin is of paramount importance, and then the yard; she does not describe the outside of the house, because that is not a child's view. In *Little House in the Big Woods,* Laura is at an undefined, but very young, age. Wilder mentions the trundle bed Laura sleeps in before observing the "solid log walls" that surround her and keep her safe. She then describes the interior of the house, noting that it has two rooms, one of them a small bedroom with a glass-less window and the other, the "big room," with two glazed windows and two doors. There is also a large attic to play in. She then expands outward to describe trees in the yard (plate 7). In the course of the book, the family makes one trip to the town of Pepin, Wisconsin, seven miles away. Laura had never seen a town before, or a store, or buildings that were not made of logs.[17]

Little House on the Prairie begins with the Ingalls family's departure from their house in Wisconsin, because "Pa said there were too many people in the Big Woods now." They settle on the Kansas prairie, on land that was part of the Osage Diminished Reserve. In Kansas Laura is old enough to be more aware of her surroundings and to observe the construction of their log cabin. Wilder eloquently describes the treeless plain and notes that Pa has to haul logs from the river banks. He saddle-notches the logs: "Now with his ax he cut a wide, deep notch near each end of these logs. He cut these notches out of the top of the log, but with his eye he measured the sills, and he cut the notches so that they would fit around half of the sill. When the notches were cut, he rolled the log over. And the notches fitted down over the sill."[18] He builds the cabin three courses high, then enlists the help of his wife to hoist the logs. But a log falls on Ma's foot, spraining her ankle, so Pa gets a neighbor, Mr. Edwards, to help instead.

The men finish the walls, then build a "skeleton roof of slender poles." Wilder describes the effect from a child's point of view: "Stripes of sunshine came through the cracks in the west wall, and stripes of shadow came down from the poles overhead. The stripes of shade and sunshine were all across Laura's hands and her arms and her bare feet. And through the cracks between the logs she could see stripes of prairie."[19] Pa initially covers the pole roof with the canvas from their covered wagon, then diverts his energies from the house to build a stable to shelter their horses. After wolves threaten the family, Pa builds a door for the cabin. He splits logs into slabs but has no nails, so he pegs horizontal cross-pieces into the vertical

Figure 62. The Little House on the Prairie, as depicted in the 1953 edition. Wilder carefully describes the construction of this log cabin. In this view, Laura and her sister Mary are picking up every nail that Pa drops. (Garth Williams, delineator, 1953, *Little House on the Prairie,* p. 125; text copyright 1935, 1963 Little House Heritage Trust; used by permission of HarperCollins Publishers)

slabs to hold them together. For hinges he uses leather straps that he pegs to the door. He builds a fireplace from river stones, mortared with clay and water. For the chimney, though, he uses cribbed sticks and mud.

Concern over the danger of sparks from the chimney igniting the canvas roof leads Pa to borrow nails from Mr. Edwards so that he can put on a slab roof. He borrows only reluctantly, saying, "I've never been beholden to any man yet, and I never will be. But neighborliness is another matter, and I'll pay him back every nail as soon as I can make the trip to Independence," the nearest town. Laura and her older sister, Mary, retrieve every nail that falls astray, and Pa straightens out the bent ones; "It would never do to lose or waste a nail" (fig. 62).[20] Pa then lays a puncheon floor and chinks the walls with strips of wood and mud. Later in the fall, Pa goes to town and brings back, among other items, eight panes of glass for windows. Finally, three quarters of the way into the book, the house is complete.

Wilder's description of process is characteristic of these books. She also describes

Plate 1. Caldwell-Hutchison Farm, Lowndesville, South Carolina. Newspapers cover the walls of the living room of this log house, built about 1800. (Dennis O'Kain, photographer, 1980, Historic American Buildings Survey, Library of Congress)

Plate 2. Campaign textile. Chintz cloth with images of William Henry Harrison and a log cabin created for Harrison's presidential campaign in 1840. (Library of Congress)

Plate 3. Abraham Lincoln Birthplace National Historical Park, Hodgenville, Kentucky. The log cabin is the only item on display inside the temple. (Postcard in author's collection)

Plate 4. Lincoln Logs. This toy developed by John Lloyd Wright in 1918 takes advantage of the association of Lincoln with log cabins. (Photograph by the author, 2012)

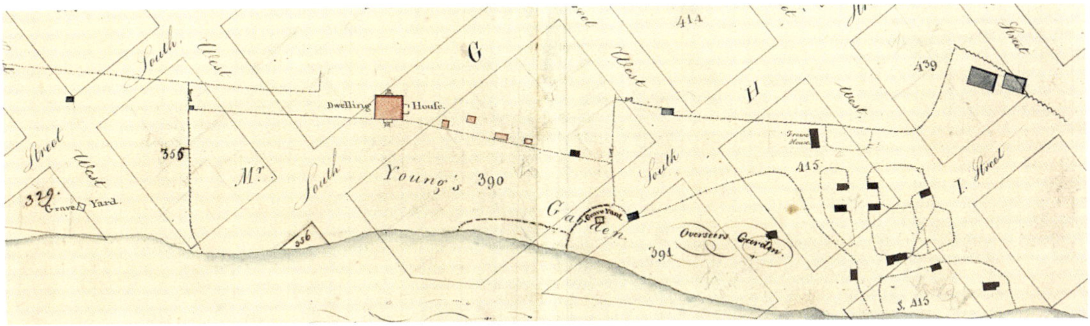

Plate 5. Notley Young property, District of Columbia. Young, the largest slaveholder in the District, housed his slaves in a dozen buildings, most of which were log. The surveyor has drawn the new street plan over the existing plantation. (Nicholas King, delineator, 1796, Library of Congress)

Plate 6. Slave quarters, Carter's Grove, James City County, Virginia. Staff at Colonial Williamsburg designed and built these reconstructions in the late 1980s. Only one log cabin survives today. (Courtesy of Jeffrey E. Klee, 2007)

Plate 7. The Little House in the Big Woods, as depicted in the 1953 edition. The size of the tree trunk, dwarfing the little log cabin, emphasizes how small Laura Ingalls felt in the midst of such woods. (Garth Williams, delineator, 1953, from *Little House in the Big Woods*, p. 1; text copyright 1935, 1963 Little House Heritage Trust; used by permission of HarperCollins Publishers)

Plate 8. Richard Proenneke building his cabin, Twin Lakes, Alaska. Proenneke photographed and filmed himself while he was building his cabin in 1968. (Courtesy National Park Service, Lake Clark National Park and Preserve, LACL-3522)

Plate 9. Richard Proenneke Cabin, Twin Lakes, Alaska. Proenneke thought the chimney added beauty to the cabin. Twin Lakes is in the background. (Richard Proenneke, photographer, 1969, courtesy National Park Service, Lake Clark National Park and Preserve, LACL 3522)

Plate 10. New England Coffee Shop, Los Angeles, California. The concrete log construction was intended to remind customers of New England in this 1930s commercial building, now a Mexican restaurant. (Photograph by the author, 2015)

Plate 11. My Grandfather's House Antique Shop, McMinnville, Tennessee. Formed from an early nineteenth-century log house moved to the site in the late 1920s, this antique shop advertised its goods through its building material. (Postcard in author's collection)

Plate 12. Log cabin in Twitter offices, San Francisco, California. In 2014 the company moved two log cabins from Montana to its offices in San Francisco to serve as spaces that were separate and identifiable. (Jasper Sanidad, photographer, 2014)

Plate 13. Camp Santanoni, Newcomb, New York. Six log buildings connected by porches face onto Newcomb Lake. The kitchen and service building is in the foreground in this view. (Paul Malo, artist, ca. 2000, courtesy of The Adirondack Museum, Blue Mountain Lake, NY)

Plate 14. William Allen White Work Cabin, Rocky Mountain National Park, Estes Park, Colorado. White, a newspaper editor, bought a retreat for himself in the Rocky Mountains and then in 1913 built this log cabin in which he could write. (Photograph by the author, 2014)

Plate 15 (above). Medford Lakes Lodge, Medford Lakes, New Jersey. Built in 1931, this lodge offered the "world's largest fireplace," according to this 1962 postcard. Fire destroyed the lodge in 1998. (Postcard in author's collection)

Plate 16 (left). Interior, Supervisor's Office Building, Chippewa National Forest, Minnesota. Isaac Boekenoogen supervised construction of the building, which included this rustic stairway. (Photograph by the author, 2014)

how to make items such as cheese, maple sugar, straw hats, and bullets. The Ingallses are able to survive by creating what they need out of materials at hand. Animals provide not only essential food but also the furs that Pa trades at the store for items such as sugar and a plow. Wilder also emphasizes how few material possessions the family has. Laura and her sister have to share a doll before Laura gets one of her own. They make a tea set out of leaves for the dolls, and play in the roots of a tree. For a ball they use an inflated pig's bladder. The girls are obedient—Laura's sister Mary more so than Laura—and obviously not spoiled. As in many children's books, proper behavior is an underlying message.

Wilderness, mostly defined as remoteness, is another theme. Wilder describes the setting in *Little House in the Big Woods:* "The great, dark trees of the Big Woods stood all around the house, and beyond them were other trees and beyond them were more trees. As far as a man could go to the north in a day, or a week, or a whole month, there was nothing but woods. There were no houses. There were no roads. There were no people. There were only trees and the wild animals who had their homes among them." Similarly, she describes the prairie: "There was only the enormous, empty prairie, with grasses blowing in waves of light and shadow across it and the great blue sky above it, and birds flying up from it and singing with joy because the sun was rising. And on the whole enormous prairie there was no sign that any other human being had ever been there." Critics have pointed out that these places were far more populated, with both Indians and other settlers, than Wilder indicated. Family members lived near their Wisconsin house, towns were closer than she implied, and the Ingallses interacted with more neighbors than the books mentioned.[21] But the impression that these were unpopulated spaces, that this solitary family was confronting a wilderness, was a powerful part of her story.

Wilder framed her stories around a romantic view of western settlement, in which lone families bravely established homes in isolated surroundings. Even the titles of the early books evoke this: *Little House in the Big Woods, Little House on the Prairie*—a single little house in a big place. These were the only two books built around log cabins. Subsequently, the Ingallses lived briefly in a sod house and a tarpaper shanty, but mostly in frame houses. When Wilder's father built a frame house in Walnut Grove, Minnesota, he had to engage with the market economy, buying sawn lumber, as well as "glass windows, factory-milled doors and white china doorknobs. Pa had purchased it all on credit at the lumberyard."[22]

Wilder saw her past as part of an inexorable progress from wilderness to civilization and from east to west. She articulated this view in a speech she gave in 1937: "I had seen the whole frontier, the woods, the Indian country of the great plains, the frontier towns, the building of railroads in wild, unsettled country, homesteading and farms coming in to take possession. I realized that I had seen and lived it all—all the successive phases of the frontier, first the frontiersman, then the pioneer, then the farmers, and the towns." In keeping with this process of succession, similar to the views of historian Frederick Jackson Turner, Wilder also portrayed her family's moves as inexorably westward. In reality, the Ingalls family also moved eastward, and even returned once to their house in the Big Woods, when their new ventures failed. Failure and backward movement, however, were not the themes that Wilder wanted to portray.[23]

Wilder's interaction with the wilderness was one of taming it; Pa building a house was an important part of that process. Much of the civilizing was the responsibility of Ma, though. She served as the chief disciplinarian of her children, insisting on cleanliness, tidiness, and obedience. Ma also tamed their surroundings. In *Little House on the Prairie* she defined civilization by the attainment and display of three things: a puncheon floor instead of dirt, a china figurine on the mantelpiece, and a red-checked tablecloth. "'There,' she said. 'Now we're living like civilized folks again.'"[24] In the books, Pa is always the one who insists on uprooting the family and moving on. The child's view is that Ma calmly accepts these constant upheavals, which sometimes endanger the family and leave them financially insecure. An adult reader is impressed by her fortitude.

The reader also gains a sense of the mother's heavy workload through the child's eyes. The children, who were instructed to stay close to the house, assisted their mother with her many chores, most of which concerned basic survival: preserving foods and providing meals. Ma had apparently come from a wealthier family than her husband's: "Ma had been very fashionable, before she married Pa, and a dressmaker had made her clothes."[25] The primary symbol of Ma's gentility, though, was that china figurine that traveled everywhere the family did. It was the only purely decorative item in their houses, but its importance went far beyond mere decoration. In her married life, Ma worked constantly. Besides schooling her girls in proper behavior, she spent most of the day in the kitchen, consumed with cleanliness and food production, or in the yard, doing the laundry. Her work was unrelenting.

The theme of self-reliance also haunts these books. Ma and Pa manage to forge a life for themselves and their children, combining nature's bounty with their own hard work. This aspect was perhaps most influenced by Wilder's daughter, Rose Wilder Lane, who, through her editing, emphasized individualism and freedom. Writing in the depths of the Depression, Wilder opposed government handouts and tended to amplify the self-reliant story. Wilder and Lane often excluded government aid and even wage work from the narrative. The government does not fare well in the books, first by refusing to secure the Indian Territory for white settlers and later by setting up a homesteading system that was destined to fail.[26]

The *Little House* books introduced American children to log cabins. Television shows and movies also familiarized children with log cabins, particularly in the heyday of the western—the 1950s and 1960s. But the *Little House* books endure, along with their visual impact. The original books were illustrated by Helen Sewell and Mildred Boyle, but Harper and Bros. hired Garth Williams to illustrate a new uniform edition that appeared in 1953. Williams, already a popular illustrator of children's literature, visited sites associated with the stories and consulted Wilder.[27] Williams's lyrical drawings continue to interpret Wilder's text for editions published today.

Little House aficionados can also visit the sites of the two log cabins, although neither survives. At both sites, local nonprofit organizations built reconstructions in the 1970s, once the TV show reintroduced a new generation to the books. Given the lack of specificity in the books, the reconstructions are highly inferential. The Little House in the Big Woods, near Pepin, Wisconsin, is a three-room house measuring about 21 by 19 feet, with partition walls of log (fig. 63). Although Wilder described the house as having two rooms, she also mentioned a pantry, but it is unclear where it was located; this reconstruction allocates a sizable room to it. Little House on the Prairie, near Independence, Kansas, is one room, measuring 13 by 16 feet, with its entrance in the gable end (fig. 64). The sawn flooring, shingle roof, and brick chimney do not reflect Laura's description, but the unpeeled irregular logs, messy chinking, dim lighting, and small size convey the feeling of the cabin recounted in Laura's tale. More important are the settings for these houses. While the Wisconsin house is no longer in the woods, and the Kansas house is close to a paved road, their distance from major urban centers and highways helps evoke the remoteness that once impressed Laura.

Although the Ingallses lived in a variety of house types, the log cabins most accord with the theme of self-reliance. Pa builds a log cabin, all by himself (almost),

Figure 63. Little House in the Big Woods, Pepin, Wisconsin. The 1970s reconstruction sits on land that is no longer heavily wooded. Instead, fields stretch out in all directions. (Photograph by the author, 2014)

Figure 64. Little House on the Prairie, Independence, Kansas. Also a 1970s reconstruction, this cabin is considerably smaller and more roughly built than the one in Wisconsin. (Photograph by the author, 2015)

even without nails (almost). That action is the ultimate in self-reliance, a symbol of the ability to provide for oneself and one's family. Living in the log cabin, though, reveals the flip side of this independence—the woman's task of homemaking encounters the difficulty of establishing a genteel way of life beyond the reach of civilizing influences and material goods.

WINNING THE WEST

Theodore Roosevelt, a famously gregarious New Yorker, might be an odd choice to exemplify log cabins in the wilderness, but his experience was emblematic in many ways (fig. 65). Roosevelt saw in his life on the western frontier a direct connection to pioneers of the eighteenth century in the East. While acknowledging broad differences between "the life of a cattleman on the Great Plains and among the Rockies" with that "led by a backwoodsman in the Alleghany forests a century before," he also highlighted the similarities: "We guarded our herds of branded cattle and shaggy horses, hunted bear, bison, elk, and deer, established civil government, and put down evil-doers, white and red, on the banks of the Little Missouri and among the wooded, precipitous foot-hills of the Bighorn exactly as did the pioneers who a hundred years previously built their log-cabins beside the Kentucky or in the valleys of the Great Smokies. The men who have shared in the fast vanishing frontier life of the present feel a peculiar sympathy with the already long-vanished frontier life of the past."[28] Roosevelt's four-volume *The Winning of the West* celebrated the role of the frontiersmen in bringing civilization to the continent while beating back savages. He proudly claimed the title of frontiersman for himself.

Roosevelt was a twenty-four-year-old New York State assemblyman when he headed out to the Dakota Territory on a two-week hunting trip in September 1883. He hired Joe Ferris as his guide and spent a few nights at Chimney Butte Ranch, owned by Ferris, his brother, Sylvane, and their partner, William Merrifield. Taken with the raw beauty of the landscape and the ranching way of life, Roosevelt bought into the ranch and renamed it Maltese Cross, based on its cattle brand. The one-room ranch house, which he described as "a log structure with a dirt roof," was a low-roofed stockaded building constructed of vertical logs.[29] Before Roosevelt returned the next year, after the death of his wife, Alice, in childbirth, Sylvane Ferris had built him a new house (fig. 66).

Figure 65. Theodore Roosevelt in buckskins. Roosevelt dressed the part while hunting and ranching in North Dakota. (George Grantham Bain, photographer, 1885, Library of Congress)

Figure 66. Maltese Cross Cabin, Medora, North Dakota. Roosevelt had this cabin built for himself in 1884. (Roosevelt 560.14-062 olvwork421096, Houghton Library, Harvard University)

Like its predecessor, the new Maltese Cross Ranch house was built of a rare commodity: logs. In the sparsely wooded Badlands of western North Dakota, cottonwood trees growing along streams were usually the best option for construction. Instead, for this house, Ferris collected Ponderosa pine logs that had been stranded along the Little Missouri River when contractors for the Northern Pacific Railroad had tried to float them downstream. The contractors had cut them as far as two hundred miles away.[30] Ferris hewed the logs square and joined them with rough saddle notching. He built an uncharacteristic, steeply pitched roof covered with cedar shingles; local tradition preferred a flatter roof covered with dirt and scoria, a volcanic rock found in the region.

As basic as this cabin appears, it was grander than most ranch cabins. On the first floor, the house had three whitewashed rooms: living room, kitchen, and bedroom. The attic space served as a sleeping area for employees. The glass windows, flooring, division into rooms, and whitewashing made this 25 by 18–foot

Figure 67. Elkhorn Ranch, north of Medora, North Dakota. In 1885 Roosevelt had this log cabin built for himself in a more remote location. He wrote fondly of the rocking chairs on the front porch. (Roosevelt 560.14-062 olvwork421096, Houghton Library, Harvard University)

cabin exceptionally civilized. By contrast, the original ranch house on the site had contained one room with three bunks. In this new cabin, Roosevelt had his own bedroom.

While running the cattle operation and helping the more skilled cowboys on the ranch, Roosevelt was also writing a book. The Maltese Cross Ranch was just seven miles south of the boomtown of Medora, and the traffic past his door annoyed someone who sought solitude. Accordingly, Roosevelt bought a new ranch some forty miles north of the Maltese Cross. He brought out two woodsmen whom he knew from Maine, William Sewall and Wilmot Dow, to partner with him, and during the winter of 1884–85 they built him a new cabin on the ranch they called the Elkhorn (fig. 67).

The Elkhorn Ranch house was much larger than the Maltese Cross, measuring 30 by 60 feet, with a hallway down the middle. Sewall and Dow built it of cottonwood logs, hewn square and half-dovetailed at the corners. They reused pine boards from the ghost town of Little Missouri, fifty miles away. The house had eight rooms and a porch on the front. Roosevelt described it as "a long, low ranch house of hewn logs, with a veranda, and with, in addition to the other rooms, a bedroom for myself, and a sitting-room with a big fire-place. I got out a rocking-chair—I am very fond of rocking-chairs—and enough books to fill two or three shelves, and a rubber bathtub so that I could get a bath. And then I do not see how any one could have lived more comfortably."[31]

Roosevelt traveled back and forth between his Dakota ranches and houses in Albany, New York City, and Oyster Bay, Long Island. He remarried in late 1886 and toured Europe with his new wife, Edith. The exceptionally hard winter of 1886–87 killed as many as three-quarters of his cattle, after which his ranch visits became infrequent. By the end of the century he had sold both ranches. Although his western sojourns lasted only a few years, they affected him deeply. He also used them to sell books, polish his persona, and hone his credentials for public office.

Roosevelt published three books about his experiences. *Hunting Trips of a Ranchman* (1885), *Ranch Life and the Hunting-Trail* (1888), and *The Wilderness Hunter* (1893) celebrate ranch life and hunting. The first describes the Elkhorn Ranch house tersely: "the story-high house of hewn logs is clean and neat, with many rooms." But life on the front porch he recounts elegiacally: "The low, long veranda is a pleasant place in the summer evenings when a cool breeze stirs along the river and blows in the faces of the tired men, who loll back in their rocking-chairs (what true American does not enjoy a rocking-chair?), book in hand—though they do not often read the books, but rock gently to and fro, gazing sleepily out at the weird-looking buttes opposite, until their sharp outlines grow indistinct and purple in the after-glow of the sunset." The interior harbors a haven of masculinity, replete with guns and animal parts: "The rifles stand in the corners of the room or rest across the elk antlers which jut out from over the fireplace. From the deer horns ranged along the walls and thrust into the beams and rafters hang heavy overcoats of wolf-skin or coon-skin, and otter-fur or beaver-fur caps and gauntlets."[32]

For Roosevelt, the life of the ranchman was elemental and liberating: "Civilization seems as remote as if we were living in an age long past. The whole existence is patriarchal in character: it is the life of men who live in the open who tend their herds on horseback, who go armed and ready to guard their lives by their own prowess, whose wants are very simple, and who call no man master." Roosevelt claimed that he usually hunted out of necessity, not for sport, and noted that the wilderness hunter should demonstrate "the qualities of hardihood, self-reliance, and resolution needed for effectively grappling with his wild surroundings." As he introduced himself in his third book, *The Wilderness Hunter,* "For a number of years much of my life was spent either in the wilderness or on the borders of the settled country—if, indeed, 'settled' is a term that can rightly be applied to the vast, scantily peopled regions where cattle-ranching is the only regular industry."[33] In each book he mentioned the log building he inhabited, helping to establish his bonafides.

Whether Roosevelt's sojourns as a ranchman were a calculated political ploy or a sincere effort to regain his physical and mental health, there is no doubt that they changed him. Asthmatic and sickly as a child, he took up boxing and taxidermy as manly endeavors. His scientific interest in the natural world lasted through his lifetime and crossed easily into an interest in hunting. Because of his thick spectacles and high-pitched voice, critics perceived him as effeminate as he entered political life. His expeditions in the West, publicized in his books, counteracted that perception. Yet as fond as he was of publicity, his enthusiasm for "cowboy land," as he termed it, was genuine. His fellow ranchmen admired his perseverance and tenacity as well as his unmitigated joy in the great outdoors. Further, he went west when he was feeling ill, and especially when mourning his first wife; in the clear air and wide-open spaces he regained not only his composure, but also his natural ebullience.

Roosevelt used another log cabin to promote his ideals more directly. On May 15, 1893, he was on hand to dedicate the Hunter's Cabin at the World's Columbian Exposition in Chicago (fig. 68). That cabin, built of round logs saddle-notched at the corners, with a log chimney on one end, was a project of the Daniel Boone and Davy Crockett Club, established in 1888 by Roosevelt and George Bird Grinnell, a naturalist, editor of *Forest and Stream,* and founder of the Audubon Society. Founded as a hunting club with Roosevelt as its president for its first six years, the Boone and Crockett Club rapidly became a conservation organization. Its membership, a group of well-connected New York hunters, forged an organization exceptionally effective at what it eventually determined to do: ensure legal protections for vast swaths of wilderness.[34] Roosevelt's experience in the West framed his interest in conservation issues and influenced the club's move toward these issues as well.

The descriptions of the Hunter's Cabin at the Fair do not indicate that the club

Figure 68. Hunter's Cabin, World's Columbian Exposition, Chicago, Illinois. Roosevelt supported the exhibit of a log cabin at the Chicago's World's Fair in 1893. (*The Dream City: A Portfolio of Photographic Views of the World's Columbian Exposition* [St. Louis: N. D. Thompson Publishing Co., 1893])

highlighted the conservationist message, however. Instead, it presented the cabin as "a museum and memorial in honor of Daniel Boone and Davy Crockett." Nostalgia seems to have been its greatest virtue: "On chilly days a fire blazed in the broad fireplace, and in that regard the interior exactly resembled the houses of pioneers in timbered regions forty years ago. . . . The skins of wild animals covered the floor, and beds and settees were made of stretched skins." Like many of the anthropological exhibits at the fair, which were staffed by natives, this cabin had its own frontiersman living there: "a hunter in long hair and wide-brimmed felt hat," who answered the questions of curious fair-goers. Apparently a history-loving public received the cabin well: "There was a charm about the premises, pioneers loving to recall the vanished days, and younger inquirers seeming pleased to see before them the picture so often drawn in the tales of their grandsires and this chapter of their romances."[35]

The focus on the romance of the frontier, as exemplified by the Hunter's Cabin as well as in the naming of the Boone and Crockett Club, illustrates another aspect of Roosevelt's fascination with the West. His three volumes about his North Dakota experiences highlighted the romance of his western sojourn. He saw direct links in his own life to his heroes, frontiersmen such as Daniel Boone and Davy Crockett.[36]

Roosevelt's romantic view of the frontier also surfaced in his political actions. Believing that the success of democracy depended on expansion, and that the closing of the frontier thus threatened the nation, Roosevelt sought foreign markets and endorsed international expansion once he became president in 1901. During the eight years of his presidency, Roosevelt also confronted the trusts, instituted the first consumer protection legislation, and waged war in the Philippines. His conservationist record is stunning: during his presidency, he created or enlarged 150 national forests; he also created 51 bird reservations, 4 national game preserves, 6 national parks, and 18 national monuments.[37] Most of all, he elevated the presidency and made his character as important as his policies.

Small wonder, then, that attention focused on the cabin in North Dakota that had helped launch his career. Although the cabin at Elkhorn Ranch had not survived long after his ownership, Roosevelt had sold the Maltese Cross Cabin to Sylvane Ferris, one of his partners, who sold it to J. F. Snyder. Snyder changed the high roof to a low-pitched one covered with dirt and scoria. In 1903 the State of North Dakota bought the cabin from Snyder and sent it on a journey reminiscent of the travels that Lincoln's cabins took. Workers dismantled the cabin and transported it to the World's Fair in St. Louis, where they erected it in 1904 as part of the North Dakota section in the Palace of Agriculture.[38] When Roosevelt visited the cabin there, surely it occurred to him that just eleven years earlier he had provided a cabin to the world's fair that reflected his views of the past; now a portion of his own life was on display. He had gone from promoter of the West to an emblem of it.

North Dakota officials also sent the cabin to the Lewis and Clark Exposition in Portland, Oregon, in 1905. In 1906 it returned to North Dakota, first to Fargo, where the Children's Home Society exhibited it at the State Fair Grounds for two years. Although workers had carefully documented the logs before dismantling the cabin, by the time of the cabin's 1906 erection some logs were missing. In 1908 the cabin moved to the Capitol grounds in Bismarck, but it received little care and deteriorated rapidly. In 1919 a newly organized chapter of the Daughters of the American Revolution took responsibility for it. The DAR moved it to another site on the Capitol grounds, replaced the dirt roof with cedar shingles, furnished it, and opened it to the public.[39]

The centennial of Roosevelt's birth in 1958 inspired the National Park Service to assume ownership. The Park Service moved the cabin intact to Medora, about seven miles from its original site, then dismantled it to repair the logs. The Park Service rebuilt the cabin with the high-pitched roof it had had when Roosevelt occupied it. The U.S. government had created Theodore Roosevelt National Memorial Park in 1947 after several decades of advocacy and study.[40] Today, the seventy-thousand-acre national park offers the spectacular geology of the Badlands and wildlife viewing opportunities, as well as the tangible link with the "Conservationist President" through his log cabin.

Although detached from its original ranch context, and much altered through the years, the cabin adds a human and historical element to this vast national park. It also serves as an important element to the lively biography of Theodore Roosevelt. Biographers have found that his ranch experience helped form his ideas on American character and purpose and contributed to his success. Even Roosevelt himself said, "If it had not been for my years in North Dakota, I never would have become President of the United States."[41] His log cabin reminds visitors that Roosevelt's experience in the wilderness was not theoretical; it was as tangible to him as his cabin is to tourists.

ALONE IN THE WILDERNESS

In post–World War II America, the opportunities to confront the wilderness and exercise self-reliance on an ongoing basis are rare, but the fourth writer considered in this chapter is someone who sought those challenges and met them. Richard Proenneke may not be a household name, but for someone whose greatest claim to fame is that he went off alone and built himself a log cabin in the wilderness, he is widely known. A film, *Alone in the Wilderness,* broadcast frequently on PBS, has brought him and his story into the homes of many. The film is based on a book, *One Man's Wilderness,* which has gained wide readership.[42] Proenneke's own voice and persona resonate through these works, because the book is based on his daily journals, documenting his life in the wilds of Alaska, and the film employs footage that he took of himself while constructing his cabin in 1968.

Located on the shore of Twin Lakes, about 125 miles west of Anchorage, Proenneke's cabin is far beyond the road system, accessible only by float plane or by a very determined hiker. Proenneke was born in Iowa in 1916 and served in the U.S.

Navy during World War II. He first came to Alaska in 1949 and, among other jobs, worked as a diesel mechanic at the Kodiak Naval Station. He first visited Twin Lakes in 1962, when his friends Spike and Hope Carrithers built a cabin there on public land administered by the Bureau of Land Management. At the age of fifty, Proenneke built his own cabin nearby in 1967–68 and stayed for thirty years. In some winters he returned to Iowa to see his parents, but by the 1980s he stayed through the winters. In 1998, he moved to California to live with his brother, dying there five years later.[43]

Mountains surround Twin Lakes on all sides; the northernmost reach of the Aleutian Islands and the southernmost extension of the Alaska Range meet in the Chigmit Mountains. The two lakes, neither more than a mile wide, are about five and seven miles long, joined by a short portage. Although Twin Lakes sit at an elevation of 2,000 feet, they nestle in mountains that rise to 10,000 feet. The lakes are crystal clear, and the setting is spectacular. The natural beauty as well as the abundant wildlife attracted Proenneke. He filmed wildlife assiduously and produced shows in the winter for his friends back in Iowa. Grizzly bears, Dall sheep, moose, and caribou all received his attention, as well as smaller creatures such as squirrels and birds. After his first year, he stopped actively hunting, preferring to watch animals rather than kill them.[44]

Proenneke's human company at Twin Lakes included sport hunters and their guides, who stayed in their various cabins around the lake only briefly. Proenneke's main contact with the outside world was the bush pilot Leon "Babe" Alsworth, who brought in food, supplies, and mail on a regular basis. Most of the time, though, Proenneke was alone, and this formed the core of his experience.

For someone alone in a remote area, survival takes on a new dimension. Food was not a problem for Proenneke, although at times he anticipated Alsworth's delivery eagerly. Shelter assumed a greater importance, especially when Proenneke resolved to construct his own cabin using only hand tools. The choice of a log cabin was not surprising, given its predominance in the Alaska bush. It is also an ideal building for a true craftsman, because every part of the structure is visible. His mechanical aptitude was evident before he began construction, but the finished product shows his supreme carpentry skills. Proenneke did not just build a cabin on his own; he crafted it extremely well. The logs fit together snugly, the roof was tidy and weatherproof, and the interior was orderly. In perfect harmony with its setting, the cabin was a thing of beauty.

The journals and film emphasize process, and this accounts for their attraction; they give the reader the feeling that he or she could do this too. The seeming simplicity of a log cabin leads one to believe that anyone could build one. Proenneke's journals encourage this view, describing his ability to work through every obstacle, but they underplay the difficulties—first, the physical strain of hauling logs, poles, gravel, sand, and rocks to the site and, second, the craftsmanship necessary to get a crooked, tapered log to fit, or to make a wooden hinge. The description of the process fascinates anyone who has ever thought of building a log cabin.

In the summer of 1967, Proenneke selected a site a quarter mile from the Caritherses, near Hope Creek on the south shore of Upper Twin Lake. He cleared a tree—as he wrote, "A tree stood where the cabin should be"—then hauled thirty buckets of gravel from the lakeshore and created a pad about 20 by 20 feet. His other task that summer was to fell white spruce trees, de-limb them, debark them, and haul them to his cabin site: "I picked trees about eight inches or a bit more at the butt. Chop them down—just as fast as the Swede saw [bow saw] and easier. I sliced a ribbon of bark from the top of the log and then loosened it a bit along the edges with the axe. I had taken a dead spruce sapling about two inches through and sharpened it to a chisel point. With this I got between the bark and the log and was surprised how easy and clean the bark came off. Sometimes the bark full length of the log would come off in one big sheet. In about 30 minutes I could cut, limb and peel a 26 footer." Although he originally intended to wait until his brother arrived later in the summer to help him move the logs, he grew impatient. He skidded his fifty logs three hundred yards to his cabin site, making as slick a path as he could.[45] There he left them to season for the winter.

Proenneke had a rough idea of the design of his cabin before obtaining the logs, but it was not until a couple of days later that he put pen to paper: "Worked on a floor plan for the cabin. I think the best I can do is 12' x 16'. A door and four windows. One at least two by three feet. I don't like to leave the door open to get enough light. A fireplace would be no problem. Sand is close and so is plenty of rock the right size. Double deck bunks to save space. Stove out where you can walk around it. A good roof. I like moss which is good insulation but a fire hazard in early spring. Cedar shingles would be second choice. . . . It is interesting to think and plan what one can do with nothing but a few tools."[46]

When Proenneke returned to Twin Lakes the following May, he began first by sharpening his tools and making wooden handles for his auger, chisel, and files.

Then he started work on the walls. He hewed crooked logs straight but left them in the round. He also coped with the taper of each log, reversing them every course. As he noted, "The black spruce works real nice with axe and draw knife. Next, two end logs and the notches marked. I plan to make it eleven foot by fifteen foot on the inside." He saddle-notched the corners, using a marker that he had made out of spruce: "They are nothing more than a pair of dividers with a pencil on one leg." He recounted his technique for making the notches: "Rough out the notch with saw and axe then finish it in short order with the chisel." By the time Proenneke got to the eave logs, he was working over his head. This is where help is usually desirable, but Proenneke managed the task alone by resting one end of the eave log on the projecting logs at the corner, and then lifting the other end.[47]

The eave logs, purlins, and ridge pole were all twenty feet long, not sixteen, because Proenneke extended the roof past the front of his cabin to create a covered area. The framework of the roof consisted of these members, which rested on gable logs that decreased in length as they went up. On June 6, with the walls and roof structure completed, he assessed his progress: "Ten days from the time I cut the first notch. I do need window and door frames and roof poles if I can find some. My logs came out just right. Only four full length leftover and only one of them was a halfway decent log."[48]

For window and door frames, Proenneke split boards 1¾ inches thick, which he smoothed with a draw knife. To make boards for the door, window ledges, and shelves, he used a rip saw. He chinked the cabin with moss and oakum, a tarred fiber used for caulking: "I used straight oakum in the narrow seams and the mixture of oakum and moss where the opening was more than quarter inch." The floor required no construction; the gravel pad sufficed until 1979, when Proenneke added carpeting.[49]

Proenneke designed a modern variation of a traditional roof, which had poles extending from ridgepole to eave log, tightly packed, and covered with a layer of moss. Because Proenneke covered his roof poles with tarpaper and plastic, he could space them out a bit (plate 8). The gathering and debarking of the one hundred poles was laborious and provoked one of the few complaints in his journal: "Seems a pole roof takes a lot of time but then there is a lot of work involved and all of it slow." He then covered the poles with tarpaper and a layer of polyethylene—some of the few materials that were not indigenous. He cut moss in chunks 18 inches by

36 inches by 8 inches thick, then hauled them in a carrying rack that he made. The roof required more moss than he expected: "Man, I have cleared two acres of moss it seems and yet it isn't covered." But once the moss was in place, he was pleased: "She is really looking up now. The roof helped more than any one thing to finish it off."[50] He then laid poles on top to hold the moss in place until it grew together.

Proenneke fashioned strap hinges out of wood, inventing as he went along. As he noted, "I was anxious to try this business of making hinges." He had a model, of a sort—"Frank Bell had made some for his cabin but they were very crude"—but his extensive discussion of them in his journal indicated his meticulous attention to detail. Once the hinges were made, hanging the doors tested his expertise: "Now the door. I checked and rechecked my hinges to see that they were in line. I put the door in the opening and fastened the top and bottom hinge. Swings good but squeaks a bit—some soap will fix that. Now, No. 2 & 3 hinge. Close together and they have to be on the money. No. 3 wasn't quite good enough, so I pried it off and planed on the seating surface a bit. Not quite enough, so I gave it more. Give it a try. So I daubed on some glue and nailed it fast. The door still worked good with all four hinges secure." Then, still concerned, he cut the door in half to create a Dutch door. As he noted, "If I haven't been accurate enough with my work it will look like a sloppy job except when closed." He took the door off the hinges, cut it nearly through, then rehung it and finished the cut. "I swung it back and was real happy. It wasn't perfect but very close. Plenty close for rural work. Now I had a Dutch door and a real cute looking door at that. With soap on the joints and pins it is entirely silent. Works just as nice as a door on a bank vault."[51]

The stone fireplace and chimney provided another challenge. He did not need a fireplace—he already had a stove and stovepipe—but it was something that he knew would add beauty to the cabin. Proenneke did not often articulate his desire for a beautiful end product, but implied it in his craftsmanship. On occasion he added finishing touches that were not entirely necessary, such as a half pole to cover the ends of his roof poles. As he explained, "Something had been bothering me. Those roof pole ends on the cabin didn't look very professional. Why not rip one of my twenty foot poles from Lofstedt's and put half on each side to cover the ends so—I ripped her and it didn't take so long. Just what the doctor ordered. They helped the looks of the cabin 100%." He could also be disparaging about other cabins, describing a neighbor's cabin: "A chainsaw cabin and not much for workmanship. If it is called completed, it is a sorry job of building."[52] One thing that he liked about that cabin, though, was its finishing coat of polyurethane, which he put on his own cabin.

He started gathering rocks for the fireplace and chimney in the fall of 1967. A year later, somewhat reluctantly, he cut into the end wall to create a fireplace: "I wouldn't cut that hole too high until I found out how this rock laying is going to go. I took out the bottom two logs. Plenty room to lay the base." That seemed to work, so two days later he enlarged the opening: "Today was the day. Cut the other five logs out and let the sunshine in." He mixed cement with sand and water to create a mortar, devised a form for the arch over the fireplace, and made a collapsible form for the chimney. Proenneke carefully selected the keystone, and it is clear that the appearance of the stonework mattered. When he finished it, he wrote: "Say! That fireplace makes the rear of the cabin as attractive as the front which I have favored in all my pictures"[53] (plate 9).

Proenneke made all the furniture for the cabin: a double bunk, tables, chairs, shelves, cabinet. He also fashioned pots and pans out of gas cans and carved serving utensils out of wood. He built a 12 by 8–foot combination woodshed and privy in 1968 and cut logs for a cache to season over the winter. The cache, an elevated structure common in Alaska, keeps food out of the reach of bears and other animals. In the spring of 1969 Proenneke built his 6 by 4–foot cache of saddle-notched logs, much like his cabin, on the ground. He then dismantled it and reerected it 9 feet off the ground on posts, finishing it with a pole-and-moss roof and a strap-hinged door.

Like most daily journals, Proenneke's explains the *what* and *how* better than the *why*. Besides keeping up extensive correspondence, he wrote in his journal every night, sometimes a thousand words a day. Proenneke's first audience for the journals was Helen White, a friend in Anchorage to whom he sent each notebook as he completed it. The journals then circulated among a small group of friends, but it was Sam Keith's book based on his journals that garnered a broad readership. Keith, a Massachusetts school teacher and administrator, had known Proenneke since 1952 when they both worked at Kodiak. He visited Proenneke at Twin Lakes in 1970 and, impressed by what he saw, borrowed the journals. His book, *One Man's Wilderness,* written as if they were Proenneke's journals, paraphrased them and also included material not in the journals, somewhat to Proenneke's dismay.[54] In turn, the film produced by Bob Swerer drew more on Keith's book than on the original journals. Narrated by Swerer speaking Proenneke's words (or Keith's interpretations of them), the film echoes the viewpoint of Keith's book, with the same narrative arc following Proenneke's first year at Twin Lakes.

Although Proenneke never explained in his journals what drew him to build a log cabin on Twin Lakes, Keith put together a plausible explanation. The attraction of the place was clear: "It was good to be back in the wilderness again where everything seems at peace. I was alone. It was a great feeling—a stirring feeling. Free once more to plan and do as I pleased." Keith interpreted the adventure as a test: "I suppose I was here because this was something I had to do. Not just dream about it but do it. I suppose, too, I was here to test myself. . . . What was I capable of that I didn't know yet? What about my limits? Could I truly enjoy my own company for an entire year? Was I equal to everything this wild land could throw at me? I had seen its moods in late spring, summer, and early fall, but what about winter? Would I love the isolation then, with its bone-stabbing cold, its brooding ghostly silence, its forced confinement? At age fifty-one I intended to find out."[55]

Proenneke's journals do not demonstrate this kind of introspection. When he returned to Twin Lakes in May 1969, he noted only: "It was good to be back in the wilderness which always seems to be at peace with the world." In 1990 Proenneke observed that the longest period he had been alone, without seeing another human being, was ten weeks. But he stated it as fact and did not delve into his feelings about the solitude. When Keith's journal entry went on to contemplate the "how and when of projects"—"Could I really build the cabin with just hand tools to the standards I had set in my mind?"—it sounded much more like Proenneke, whose mind immediately turned to the means of accomplishing a task.[56] Proenneke's plainspokenness and directness, which Keith also captured, added to the appeal of the book.

Keith wrote: "The most exciting part of the whole adventure was putting self-reliance on trial."[57] The idea of self-reliance, borne out in a harsh climate by a solitary man, witnessed through journals and film, probably accounts for the popularity of Keith's book and Swerer's film. Many people like to believe that they are capable of such strength of character, and it is unknown how many headed off to the wilderness, *One Man's Wilderness* in hand, to test themselves. More likely, most readers just dreamed about it. But the popularity of the book also meant that Proenneke became something of a folk hero, attracting visitors even to his remote cabin site—and thereby making it a bit less remote.

Figure 69. Richard Proenneke Cabin, Twin Lakes, Alaska. Recently delivered groceries sit outside this meticulously crafted cabin. (Photograph by the author, 1982)

In 1980 the U.S. government created several new national parks in Alaska as part of a long-simmering settlement of Alaska Natives' land claims. Lake Clark National Park and Preserve surrounded Proenneke's homestead. The parks proved controversial within Alaska, stirring up fears among some inhabitants that the federal government was "locking up the land," not leaving it open for homesteading, hunting, and other uses. Proenneke, as the face of Alaskan wilderness to the Outside, implicitly helped make the case for the importance of these lands to the American public. He also actively supported the park, working with park staff and volunteering for various projects. In 1978, as the national park debate was raging, he appeared on PBS in a Nova show about Alaska, arguing for the preservation of Twin Lakes. His dislike of commercial hunters and his affinity with people who trod lightly on the land—the kind of people who would be attracted by a national park—contributed to his support of the park. In 1998, after he left his cabin for the last time, he donated it to the National Park Service.[58]

Proenneke's cabin is not easy to reach. From Anchorage, a visitor flies 170 miles through Lake Clark Pass to Port Alsworth, then takes a float plane 35 miles north to Twin Lakes. Nonetheless, Proenneke's cabin received about seven hundred visitors in 2012, more than double the number of ten years previously. At this pilgrimage site for aficionados of the book and film, grown men cry when they see the cabin. The National Park Service has maintained the cabin with a light touch (fig. 69).[59] In summers, park volunteers live near the cabin to host visitors.

Although both the book and film use "wilderness" in their titles, and both open with Proenneke's return to his remote site, wilderness in the abstract did not interest him. The raw physical beauty of the place and the wildlife clearly enchanted him, but he also noted every plane that flew into Twin Lakes and speculated on people's comings and goings. He valued good company, either in person or through letters. He observed wildlife, described dramatic geologic features, and tracked the weather. Proenneke spent less time worrying about the wildness of his place than with appreciating his front seat at nature's splendor. His log cabin enabled his engagement with his Twin Lakes wilderness and also served as his well-considered and carefully crafted contribution to the place.

The masculine view of log cabins that Teddy Roosevelt and Richard Proenneke described—living an independent lifestyle amid great natural beauty—plays into Americans' romantic view of log cabins. The reality of making a home in such a place, as evoked by Caroline Kirkland and Laura Ingalls Wilder, receives less attention in the public imagination. But it would not be a romance if it did not ignore harsh realities. The log cabin of the imagination relies on a preference for independence and remote locations.

5

TWENTIETH-CENTURY LEISURE

When a Log Cabin Is Not a Log Cabin

By the early twentieth century, log cabins had become unusual enough to an increasingly urbanized nation that they began to be used in noncabin functions. While in the nineteenth century and earlier log construction had served for buildings other than cabins—such as barns, schools, churches, and stores—this new incarnation was different. Earlier, log construction was used for all kinds of buildings because it was expedient and inexpensive, but the leisure-related log construction harkened back to the log cabin in a deliberate reference to America's past. The log cabins of the nineteenth century might have been used to symbolize independence, resourcefulness, or compatibility with nature, but in leisure settings they were used to connote a departure from the norm, even as they served as homages to the old values. Restaurants, gift shops, antique shops, and clubhouses traded on the image of the log cabin—not the log store or log church—to impart associations to history. Log cabins were popular, not as icons of the builder's resilience and independence, but as an eye-catching departure from the norm.

Several concurrent societal shifts helped spur the new popularity of log cabins. The growth of the middle class contributed to an increase in tourism, aided by two factors: the automobile and the vacation. Ownership of motorcars rose from 0.5 million in 1910 to more than 8 million in 1920 to 26.5 million in 1929, and the declining cost of the automobile meant that middle-class Americans were more likely to be able to afford one. The automobile established new patterns for tourism, freeing the traveler from the confines of railroad lines. At the same time, vacations, which had been rare events for the middle class in the nineteenth century, became more common, giving tourists the time to motor to destinations.[1] The shrinking work week also provided leisure time, maybe for an afternoon in the country or a trip to a local historic site.

As vacationers ventured forth, they carried with them new attitudes toward log cabins. By the twentieth century, the presence of log cabins on the American landscape was diminishing. This ordinary building, once the norm throughout rural America, had become exceptional due to its relative scarcity. Although still serving as primary residences, especially in remote areas where they were practical and even optimal, log cabins were increasingly alien to many Americans. Log cabins also conveyed informality to the burgeoning middle class, which made cabins ideal for club members or vacationers. Log cabins became a shorthand image for "old"—a generalized antiquity that could mean colonial times or just a few decades earlier—and sometimes for "the West," a vaguely defined area. In these latter connotations, the log cabin was not of the same time or place as the viewer. All of these qualities, applied to the log cabin, made it appropriate for noncabin uses in which conspicuousness and attraction were desirable, such as restaurants, gift shops, visitors centers, and clubhouses.

As log cabins found new uses in the early twentieth century, the log quality changed as well. Expedient ways of simulating log construction, such as half logs nailed onto wood frames, and less skilled methods of notching, such as square notching, became more popular. And when whole logs were used in commercial applications, they were more often big, round, and saddle-notched—the most obvious kind of log construction.

This chapter begins with a discussion of the architectural trends that were making log cabins acceptable, or even of interest, to the architectural establishment. The discussion then turns to two forms of log noncabins—roadside establishments and clubhouses. The next chapter also looks at leisure uses, specifically second homes and vacation lodging. Chapter 7 explores yet another type of destination—parks and forests—rounding out this examination of log cabins as buildings for leisure.

Much of the log cabin's newfound popularity in the late nineteenth and early twentieth centuries was due to two movements that are identified with architectural styles and extend into broader realms. The Colonial Revival and the Arts and Crafts movements framed Americans' understanding of historical styles in this period. In a way, these two movements intersected at the log cabin: the Colonial Revival's promotion of the past and the Arts and Crafts' elevation of the handcrafted. For both, the log cabin functioned as an extraordinary building, conspicuous in its reference to the preindustrial past.

The Centennial Exposition held in Philadelphia in 1876 was a catalyst for the Colonial Revival movement. There the display of a New England kitchen caught the imagination of fairgoers. Known as the New England Farmer's Home and Modern Kitchen, the exhibit occupied two adjacent buildings (fig. 70). The "Farmer's Home" was a one-story log cabin constructed of round logs with the bark still on and a porch across the front. Logs with knots and branches supported a hood over the entryway for an additional rustic effect.

The use of logs for this building was somewhat incongruous, given New England's lack of historical experience with the log cabin, but apparently by 1876 the identification of the English colonial experience in America with the log cabin was complete. Although there were detractors, including one who thought the log cabin looked more like Ohio than New England, in general the claim that it was made "in exact imitation of the country dwellings of a hundred years ago" convinced fairgoers. As one guidebook reported, it was "built and arranged in the style of the New England Farm-houses of a century ago. It contains a parlor, or 'settin-room,' a kitchen, and bed-rooms, all of which are furnished with veritable heirlooms contributed by the people of New England." The guidebook found it to be a realistic reproduction, evocative of the moment the Minute Men left to join the Revolution, leaving the women behind. The account noted, "The farm-house is occupied only by ladies, who are dressed in the quaint costumes of their great-grandmothers, and who conduct visitors through the house and explain to them the story and uses of its contents." The contents were a treasure-trove of relics ranging from Pilgrim to Revolutionary times: John Alden's desk, the cradle used by a baby born on the *Mayflower,* a silver pitcher used by the Marquis de Lafayette in Boston, a four-hundred-year-old clock, and so on. The adjacent "Modern

Figure 70. New England Farmer's Home and Modern Kitchen, Centennial Exposition, Philadelphia, Pennsylvania. In 1876 New Englanders exhibited a log building, in a reference to olden times. (Free Library, Philadelphia, PA, USA/Bridgeman Images)

Kitchen," a contemporary wood-frame stick-style building with striped awnings, offered traditional New England boiled dinners with baked beans, brown bread, and "old-fashioned puddings" served "in real old-fashioned style" daily from noon until 3:00.[2]

The New England Farmer's Home's broad interpretation of 1776—that it included Pilgrims and log cabins and baked beans—reflected an open mind toward the past. Anything with the "ripe flavor of antiquity" merited appreciation as Americans looked to their history.[3] Increasingly through the end of the nineteenth century and into the twentieth, architects drew inspiration from colonial dwellings, purveyors of furniture and decorative arts looked to the past, people famous in American history attracted more interest, and historic sites that could be related to the nation's founding became popular. Log cabins rode these trends. At the Columbian Exposition of 1893 in Chicago, at least eight log cabins were on view, including the Hunter's Cabin promoted by Theodore Roosevelt, discussed in the preceding chapter. The New England Kitchen idea was revived, and the New England Log Cabin—this time with shed-roofed dormers—was located on the Midway, adjacent to a barn-like structure advertising "Old Tyme Farmers

Dinners." Log cabins with associations with Abraham Lincoln and Sitting Bull attracted fairgoers, as well as the Idaho State Pavilion, a Michigan logging camp, and two exhibits by Kentucky distillers, all of which were log.[4]

One aspect of the Colonial Revival movement that the log cabin shared was an implied Anglo-Americanism. Restoration of grand English Colonial houses was a cornerstone of the Colonial Revival movement, and log cabins often played a role in these historic sites. The identification of the log cabin with English colonists had begun with rhetoric surrounding Harrison's 1840 campaign and became written into history with an 1841 description of the Pilgrims' settlement in Plymouth, Massachusetts, as log huts. By the time of the tercentenary of the Pilgrims' landing, celebrated in 1921, the idea was firmly fixed. Besides a pageant with a cast of thousands (which included a line about the Pilgrims' "houses of hewn trees") and a parade with a number of floats carrying log buildings representing sites of significant events, a log cabin built near the original landing site reminded visitors of the Pilgrims' first dwellings, as they were then understood. Frank M. Gregg, a banker in Cleveland, contracted with a local builder, Arthur Emond, to construct a building that he hoped would "duplicate the Common House which the Pilgrims built in 1620 when they first landed" (fig. 71). He cautioned his builder against making it too finished or fancy: "I do not want any finishing touches, I want it just as people would build it in the mid-Winter without many tools to do the job. . . . It was a rough crude affair as they did not have any time to give to appearances. The floor is to be dirt."[5]

By the early twentieth century the log cabin's identification with English colonists was so complete that the log cabin often signaled a reference to old-stock Anglo-Americans, who were the preferred clientele of many commercial establishments. Recent immigrants, such as Scandinavians who were establishing farmsteads with log cabins in the northern Midwest during this period, would not have seen the charm of a log tea room. Only those for whom the log cabin was out of the ordinary—middle- and upper-class urban dwellers—found it quaint and attractive, while flattering their supposed historical connection with the building type. In a society faced with an influx of immigrants, the Colonial Revival movement marshaled log cabins and other historical traditions to reinforce the Anglo-American elite.[6]

While the Colonial Revival awakened Americans' interest in the past, the Arts and Crafts movement directed their attention to the virtues of handcraft. The Arts

Figure 71. Log cabin, Plymouth, Massachusetts. At the 1921 tercentenary of the landing of the Pilgrims, a Cleveland banker financed the construction of a log cabin to represent their initial housing. (Plymouth Antiquarian Society)

and Crafts movement arose in Great Britain in the nineteenth century, where the work of John Ruskin, an architectural critic who argued for "truth" in architecture, gained followers. Ruskin's advocacy of honesty of expression in architecture, particularly in structure and materials, influenced the Arts and Crafts movement, which involved architecture, art, decorative arts, and politics. In the United States, followers of the movement were particularly interested in materials and their relationship to nature as an expression of truth. At a time when more and more items were produced by machines, the Arts and Crafts movement valued the handmade.

One of the best-known proponents of the Arts and Crafts movement in America was Gustav Stickley, a furniture maker who published the *Craftsman* magazine in the early twentieth century. Along with an esthetic of simple forms and handcrafted work, the magazine helped promote the bungalow, a low structure with porches and a tangible relationship to nature.[7] Stickley's insistence on exposed structure and closeness to nature also led him, inevitably, to the log cabin.

In 1907 an unsigned article in the *Craftsman* discussed the pluses and minuses of

Figure 72. Clubhouse, Craftsman Farms, Morristown, New Jersey. In 1911 Gustav Stickley built a log house for the new settlement he envisioned. Entrance is through the porch to the left, while the kitchen is in the lower portion on the right. (Photograph by the author, 2014)

log construction. Its advantages included picturesqueness, harmony with nature, and a sort of primitive memory: "All sorts of traditions and memories of adventure and heroism and the joy that comes from wrestling strongly with the forces of Nature on her own ground are associated with the log house." Drawbacks included the aptitude of logs to rot; the "crude clumsiness of construction" that often looked out of place among other forms of architecture; and the difficulty of bringing the interior into harmony with the exterior. Nonetheless, Stickley claimed to have solved these problems in the three designs he published in that issue of the magazine.[8] A few years later, Stickley began construction of a log building at the settlement he founded, Craftsman Farms, near Morristown, New Jersey (fig. 72). The design was initially for a clubhouse, or "general assembly house," with large spaces for gathering, but when it was completed Stickley moved in with his family and stayed for six years.

In a 1911 article in the *Craftsman,* Natalie Curtis waxed poetic about the Stickley log house, calling it "a log cabin idealized." She lauded the "instinctive feeling of kinship with the elemental world" that log buildings evoked, while also acknowledging their aesthetic appeal—"the bare beauty of the logs themselves with their long lines and firm curves" and the "open charm of the structural features." The

Figure 73. Detail of notching, Clubhouse, Craftsman Farms, Morristown, New Jersey. The logs, hewn to rustic effect, were not staggered. (Photograph by the author, 2014)

building's logs were from chestnut trees that had been harvested from the site and hewn on top and bottom for a tight fit (fig. 73). The building sat on a stone foundation, and wooden shingles covered the wood-frame second story. Stickley divided the main block of the building into three spaces, each extending the fifty-foot width of the structure: porch, living room, and dining room. The kitchen was in a rear ell. Set on a hillside, the low building with expansive roof nestled into nature, while the band of windows enclosing the wide front porch erased boundaries between indoors and out. Curtis concluded, "To the strength, the courage and the honest effort typified by the primitive log cabin, art has here added the grace of beauty, and science the requisites of comfort."[9]

The resurgence of log cabins in the early twentieth century was not always welcomed by the architectural establishment, however. In 1912 critic Montgomery Schuyler sniffed at the shift in the log cabin's role from "the most practical and utilitarian of all possible constructions to that of a mere toy." He admired the resourceful pioneer and saw the log cabin as the worthy product of his endeavor, but Schuyler disdained the log cabin built for leisure. This, in which "the dwelling be itself a toy," such as "in the Adirondacks and other still wooded regions in which rusticating citizens have built for themselves cottages or 'camps'" loosely based on the log cabin, did not qualify as serious architecture.[10] The log cabin's reputation as being outside the architectural canon only served to increase its allure as a building that was slightly exotic.

Even though exotic, the log cabin was definitely American. Despite their references to England, both the Colonial Revival and the Arts and Crafts movements claimed to promote a national style peculiarly suited to America. At the intersection of these two movements, the log cabin also had a claim on national pride. Natalie Curtis wrote: "Since the log house has played so important a part in our history its development into a definite and characteristic type of architecture might give us something national, something peculiarly American in suggestiveness."[11] With a long history in this country—and one that was identified with good, patriotic qualities of self-reliance and individualism—as well as an honest, unornamented appearance, the log cabin gained new proponents in the early twentieth century. It may not have been suitable for urban or suburban homes, but for Americans who took to the road in search of something a little out of the ordinary, it provided a worthy destination.

ON THE ROADSIDE

To serve the new touring population that emerged in the early twentieth century, new building types emerged, such as motels and informal restaurants. To attract tourists, visible and memorable designs proved to be effective. Needing a conspicuous construction to gain the attention of motorists, entrepreneurs used the very buildings that housed their businesses to advertise them. One of the most common images was that of a home, often sporting large chimneys, dormer windows, shutters, and expansive roofs.[12] And one of the most familiar such homes was a log cabin, which also had associations of history, rusticity, and the wilderness. Tea rooms, gift shops, visitor centers, and antique shops were some of the facilities that found particular resonance in log cabins.

The Colonial Revival connection to tea rooms is particularly clear at George Washington's birthplace, a plantation named Wakefield, on the Northern Neck of Virginia, where the 1930s reconstruction of the house in which Washington was born created the need for another building to serve visitors. This building was log. The Wakefield National Memorial Association, founded in 1923 by a collateral Washington descendant named Josephine Rust, hired architect Edward W. Donn Jr., known for his expertise with Colonial Revival architecture, to design the birthplace reconstruction. Donn provided drawings for a one-and-a-half story, center-hall brick house, although there was no evidence that Washington's family had lived in such an elaborate dwelling. The association arranged for the National Park Service to assume ownership and operation of the birthplace once construction was complete in 1931.[13]

Washington's birthplace was in a remote area, though, thirty-eight miles from the nearest city, Fredericksburg, Virginia, and ninety-five miles from Washington, DC. Realizing that visitors would need to be provided for, the association also planned a facility to provide light meals to tourists, as well as a few rooms for overnight lodging. At the association's request, in 1927 Donn designed this building—a log structure with gabled dormers, a porch across the front, and a picket fence. There were several explanations for its log construction. The association's first meeting in July 1923 noted that "a log cabin as emblematic of the first settlers" would be part of its construction program. Later, Josephine Rust explained that "a log house stood on this tract originally and we wish to build a similar structure, thus giving the spirit of the earlier period of American life as well as that of George Washington's boyhood."[14] Apparently she had in mind a seventeenth-century dwelling to contrast with the more finished early eighteenth-century house of Washington's childhood.

As built, the Log House embodied a number of contradictions (fig. 74). The first was its materials: although the walls appeared to be hewn logs, dovetailed at the corners, they were in fact a 6-inch thick veneer, laid against a stud frame with diagonal sheathing. At the windows and doors, round pegs, 1½ inches in diameter, were driven through the logs to attach them to the stud frame, and it is presumably this feature—highly visible pegs—that necessitated painting the building. Upon completion, the Log House was painted white. Secondly, the form of the building was atypical. The broad front, nearly 43 feet long, resembles in some respects the reconstructed birthplace home, not a seventeenth-century dwelling. Like the

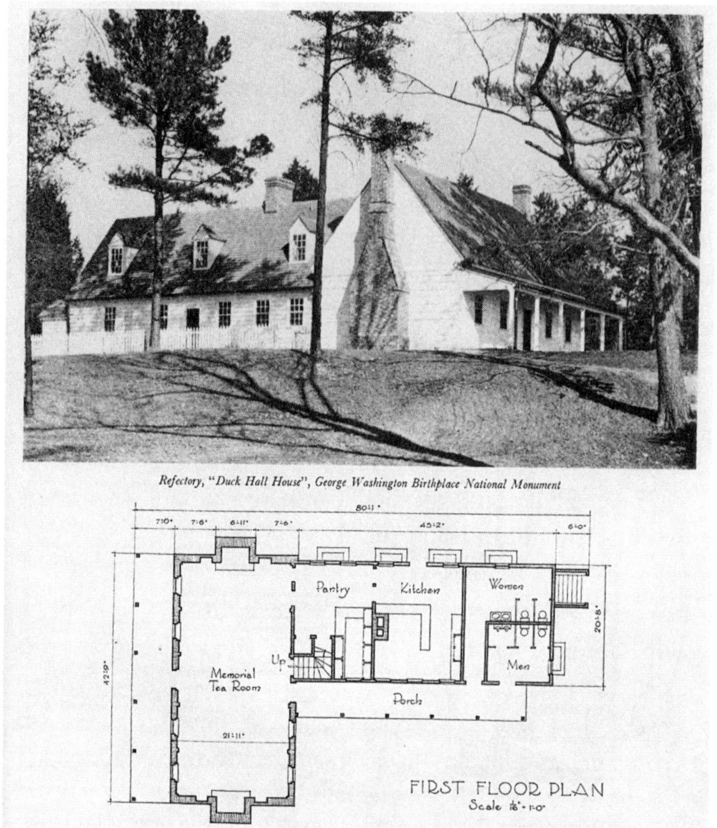

Figure 74. Log House, George Washington Birthplace National Monument, Colonial Beach, Virginia. Edward W. Donn Jr. designed the log tea room and meeting place for the Wakefield National Memorial Association. It opened for business in 1932 and appeared in a National Park Service publication a few years later. (Albert Good, *Park and Recreation Structures* [1938], 2:77)

50-foot wide main house, the Log House has a five-bay front and center door. A one-story porch across the front adds an air of informality to the log building. Inside, the unpretentiousness implied in the log construction is abandoned in favor of a large room, 40 by 20 feet, with a high open ceiling supported by arched trusses. With fireplaces at both ends and paneled walls, the space resembled a great hall and functioned well as a tea room and meeting space. The Log House opened for business on December 1, 1932, and offered meals and rooms through the 1930s. While the log building's appearance might have seemed inappropriate for this early eighteenth-century landscape, it was clear that the birthplace site's sponsors sought an evocation of Washington's time and place, not a reproduction, a view consistent with much of the Colonial Revival movement.

Tea rooms were a byproduct of the motor age. The public who drove out to the countryside looking at historic sites, for instance, needed a place to eat, and the tea room arose to fill this need. As an informal alternative to a hotel dining room, the tea room offered direct entry, not filtered through a lobby; light, simple meals, not heavy multicourse concoctions; and feminine, airy décor, not heavy upholstered furniture. Tea rooms appeared in the 1910s, often operated by women in a world that until then had been run by men, targeting women and families as the desired patrons. The name "tea room" signified not that only tea was served, but more importantly that no alcohol was—this was not a saloon. Tea rooms were popular in cities, but as automobile ownership increased, they also took root in the countryside. As the trade publication *Tea-Room Management* declared, "The house itself must be quaint, or picturesque, or distinctive in some way, so that the eye is arrested and the passerby is made anxious to investigate further." For quaint, picturesque, and distinctive, log cabins often fit the bill, and as a tea room, the Log House at Washington's birthplace was to some extent typical. Many tea rooms were operated by women and had associations with historic buildings.[15]

The use of log for tea rooms and restaurants may have also sent subtler messages than just a fondness for the historic. A California chain of White Log Taverns and Coffee Shops featured a rustic wooden sign that noted, "White Taverns are strictly American of New-England descent." It is unclear what was New England about the buildings; Kenneth Eaton Bemis, the founder of the chain, was born in Minnesota. Bemis came to Oakland, California, in 1930 and developed an easily fabricated and sanitary prototype: a "log cabin" constructed of steel frame and concrete formed to look like logs (plate 10). By 1936 he had 62 coffee shops spread over 8 chains and 9 companies, each owned by a different family member. The names of each chain's restaurants indicate the associations Bemis was seeking with his "log" cabins: New England Coffee Shops (Los Angeles), Log Coffee Taverns (Los Angeles), Colonial Coffee Shops (San Francisco), Pioneer Coffee Shops (Alameda and Oakland), Lincoln Coffee Shops (northern California), White Log Coffee Shops (Portland and Seattle), and Mayflower Coffee Shops (Oakland and Berkeley). These names conflate Puritans, pioneers, and Lincoln into one memorable image: the log cabin. Promoting general historical associations as well as a specific Anglo-Americanism, Bemis's log cabins were also unusual and memorable in their West Coast, urban settings—exhibiting what would be seen today as effective branding.[16]

Figure 75. Fort Rosalie gift shop, Natchez, Mississippi. This gift shop and ticket office was built in 1941 for a nearby reconstruction of a French colonial fort. Its log material evoked the past and associated it with the fort. (James Rosenthal, photographer, 2006, Historic American Buildings Survey, Library of Congress)

Because of their historical implications, log cabins served for all sorts of buildings ancillary to historic sites, such as the gift shops adjacent to the two Lincoln sites, discussed in chapter 2 (see fig. 37). Other auxiliary buildings had more complicated associations with log construction. A gift shop and ticket office still stands at Natchez, Mississippi, although its associated historic site—a reconstructed fort—is long gone. Jefferson Davis Dickson, a sports promoter active in France, returned to his Natchez birthplace in about 1940 and decided that in order to celebrate its French heritage, the city needed to reconstruct its French colonial fort. The fort, an earthworks surrounded by a moat, did not survive into the nineteenth century, and little is known of its buildings, but Dickson plunged ahead and built eight structures, including a three-level log blockhouse, surrounded them with a stockade fence, and located a log building housing the gift shop and ticket office outside the fence.[17]

The one-story gift shop, measuring 46 by 19 feet, had saddle-notched log walls (fig. 75). Shakes covering the hip roof and strap hinges and a thumb latch on the door added to the historical character. Dickson's Fort Rosalie opened in 1941, but it closed during the war and never reopened; only the gift shop remains today.[18] It has had several commercial occupants over the years and since 1989 has been the

Figure 76. Fort Ticonderoga gift shop, Ticonderoga, New York. Built in 1920, the log gift shop and ticket office contrasted with the massive stone fort that it served. (Photograph by the author, 2015)

home of Fat Mama's Tamales. Once again a log building has provided a congenial home for a restaurant.

Fort Rosalie's log gift shop was similar to the reconstructed fort buildings, but at another fort the gift shop was deliberately different. In New York, Fort Ticonderoga on Lake Champlain, built by the French in 1755 and later occupied by the English before being seized by the Americans in 1775, was a massive stone fortification. Having deteriorated through the nineteenth century, the fort became the focus of one of the country's first historic reconstruction efforts. Stephen H. P. Pell and his wife, Sarah Gibbs Thompson Pell, began a reconstruction of the fort in 1909. In 1920 they built a log cabin outside the walls to serve as a gift shop and ticket office (fig. 76). In the 1930s, they expanded it to accommodate a restaurant. The building has round logs, saddle-notched at the corners, and a broad gable roof; a cross gable marks the restaurant addition. Exposed logs on the interior, along with stone fireplaces and chimneys, maintain the rustic appearance throughout the building.[19]

The choice of log for this building served to set the ticket office apart from the stone construction of the fort, while still conveying the idea of "old." Historical precedent for log buildings here was cited by restoration architect Alfred C. Bossom, in reference to a nearby log playhouse, which he claimed "was built in the same form as the settlers built their log-cabins, under the protection of the fort."[20]

In addition, the log building seems to have been a reference to the Adirondack setting of the fort and to the prevalence of forests nearby. Reflecting the Pells' interest in the Colonial Revival movement, the log building seems calculated to represent history in a broad sense, not specific to the site. It indicated a different, nonfort function. Directing visitors to buy their tickets in a log cabin is much easier than in a bland building that might blend in with the setting.

A gift shop and ticket office provided some of the same functions as a visitor information center, intended to orient tourists to multiple sites. Visitor information centers were also located in log cabins, especially in northern, wooded areas. Designed to serve motorists, the cabins advertised their place through their architecture, attracted tourists with their home-like appearance, and to some extent promised the exotic. A visitor information center in the Upper Peninsula town of Ahmeek, Michigan, illustrates this. Poised at a prominent Y-intersection, the cabin is highly visible, serving as the gateway to the northern county of Keweenaw. Across the street stood a row of hewn-log cabins built by a mining company for its workers, and behind it was a mining operation that still functioned when the tourist information cabin was built in 1936 (fig. 77). Hard-hit by the Depression, Keweenaw County foresaw the decline of the regional copper-mining industry, and beginning in the late 1920s it shifted its resources toward tourism, taking

Figure 77. Visitor information center, Ahmeek, Michigan. Workers funded by the Works Progress Administration built this facility in 1936, when county officials saw tourism as the future of a faltering copper-mining area. (Photograph by the author, 2014)

Figure 78. Visitor information center, Anchorage, Alaska. The sod-roofed log cabin, built in 1954, stands in sharp contrast to downtown Anchorage but conveys the qualities that tourists seek. (Jet Lowe, photographer, 1991, Historic American Buildings Survey, Library of Congress)

advantage of its location on the shores of Lake Superior. In order to attract the motoring tourist, county workers built roads, roadside parks, mountain drives, and a golf course accompanied by a lodge and log cabins for overnight guests. The visitor information center in Ahmeek attracted potential tourists and sent them northward. Workers funded by the Works Progress Administration built the six-sided cabin out of round logs, stained brown and saddle-notched at the corners. A large fireplace of native stone dominated the interior. The cabin thus sent signals of wilderness vacation, of something different from the mining landscape, and of a welcoming home through its hearth.[21]

In Alaska log cabins resonated with tourists who came to see the Last Frontier. In 1954 the City of Anchorage built an information center in the form of a log cabin (fig. 78). Its setting could not be more anomalous, located as it was on a grid plan among low-rise masonry commercial buildings. The front-gable building with extended purlins has a luxurious sod roof, typical of Alaskan log cabins, but its stone chimney and fireplace were uncommon in Alaska. The building has round logs, saddle-notched at the corners.[22] Anchorage developed as a railroad town, beginning in 1915, and most of its early buildings were of wood-frame construction. But log cabins were what tourists expected to find in Alaska, so the city constructed a building that was conspicuously different from the rest of downtown. Log cabins serve as visitor information centers along the highway in other Alaskan communities too, notably Palmer, Nenana, and Fairbanks.

Another roadside attraction, one that contained historical objects rather than being associated with other historic buildings, was the antique shop, which experienced a new popularity in the early twentieth century. Fostered by the automobile's easy trips into the countryside and the general enthusiasm for American artifacts, amateur antique collectors ventured forth. By the 1920s, the *Saturday Evening Post* treated the phenomenon as a veritable trend by publishing articles with titles like "Antiqueering" and "Antiquamania." One of these articles explained that outside major cities, "there is a circle of country antique dealers. . . . They travel out into their districts, buying the old pieces directly from the farmers, village and town people and from auction sales." This and similar articles contained advice on how to buy from these dealers, as well as stories both on great bargains and on shockingly high prices. One anecdote involved a Log Cabin bottle from Harrison's 1840 campaign, which a friend bought for $12 four years before a similar one sold at auction for $100—thereby feeding the antiquing frenzy.[23]

To attract these shoppers, a building that looked old was effective, and the log cabin was the best advertisement. In 1929 Daisy Cleopatra Womack opened an antique shop in McMinnville, Tennessee (plate 11). Womack bought the log building her great-grandfather, Abner Womack, had built in 1817 and then had it dismantled, moved about twelve miles, and reerected on a site near the intersection of the Nashville Highway and the Old Post Road. The two-story house, of hewn logs with irregular half-dovetail notching, had two pens, one about 22 by 18 feet and the other 24½ by 18 feet, with a central brick chimney. Two log additions on the rear expanded the space, which also served as Womack's residence. For forty years she sold antiques out of this shop, which she called My Grandfather's House. Initially, she obtained antiques from the local area and then expanded her range as her business became more successful. Womack also collected a number of log outbuildings, moving them to the heavily wooded site.[24] Her interest in log cabins was consistent with her passion for antiques—both represented the past in obvious ways—and the log building was an appropriate advertisement for a place that marketed the past.

The employment of log cabins along the roadside demonstrated shrewd marketing: catch the traveler's eye with a distinctive building, promise historical and local things inside, and offer familiarity and comfort in a house-like building. This worked for restaurants, gift shops, visitors centers, and antique stores, or anywhere the combination of unusual and familiar resulted in an effective appeal to the customer. It also worked for nontravelers, those who sought only to get out of their own house for a while and into a club of like-minded people.

CLUBHOUSE

Also taking advantage of log buildings' out-of-the-ordinary appearance, clubhouses of various sorts appeared in the form of log cabins. Besides offering distinctiveness, particularly in urban settings, the log construction created an informal atmosphere that fostered a collegial, can-do attitude among a club's members. The use of log for meeting halls recalls the "council houses" built for William Henry Harrison's Log Cabin campaign. Temporary buildings, these large log structures provided noticeable places to meet.

As Alexis de Tocqueville found in his 1830s tour of the young nation, the United States was a nation of joiners, which he identified as an important factor in its democratic structure. Clubs have always attracted Americans, whether they were organized around a purpose, such as temperance or gay rights; an activity, such as fishing or reading books; or common experiences, such as veterans or single parents. The greatest growth of voluntary associations, measured in both numbers of organizations and numbers of members, occurred in the last third of the nineteenth century and then leveled off before dipping in the 1930s.[25] It was in the 1920s and 1930s, though, that organizations seemed most likely to build their clubhouses of log, perhaps influenced by the proliferation of rustic retreats for vacationers.

One organization that seemed to take particular interest in log cabins as clubhouses was the American Legion. A veterans' group founded just after World War I, the American Legion operated through chapters established across the country—more than ten thousand by 1930. Concerned with combatting the influence of radical organizations such as the International Workers of the World and the Communist Party, the American Legion promoted patriotism through parades, respect for the flag, and advocacy of the national anthem. The legion also sponsored activities for youth such as Boy Scouts, parks and playgrounds, and junior baseball leagues.[26]

When chapters decided to build their "huts," as they were termed, they often selected log as the material. Its identification with American-ness probably led to its popularity, or maybe it was just the clubby feel that logs had come to impart. In the 1920s, local American Legion chapters built huts of log construction in places as distant as Yarmouth, Maine, and Jackson, Wyoming. In Fillmore, Utah, the newspaper specifically noted that the building constructed in 1925 was "fashioned after the large log structures in Yellowstone National Park." Octagonal in plan, the hall had round logs, saddle-notched at the corners, and cobblestone chimneys (fig. 79). The building stood on the public square and, among other uses, hosted high school proms until the local high school built a gymnasium in 1935. It also accommodated meetings of the rod and gun club, Boy Scouts, and events sponsored by the American Legion's Ladies' Auxiliary.[27]

Because American Legion halls served as community centers as much as the organization's meeting places, chapters were able to tap into federal funding in the 1930s. Arkansan chapters demonstrated particular success with this, using Works Progress Administration–funded labor to build their new facilities. Often municipalities donated the land, sometimes members donated materials, and volunteers occasionally aided construction. At least seven of these new American Legion halls built in Arkansas in 1933–35 utilized log construction. They varied widely in appearance—vertical and horizontal logs, saddle-notched and square-notched corners, and rectangular and T-shaped plans—indicating a lack of centralized planning, but they all had big open rooms and prominent fireplaces. Besides legion meetings, the halls also provided space for the City Council in Newport, Arkansas, the county library in Rison, Arkansas, and dances in most of them. In Paris, Arkansas, the legion hall was part of a park that also contained cabins for the Boy Scouts and Girl Scouts, rock walls, and a path with stone steps, all constructed by WPA-funded labor.[28]

Log cabins suited Boy and Girl Scouts, offering a cozy setting, an "outdoorsiness" appropriate for camping, and an informal atmosphere. In the working-class suburb of Woodlynne, adjacent to Camden, New Jersey, workers funded by the Works Progress Administration built a log building for Boy Scouts and other community groups in 1938–39 (fig. 80). The 50 by 40–foot building sat behind the

Figure 79. American Legion Hall, Fillmore, Utah. The octagonal plan and log construction set this 1925 American Legion Hall apart from the rest of the buildings in town. (Utah State Historic Preservation Office, 2010)

Figure 80. Boy Scout cabin, Woodlynne, New Jersey. Boy Scouts in this working-class suburb of Camden received a log cabin, built with labor funded by the Works Progress Administration in 1938–39. (Photograph by the author, 2014)

Cooper Mansion, which was then being used as the Borough Hall, to form a small civic center. Semi-detached houses line the adjacent streets, forming a distinctively urban setting for a log building. The building housed the police station while a new Borough Hall was under construction in 1973–74 and later accommodated the borough's library. The building has round logs, saddle-notched at the corners, and a prominent stone fireplace.[29]

At Fort Ticonderoga, a youth-oriented log building provided play space for children. Stephen and Sarah Pell, who were restoring Fort Ticonderoga, also restored a Neoclassical mansion built in 1826 for their own use. Nearby, they built a log playhouse for their two sons (fig. 81). Called the "Y-D House," for "Yes, Do," in contrast to all the warnings against touching in the main house, the playhouse was intended to be a place where boys could roughhouse and enjoy themselves, and the rustic, informal appearance reinforced that. The playhouse was as large as any log

Figure 81. Pell Playhouse, Ticonderoga, New York. Stephen and Sarah Pell built this log cabin for their two sons, calling it the "Y-D House," for "Yes, Do"—a place where boys did not have to behave properly. (Photograph by the author, 2014)

cabin intended for adults, with multiple rooms, a cross-gable roof, and a T-shaped plan. Round logs of varying diameters, saddle-notched at the corners, and a rough rubble stone chimney contribute to its irregular appearance.

One of the most extreme cases of a Boy Scout cabin must surely be the one in Buffalo, New York, which was built in the basement of a church in 1928. Actually wood-frame construction with unpeeled slabs on both exterior and interior, the cabin provided a transcendent meeting place for urban Scouts. As one veteran remembered this Scout cabin some fifty years afterward: "It was dimly lit and the floor so dusty you could imagine it was dirt. I was a kid in a magical log cabin in the middle of the city that I thought was perhaps built by Abraham Lincoln."[30] The disconnect between the red sandstone Romanesque church and the log cabin in its basement demonstrates the desirability of a rustic meeting place for Scouts. The log cabin's ability to trigger the imagination and bring some of the outdoors inside made it the perfect clubhouse.

Log clubhouses were not solely the provinces of men and boys. The Hermitage Ladies' Association, which administers Andrew Jackson's home near Nashville, Tennessee, built a log clubhouse in 1940. Complicating an already complex history of log buildings on the plantation, with the log house occupied by Andrew Jackson and his wife having later served as slave quarters, the association members added yet another log building to the site when they constructed a hewn-log structure with half-dovetailed notching and large stone fireplaces to serve as their meeting place.

Log cabins now serve Twitter employees. Two nineteenth-century hewn-log cabins with dovetailed notching were moved from Montana to the interior of Twitter's modern headquarters building in San Francisco in 2014 (plate 12). Reconstructed without their roofs or windows, the cabins provide separate areas for eating and watching television, but also function as special places, creating a clubhouse feel. A Twitter spokesman hailed them as a kind of reuse or, as an article termed it, "creative up-cycling."[31] Twitter's embrace of log cabins, even as design elements, adds a touch of hipster cool to a very old building type.

Although these examples of clubhouses varied in clientele and purpose—American Legionnaires, Hermitage Ladies, Boy Scouts, privileged children, and Twitter employees—they all sought a place that set itself apart from the rest. The log cabin was distinctive in appearance and also created unusual surround-

Figure 82. Towle's Log Cabin Syrup advertisement. Log Cabin Syrup, still on the market today, first appeared in a distinctive log cabin tin in 1897. (*Ladies' Home Journal*, February 1920, p. 123)

ings, inspiring collegiality, informality, and creativity, while containing at least an oblique reference to an admirable American past.

Along with new uses for the log cabin, such as gift shops and tea rooms, log cabins also appeared in the popular culture of the early twentieth century. One of the longest-lasting products with log cabin associations is Log Cabin Syrup. In 1887 a Chicago grocer, Patrick J. Towle, who mixed maple syrup and sugar cane syrup to create an affordable maple-flavored syrup, moved to St. Paul, Minnesota, and established the Towle Maple Syrup Company. He named the syrup Log Cabin after his hero, Abraham Lincoln. In 1897 the syrup first appeared in distinctive log-cabin shaped tins, which served as toys (and later as collectibles) after they were emptied of their syrup (fig. 82). By the early twentieth century, Towle marketed his syrup as "Towle's Log Cabin Syrup," not mentioning maple in the title. The company that would become General Foods acquired Towle's syrup in 1927

Figure 83. Theodore Roosevelt at the Grand Canyon. This ca. 1913 campfire scene includes the distinctive Log Cabin Syrup tin in the lower left, on the ground in front of the burlap bag. (Nicholas Roosevelt Collection, Grand Canyon Museum Collection, #10694)

and stopped selling the syrup in tins during World War II, although occasionally vintage tins are produced.[32] Today, Log Cabin Syrup appears in plastic bottles with log cabin imprinting on a standard bottle shape.

Towle did not make an explicit reference to Lincoln, nor did he make an association between syrup from trees and the logs in the cabin. Instead the log cabin shape served as a novelty, a memorable advertising gimmick. And it was effective; by the 1930s Log Cabin was the best-selling breakfast syrup in the United States. The log cabin was also recognizable, so that a photograph of Theodore Roosevelt at a campsite at the Grand Canyon shows a tin that can only be Log Cabin Syrup (fig. 83). And in a self-referential discovery, an archaeological excavation of an early twentieth-century prospector's log cabin northeast of Fairbanks, Alaska, found a Towle's Log Cabin syrup tin—a log cabin in a log cabin.[33]

With commercial branding such as this, the universality of the log cabin becomes apparent—recognizable, nonthreatening, all-American. The life-size log cabin held equal appeal. For most Americans, log cabins contrasted with their quotidian surroundings, promising escape, closeness to nature, and a brush with history. They convinced the visitor that he or she was on vacation, not at home, away from the ordinary. Along the highway, log buildings caught the motorist's eye, offering a shop or restaurant that seemed to connect with its place. Even for those not on vacation, but maybe just getting out of the house to socialize with fellow club members, the log cabin provided a suitably out-of-the-ordinary context.

6

"ALL THE PLEASURES OF PRIMITIVE LIVING"

The Log Cabin on Vacation

Continuing a long tradition, in the early twentieth century log cabins still served as lodging, even if not always as the primary residence. Along the roads, log cabins served as motel units, while away from roads they served as lodges, camps, summer homes, and dude ranches. Touring Americans found log cabins reassuring and home-like, appropriate for vacation lodging, while at the same time slightly exotic, given that Americans' experiences were growing farther away from log cabins. The combination of informality and difference made log cabins ideal vacation accommodations, particularly in woodsy areas.

SECOND HOMES

In the nineteenth century, summertime on the East Coast meant that some who could afford vacations found them where the temperatures were cooler and the surroundings informal. The Adirondack Mountains of New York were one such place. Through the creation of private preserves and clubs, New York elites were able to gain control of vast swaths of forested land on which to build their own retreats. William West Durant, heir to a railroad fortune, was one of the first to recognize the resort potential of the area. Beginning in 1876, he built several camps, then sold them to men such as J. P. Morgan, Collis Huntington, and Alfred G. Vanderbilt. Clubs such as the North Woods Club, founded in 1887, and the Adirondack League Club, founded three years later, provided common dining and recreation facilities for their members, who built their own cabins to sleep in.[1]

Architectural precedent for these woodsy retreats did not exist, but builders soon settled on a comfortable rusticity that featured natural wood walls and stone fireplaces. The lodges, the main communal gathering place of these complexes, often had high-ceilinged living rooms and overscaled fireplaces, while the residential cabins were more modest in scope. Composed of a collection of single-purpose buildings, "camp" was the term most often applied to these retreats. While many of them were modest, the Adirondack camp is most readily identified with large rustic buildings, and for these logs helped to impress—not only log walls and wood shingles, but also bark wall covering, log posts, branch railings, tree-crook brackets, stump tables, half-log benches, and twig light fixtures. Dramatic fireplaces and chimneys of local stones often dominated the central living room, which might be further enhanced by elaborate log trusses. And the camps often strayed from the merely utilitarian in their facilities as well as their decor. As a 1903 newspaper article described Alfred G. Vanderbilt's Sagamore Lodge, which Durant had built in 1897–98, "What would 'Honest Abe' Lincoln have said of a log cabin containing an up-to-date bathroom, a dining room furnished with upholstered chairs and a lady's boudoir, fitted up with luxurious bed, soft rugs and other accessories of civilization?"[2] "Honest Abe" might also have objected to the structure, which was wood frame covered with half-logs. The twenty-seven buildings at Sagamore Lodge included residential cabins of various sizes, as well as the main lodge, dining hall, playhouse, and even a bowling alley (fig. 84).

At Santanoni, in Newcomb, New York, Robert C. Pruyn, an Albany banker, and his wife, Martha Anna Williams, built an unusual complex of log buildings in 1892 (plate 13). Six saddle-notched log cabins formed the core of the complex. Five of them faced Newcomb Lake, with the main cabin in the center and the flanking residential ones slightly set back to permit scenic views as well as privacy. Behind the main cabin was the kitchen and service building. Covered porches connected all six cabins to facilitate movement between them. By creating separate cabins and dividing them into separate pens, architect Robert H. Robertson designed a large camp in which few walls were longer than a thirty-foot log. The many short walls accommodated the nature of log construction, and the many notched corners added to the rustic effect. In the main lodge room, the wainscoting was of

Figure 84. Camp Sagamore, Raquette Lake, New York. Although this large camp building, dating from 1897–98, looks like a log building, it is constructed of a wood frame onto which half-logs have been attached. (Photograph by the author, 2014)

diagonally laid small split logs, while the upper part of the wall and the ceiling were covered with large sheets of birch bark, held in place by battens of half logs.[3]

The Adirondack camps led the way in terms of grand log dwellings, but the idea of the more modest log cabin as a wilderness retreat also became widespread. One proponent of this was William S. Wicks, an architect with long experience camping in the Adirondacks. He was also a member of the elite Adirondack League Club, whose first clubhouse he designed. Educated at MIT and the Ecole des Beaux Arts in Paris and a partner in the prominent Buffalo firm of Green and Wicks, Wicks published *Log Cabins: How to Build and Furnish Them* in 1889. This heavily illustrated book, which went through several editions over the next thirty years, instructed readers how to build a modest log cabin, not a sprawling Adirondack camp (fig. 85). Even so, it is clear that Wicks's intended audience is not a person whose only alternative is a log cabin; rather, his book is directed at someone

Figure 85. "Cabin in Herkimer Co., N.Y." In 1889, William S. Wicks wrote a popular book called *Log Cabins: How to Build and Furnish Them,* with illustrations such as this. (Special Collections, University of Virginia, Charlottesville, VA)

who returns to "the forest primeval" with at least a few "traces of his civilization." Wicks declares that "one essential of both a log cabin and its furniture is that as far as possible both must be made on the spot and with the material at hand," but then he advises the reader to purchase flooring, window sash "already painted and glazed," and fire brick. He describes cabins of round logs, left unpeeled, and joined with V-notching. In the 1908 edition of his book, he adds double notching, noting that "this is the Swiss or Norwegian way," perhaps having been influenced by Scandinavian immigrants who were using that technique. For caulking he recommends oakum, moss, or cement. "If the cabin is to have the dignity of a chimney or fire-place," he advises brick or stone, although in the 1908 edition he adds a stick-and-clay chimney option, noting its picturesqueness despite its hazard. Aesthetics are clearly a priority for this architect: "the structure should be the outgrowth of, and harmonize with the site, so that when your cabin is completed it shall be a new object added by the hand of man to perfect and beautify its surroundings; and the whole when viewed shall produce an agreeable effect, like harmony in music and rhythm in poetry."[4]

In terms of identifying a trend toward log cabins serving as vacation retreats, Wicks was perceptive. Americans have long been interested in retreating into more rustic surroundings. Thomas Jefferson's Poplar Forest in Piedmont Virginia and Henry David Thoreau's rough shack at Walden Pond were two early examples, but the trend intensified in the late nineteenth century as the population became more urbanized and cities became more crowded and unhealthy. With paid vacations becoming more common in the 1920s and the automobile permitting travel to remote sites, the ease of escaping to the wilderness meant that more people spent their vacations and weekends in second homes or lodgings built for the purpose. At the same time, the attitudes of middle- and working-class Americans toward the outdoors shifted from viewing it as a place of work, as it traditionally had been, to one of leisure. Middle-class and better-off working-class vacationers preferred housekeeping cabins or modest lodges in outdoorsy surroundings. At these lakeside or mountain retreats, the cult of simplicity prevailed, with vacationers spurning running water or electricity in favor of a more authentic wilderness experience. The log cabin, of course, was the perfect architectural representation of retreat, wilderness, simplicity, and rusticity. Although true log construction became rarer, log veneers on wood frame evoked the desired qualities. Even if the builder employed log construction, complex corner notching often gave way to simpler cornering in which logs were nailed together or into corner posts.[5]

William Allen White, a newspaperman, summered in the Rocky Mountains near Estes Park, Colorado, for thirty years. As owner and publisher of a newspaper in Emporia, Kansas, White was widely known in early twentieth-century America as a voice for Middle America. After having spent part of his honeymoon in a log cabin in the Rockies in 1893, the "Sage of Emporia" bought a cabin there nearly twenty years later. Involved in Progressive politics and Teddy Roosevelt's "Bull Moose" campaign in 1912, White found refuge in this wood-frame cabin: "It was surrounded on three sides by snowcapped mountains that looked down into a valley, a peaceful green valley through which the Big Thompson River wound its way. It cost us only a few hundred dollars. . . . And it was to be for all our lives a haven and a refuge. The cabin was only eighteen by twenty-four, with a fireplace in a little living room, two bedrooms and a kitchen." White and his wife soon enlarged the cabin, added two sleeping cabins, a privy between them, and, farther up the hill, a log cabin in which he could write.[6]

This side-gabled cabin, measuring 24 by 16 feet, was only marginally smaller than the residence (plate 14). It has a large fieldstone fireplace and exterior chimney in the center of the rear wall. The round logs are not notched, only overlapped and pinned. A wide deck surrounding the cabin on three sides and the large windows indicate the importance of views to White. The cabin has one large room, with a small bathroom in a log ell. The choice of a log building is natural for the setting—harmonious, simple, and historic—but the cabin differs from nineteenth-century cabins in the area. The side-gable roof, with the long side of the building facing the view, contrasts with the front-gable entry usually found in the late nineteenth-century West. The stone fireplace, big windows, and large deck also indicate this cabin's use as a vacation cottage, as well as a writing sanctuary.

The cabin permitted White to retreat not only from society but even from his vacationing family. The cabin functioned as a writer's retreat, a pundit's porch—White was visited by Scopes trial opponents William Jennings Bryan and Clarence Darrow, separately but on the same day—and as a place for a politically active man to regroup. In 1914 he invited his friend Teddy Roosevelt to visit this home in the Rockies: "We have a camp there, two cabins and some sleeping houses. We are nearly 9,000 feet in the air, about 40 miles from the railroad, within a few hours' walk of snow, and fairly out of the heavy tourist traffic. You and Mrs. Roosevelt could have a log cabin with a fireplace, and a tin bathtub, and a fourposter bed made of lodgepole pines. You could write, and we could tramp two or three days a week among the high Rockies. . . . At all events, it's the place for you to come to renew yourself."[7] Renewal was as important to White as it was to Roosevelt.

Like the Adirondack camps, hunting and fishing clubs drew members together in a collection of log buildings. Near the main building, which included a dining room, smaller log cabins provided sleeping accommodations. A good example of this is in the Rocky Mountains in eastern Idaho, where businessmen from Salt Lake City, Utah, established a fishing lodge called the North Fork Club. In 1904, they built a log clubhouse with eight bedrooms and a large gathering room. The kitchen and dining room were in a separate log building. After World War I, club members began to build their own individual cabins, more suited to family life (fig. 86). Constructed of logs, with large stone fireplaces, these cabins usually had porches and faced the river, permitting their residents to relax, admire the view, and, through their rustic building, feel like they were escaping modern life. As at other clubs, members continued to take their meals together in the common dining room.[8]

Figure 86. Interior, Bagley Cabin, North Fork Club, Island Park, Idaho. Some of the furnishings and rugs date from 1927, when this cabin was completed. (Thomas Carter, photographer, 2001, used by permission of the Western Regional Architecture Program Collection, Marriott Library, University of Utah)

Real estate developers saw the advantages of rustic, privately owned cabins organized around a main lodge. At Sprucewold near Boothbay Harbor, Maine, several developers sold individual lots while uniting around the idea of a log cabin settlement. In 1921 Parker Nickerson built log cabins he billed as "Nickerson's Community Camps," while George Kenniston built five log cabins, each measuring 28 by 26 feet. The developers also sold lots to private owners, who often built in log; by 1924 there were 24 log cabins at Sprucewold, and by 1930 there were more than 60. The early cabins tended to be one story with stone fireplaces and ample porches. In 1926 Nickerson built a lodge on the highest point of the peninsula. Advertised as the "largest log cabin hotel in the world," the lodge had a 45 by 30–foot lobby with a large stone fireplace and balconies all around, a dining room that was more than twice as large and seated 400, and 37 guest rooms. It was so successful that Nickerson added a 48-room log annex the next winter, followed by 15 rental log cabins

Figure 87. Sprucewold Annex, Boothbay Harbor, Maine. A large log lodge serving dozens of log cabins was the centerpiece of this summer resort area. The lodge was destroyed by fire, but this is its surviving annex, built in 1927. (Christi Mitchell, photographer, 2014, Maine Historic Preservation Commission)

(fig. 87). After the lodge was destroyed by fire in 1930, Nickerson replaced it with a modest log dining hall; the era of grand coastal lodges had ended with the onset of the Depression. The log cabin theme defined Sprucewold's identity, offering a rustic experience appropriate for a vacation. The amenity of the well-equipped lodge, though, meant that vacationers would experience "all the pleasures of primitive living with none of the penalties," as its advertising promised.[9]

While log cabins and Maine might be a natural association, log cabin communities were also found in the mid-Atlantic. Located about twenty miles east of Philadelphia in the Pine Barrens of New Jersey, Medford Lakes began as a summer resort formed on a log cabin theme. In 1927 developer Leon Todd converted the site of a colonial iron furnace and bogs into a resort area with twenty-one lakes. City planner Charles W. Darling laid out the community in a curvilinear plan designed to accommodate 1,600 cabins, many of them fronting on lakes. Todd decreed that all of the buildings would be of log, and he provided five sample designs of cabins, developed by architect William H. Kenderdine (fig. 88). All the designs depict round logs saddle-notched at the corners, low roofs, and porches. Stone fireplaces form the focal points of the living rooms. Four of the five model plans were for one-story cabins. In the two-story design, as well as Todd's own residence, the living rooms were two stories high with balconies. Purchasers were free to build to their own designs, but they seem to have followed the lead of these modest log cabins.[10]

Purchasers of lots joined the Medford Lakes Colony Club, which owned all of the public property, including the lakes, beaches, and athletic facilities. In 1931 Todd built the Log Cabin Lodge, which he claimed was "the largest full-log con-

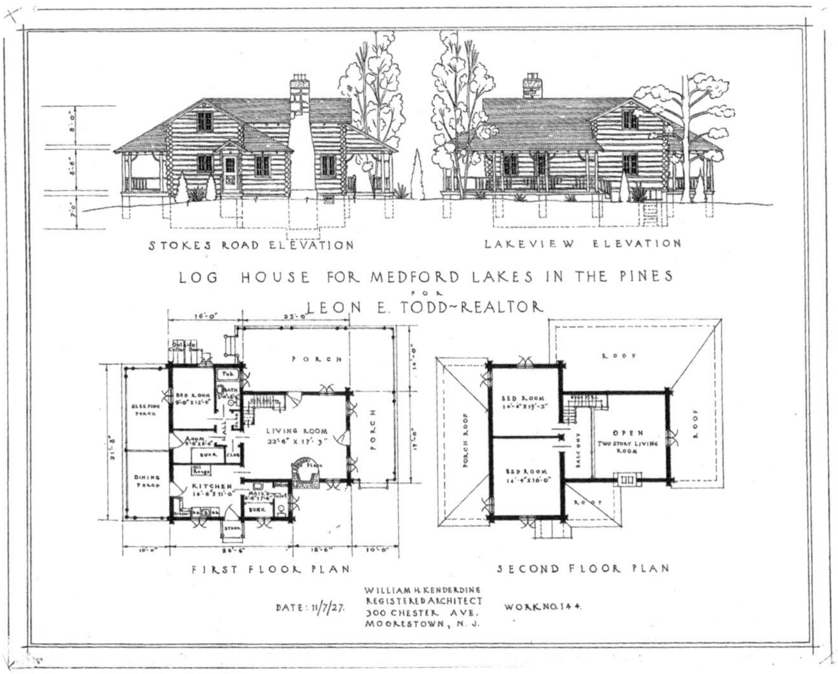

Figure 88. Design for log house, Medford Lakes, New Jersey. In 1927 realtor Leon Todd developed a community on a log cabin theme, with a large lodge, log tea room, and log churches. He also provided some suggested designs for houses, one of which is shown here. (William H. Kenderdine, architect, 1927, courtesy of Carol Cox Latti)

structed building in the United States," to provide overnight lodging for prospective purchasers (plate 15). With an impressive central fireplace and a clock with a six-foot pendulum built into the chimney, the lodge aspired to rival Old Faithful Inn, across the country in Yellowstone National Park. Other log public buildings included a community building, administration building, trading post, and a Log Cabin Tea Room, built in 1928.[11] Churches for Protestants and Catholics were log as well.

A how-to log cabin book dating from the late 1920s reflects some shifts in ideas in the forty years since Wicks's *Log Cabins: How to Build and Furnish Them* was published. Minneapolis architect Chilson D. Aldrich wrote *The Real Log Cabin* in 1928; it went through six reprintings by 1935, and there were later editions as well (fig. 89). Aldrich dedicated his book to Abraham Lincoln, "who has enshrined the log cabin in the hearts of his people," and directed his text to the American who "is going back to the good old ancestral custom—bootlegging his pioneer kick as it were—and building himself a log cabin away from the honks of man." He defines the pioneer cabin in terms similar to the rustic, although he does not use that word: "a home which looks as if it were one piece with its forest setting. One which does not flaunt its newness. One which suggests comfort and the mellow joy of living. One in which the modern concessions to convenience are skillfully hidden—if, indeed, they are present at all."[12]

Although Aldrich recommends that the cabin be built of logs cut on site and that the stone fireplace be crafted of stones gathered nearby, he also understands that nearly every other element would have to be obtained off-site. For the round log walls, saddle-notched at the corners, he advocates the frequent use of twelve-inch metal spikes, not only at the ends but also every few feet along the wall. Most of his discussion concerns small cabins without amenities, but he does include one design with a bathroom and provides instructions on water supply, septic tanks, and electricity. He notes that log cabins are not the cheapest solution—small wood-frame cottages could be built at half the cost—but he prefers log as being closer to nature. He achieves picturesque effects through low roofs, wide eaves, and "the random projection of the ax-cut ends of the logs for a few inches to two or three feet beyond the building line." By 1935, Aldrich was designing log cabins for Page and Hill, a Minneapolis firm that produced ready-cut log houses, and in its advertisements it emphasized: "the quaint charm and solid satisfaction of pioneer

Figure 89. "Pioneer Cabin in Minnesota Historical Society rooms." Chilson Aldrich included this sketch in his popular how-to guide for building a log cabin. (Chilson D. Aldrich, *The Real Log Cabin* [New York: Macmillan Co., 1935])

life... enriched by new leisure, new attitudes, and new conveniences... await you in these rustic, sturdy, correctly designed and properly built log houses."[13]

CAMPS AND DUDE RANCHES

Summer camps for children, a form of wilderness retreat, also used log cabins to reinforce the atmosphere of exotic rusticity. Evolving from tent camps to provide middle-class boys with opportunities to cultivate their masculine, outdoorsy natures, summer camps became institutions for both boys and girls, rich and poor. Reformers promoted the healthful surroundings of fresh forest air, especially in contrast to the pollution of crowded cities. By the 1920s, camp buildings had evolved from canvas tents to log cabins, particularly for those camps with a frontier theme.[14] Accompanied by associations of the pioneer past and roughing it, the cabins provided a different kind of experience for children used to urban homes. Dining halls, craft activities, and washing and toilet facilities occupied separate buildings, making the sleeping cabin a basic, single-purpose structure. Log cabins that seemed just a step removed from nature aided the emphasis on the outdoors.

A girls' camp near Lynchburg, Virginia, illustrates some of the variations. During World War I, the YWCA organized a summer camp for "industrial girls," young women who worked in the factories. In 1918, Mrs. W. G. Suhling offered a one-and-a-half-story log cabin, dubbed "Rough House," for the use of the YWCA program. By 1922, campers numbered 350, and the YWCA sought a more permanent site. It called the property it purchased Camp Ruthers, in reference to the statement "If I had my ruthers I'd ruther live in the woods." The wood-frame house on that property burned down in 1924, and the YWCA replaced it with a large, two-story log dwelling with a stone fireplace, half-log mantelpiece, and banisters of small trees (fig. 90). The building had an assembly room/dining hall and a large two-story sleeping porch. The original focus on industrial workers shifted to middle-class girls, whom the camp accommodated until it closed in 1976. The 1937 annual report, perhaps quoting a director at another camp, provided the rationale: "Camp is a community life where the chief objective is to learn the fine art of living." The statement then defined that art: "There is something about learning to build a camp fire, walking along leafy trails instead of on brick and cement, studying nature, swimming instead of going to the movies or sitting hunched over a radio. This is why boys and girls go to camp."[15] The log cabin enhanced the rural surroundings, helping to define the camp experience as different from home life.

The dude ranch was a sort of summer camp for adults. Often located in or near the Rocky Mountains, dude ranches provided nonwesterners the opportunity to experience life on a ranch. The allure of fresh air, cool temperatures, horseback riding, and simple living attracted many middle- and upper-class vacationers from the East and Midwest. Offering the right amount of rusticity and authenticity, log cabins dominated the dude ranch landscape. As one owner, Struthers Burt, described a dude ranch, "Physically it is an ordinary ranch amplified, in some sections of the country the buildings made out of logs, in others, out of adobe, or frame, or even brick. There is usually a large central ranch-house containing sitting-rooms, a dining-room, kitchens, storehouses, and so on and, scattered about the grounds, smaller cabins or houses, holding from one to four people, used as sleeping-quarters." Also scattered around the grounds were a number of outbuildings. The ensemble had to be placed so "that there is no effect of crowding or size," so as "not to destroy the impression of wildness and isolation."[16]

The establishment usually credited as being the first dude ranch was operated by Howard Eaton in the Badlands of North Dakota. Eaton took in his first paying

Figure 90. Camp Ruthers, Lynchburg, Virginia. Built in 1924, this two-story log structure was the central building at a YWCA camp, accommodating the dining hall and sleeping porches. (Travis McDonald, photographer, 2004)

guest in 1891; then a decade later he moved his operation to the Bighorn Mountains of Wyoming. Farther west, successful dude ranches were established in the area surrounding Yellowstone National Park in Montana and Wyoming. The industry picked up during World War I, when travelers found Europe difficult, if not impossible, to visit. By the 1920s dude ranches were a boom industry.[17]

To many dude ranch owners, keeping the ranch as a functioning livestock operation was key. Guests could go on trail rides and help with the care of cattle, adding authenticity to their vacation experience. The informality appealed to them; they would wear cowboy-type clothes and interact with other guests in a way that was not customary in high-end, established hotels. In 1911 Fanny Kemble Wister, daughter of famed western novelist Owen Wister, stayed at the JY Ranch in Jackson Hole, Wyoming. Many years later, she described it: "We four children had a log cabin to ourselves, and our parents had a cabin of their own next to us. Our wooden bunks were filled with pine boughs and covered with the gray blankets that we slept between. Every morning a bucket of hot water was brought to the cabin door." The informality also extended to the relationships between guests, but many dude ranches required references from their prospective guests, guaranteeing that informal interactions would remain within an accepted class of sojourners. The Valley Ranch, operated by Larry Larom, advertised, "Only the best Christian families are desired and a discriminating standard of admittance is maintained."[18]

Some familiarity with easterners was a desirable trait for a dude ranch owner; the more successful dude ranches included managers or owners who had come from the East, bringing connections and an understanding of these visitors' desires. The eastern operators also brought an appreciation for the unique qualities of western culture and maintained their sense of wonder. Larry Larom, a Princeton-educated New Yorker, was first exposed to the West by attending Buffalo Bill's Wild West shows in New York City when he was a teenager. After establishing a dude ranch southwest of Cody, Wyoming, in 1915, he built a 26 by 40–foot log building in which he held mini–Wild West shows, followed by dances. The Wild West show, a commercial event that stressed the *difference* embodied in the West, as it might strike easterners, informed his understanding and projection of the West. Westerners also impressed young Fanny Kemble Wister, who recalled, "The old wrangler filled us with awe and admiration. We hung around him as much as possible, for we knew he was the real thing. He wore high-heeled boots and leather chaps; the handkerchief around his neck was held by drawing the two ends together through a piece of ham bone. He seldom took off his ten-gallon hat."[19]

The vacationers required a delicate balance of simplicity and comfort. Log cabins and rustic furniture gave the right ambiance, but comfort was critical too; as Struthers Burt said, "if you wish to sum up the dude-business in a sentence, it consists in giving people home-made bedsteads but forty-pound mattresses." With the right amount of comfort, the log cabin was the perfect solution. As Burt rhapsodized, "Nothing is lovelier and fits more perfectly into the background from which it came than a Western log-cabin, and nothing is more comfortable. In the summer it is cool, in the winter it is warm. Its walls inside are restful to the eye, taking on a mellow ruddy patina as they get older. Moreover, they form the best of settings for anything you choose to put upon them. There is something of magic about the inevitable correctness of simplicity and usefulness."[20]

In 1912 Struthers Burt, in partnership with Horace Carncross, established the Bar BC in Jackson Hole, the broad valley at the foot of the Teton Mountains in Wyoming (fig. 91). As Burt described it, building the log cabins was not difficult, but materials such as "spikes with which to nail our logs together, various-sized nails for roofing and flooring, window-sashes, doors, hinges, and roofing-paper"

Figure 91. Bar BC Ranch, Jackson Hole, Wyoming. Built by Struthers Burt in partnership with Horace Carncross, beginning in 1912, this dude ranch expanded to forty-five buildings within a decade. (Photograph by the author, 2014)

had to be brought in. And multiple buildings were required; to accommodate fifteen tourists, Burt needed "at least seven small sleeping-cabins, fourteen by sixteen, with fireplaces, four bunkhouses, and a couple of storehouses, a meat-house, corrals and necessary fencing, a well, and a large central cabin, the last with a kitchen, a dining-room, a sitting-room, and two or more smaller rooms for writing and card-playing." Within a decade, he had expanded to forty-five buildings to accommodate fifty guests. The log buildings, generally oriented around the main lodge and dining hall in an irregular arrangement, achieved Burt's goal of avoiding a sense of crowdedness. The one-story structures, low and rambling, have round logs nailed into corner posts or square notches nailed in place. Rolled asphalt covered the roofs.[21]

The dude ranches in Jackson Hole benefited from spectacular scenery (fig. 92). The jagged peaks of the Teton Mountains provide a breathtaking backdrop that emphasized to visitors that they were far from their daily lives. Dude ranches offered horseback rides up into the mountains, as well as hunting and fishing expeditions, as a way to interact with this landscape. The ranch itself was an undeniable part of the experience, though, and the log cabins as much as the cattle identified it as a western experience.

Location in the West was not a prerequisite for a dude ranch, however, as the proliferation of dude ranches in the Adirondacks and other eastern areas showed. Beginning in 1935, entrepreneurs developed dude ranches whose proximity to

Figure 92. White Grass Dude Ranch, Jackson Hole, Wyoming. Established as a ranch in 1913, the White Grass began taking in dudes in 1919. As at the Bar BC, log buildings scattered carefully on the landscape added to the informal atmosphere. (Photograph by the author, 2014)

population areas made them cheaper for the guests. Like their western counterparts, these dude ranches offered horseback riding, clean air and cool temperatures, and an informal atmosphere, although cattle were rare. The *New York Times* termed it a "dude-ranch craze" in 1941, when there were forty-five ranches operating in the East.[22] To create the proper atmosphere, dude ranch owners brought in cowboys and Western horses, held barn dances and hayrides, and—of course—accommodated their guests in log cabins.

In 1943 Walter Isaacson bought sixty acres of forested land near Lake George, New York, with the intention of quitting his sales job in New York City and starting a dude ranch. His experience was in many ways typical of the postwar Adirondack dude rancher. Located in the heart of the eastern dude ranching area, the enterprise was a family affair, run by Walter in partnership with his brother. His wife, Betty, cooked all of the meals for the guests and staff for the first five years. As they had no experience in western ranching, their operation was more of a themed resort than a real ranching experience. But like most dude ranches, log buildings were critical in creating the ambiance.

The Isaacsons' first task was to oversee construction of the main ranch house (fig. 93). Set on a stone basement, the log building measured 70 by 36 feet, with a 16-foot wide porch across the front, and was able to seat one hundred guests for dinner. The second floor, illuminated by shed dormers, had five guest rooms, the owner's room, and a bathroom. Isaacson admitted to little experience with building in logs but cited Chilson Aldrich's *The Real Log Cabin* as inspiration. The process of constructing this log building reflected mid-twentieth-century log-building techniques. A sawmill was readily available for wood-frame construction, but the Isaacsons wanted a "real log" building to create the proper atmosphere. All of the wood, both logs and sawn lumber, came from their property. Isaacson hired local axemen to fell and prepare one hundred logs for the building, which was designed by an architect, George Breitenbucher, a close friend who donated his services. The prepared white pine logs ranged from 50 to 70 feet in length and from 8 inches to 2 feet in diameter. Hemlock suited for dimensioned lumber, such as rafters, joists, and sheathing. Once the builders laid the flooring for the first floor, they set up a mast and boom operated by a hand winch to hoist the logs into place. They saddle-notched the logs, spiked them at the corners, and then joined

Figure 93. Painted Pony, Lake Luzerne, New York. Dude ranches also appeared in the East, especially in the Adirondacks. Walter Isaacson built the main ranch house, in the background, from logs cut on the property in the 1940s. (Photograph by the author, 2014)

every three rows with reinforcing rods. The builders chinked the logs with oakum, then covered the chinking with concrete. Timber on the property also served for knotty pine paneling on interior partition walls. Isaacson and his wife pitched in where possible, such as cutting all one hundred balusters on a jigsaw.[23] Workers wallpapered the guest rooms with western scenes and made rustic furniture from timber on the property. Finally, in the spring of 1947, the ranch the Isaacsons called the Painted Pony opened to the public.

To carve out a niche for themselves in the competitive Adirondack dude ranch business, the Isaacsons decided to cater to family vacationers, recognizing that the other dude ranches appealed to the singles crowd. Painted Pony's slogan was "The East's Most Western Ranch—Where the pavement ends and the West begins." Over the next two years, Isaacson's builders added four log duplex cabins with wood-burning fireplaces. Next they built stables and a corral, followed by an arena for rodeos in 1953. Painted Pony held rodeos every Friday night through the summer. To capitalize on the crowds that attended, Isaacson built a "western town" complete with the Long Horn Saloon and Gold Nugget Dance Hall. The false-fronted wood-frame buildings, which included the Pony Express Shop where visitors could buy boots, jeans, and Indian jewelry, were designed to look like a movie set of a western town.[24] With this, the idea of the West moved from practical rural buildings—log cabins—to towns as depicted in movies.

Like neighboring dude ranches, the Painted Pony was successful through the 1960s.[25] No one was fooled by the western pretense, but the ranch offered a theme and lifestyle that appealed to vacationers. The idea of the rustic log cabin as a desirable vacation spot, which may have originated in the Adirondacks and spread west, came back to the Adirondacks in the form of the dude ranch.

SHORTER STAYS

Not all vacationers sought to retreat, however; some merely needed overnight accommodations. By the late 1920s, log cabins also served that purpose. As middle-class Americans took to the roads in the early twentieth century, they camped in tents by the roadside when they wanted to spend the night. Municipalities established campgrounds, initially free to users, to control trespassing and sanitation issues, and once campgrounds proved popular and began to charge fees, entrepreneurs entered the market. These private campgrounds provided tents

Figure 94. Log Cabin Motel, Pinedale, Wyoming. Seven two-unit log cabins built in 1929 attracted motorists on their way to Yellowstone National Park. (Photograph by the author, 2014)

and sometimes washing facilities, and as demand rose, the tents gave way to more permanent structures. With the desire to advertise through the building, cabins with character appeared—often little Colonial Revival houses, sometimes outlandish teepees, but also log cabins. In the late 1920s, individual cabins, laid out in a courtyard arrangement with parking between the units, became the norm. Offering privacy, simplicity, and economy, the cabin courts also held the romantic appeal of a small house in, or near, the country.[26]

Once again, log cabins proved to be an appropriate reference point for these overnight lodging units. Even the name—cabin—led logically to a log cabin, the familiar domestic icon. Log cabin motels, called variously motor courts, tourist camps, inns, and lodges, appeared all over the country, but especially in mountainous resort areas. The Log Cabin Motel in Pinedale, Wyoming, is a good example (fig. 94). In 1929 Walter Scott, who owned a dry goods store and the Chevrolet dealership in town, built lodgings he called "Camp of the Pines" one block off the scenic highway that led from the Lincoln Highway in southern Wyoming to the south entrance of Yellowstone National Park. He built seven two-unit log cabins in a U-shaped layout, and in the center of the U, facing the road, he built a three-room residence, also log. Behind the house, easily accessible to the cabins, was the bathhouse. Builders constructed the 25 by 14–foot cabins of round logs, saddle-notched at the corners, with a log cross wall in each. Within a few years Scott turned the double units into singles so that he could install bathrooms in each.[27]

Similar log cabin motels appeared across the country: the Log Cabin Motor Court near Weaverville, North Carolina, in 1930; the Log Cabin Tourist Camp in Hot Springs, South Dakota, in 1929; and the Log Cabin Lodge on Route 66 in Gallup, New Mexico, in 1938.[28] The geographic reach of these motels shows that log cabin iconography was a strong draw for motels nationwide in the late 1920s and 1930s. Their popularity was short-lived, though; by the 1940s lodging-owners were building connected units in a modern design, in which log cabins had no place.

As a combination of overnight lodging, retreat, club, and Colonial Revival undertaking, accommodations at a grand Virginia mansion encompassed the many functions of twentieth-century log cabins. Stratford Hall, built in the late 1730s, was the home of the Lee family, which counted two signers of the Declaration of Independence and a general of the Confederate Army among its members. In 1929 the Robert E. Lee Memorial Foundation formed to preserve the property and open it to visitors. Borrowing the governance structure from the Mount Vernon Ladies' Association, the directors were all women and represented different states. While gaining nationwide support through this arrangement, this organizational scheme had a problem: the women who came to the board meetings needed somewhere to stay. The area around Stratford Hall, located a few miles from the George Washington Birthplace National Monument in the Northern Neck of Virginia, could not provide convenient accommodations.[29]

The solution was to build a collection of log cabins. The superintendent of the site, Benjamin Franklin Cheatham Jr., suggested this in 1933 "as the most economical and suitable type of building that could be constructed and located appropriately on the property." He estimated that a one-room cabin without bathroom would cost about $100. When one of the directors offered to underwrite the cost of laying electricity and water lines, the cabins gained bathrooms and rose in cost, although the superintendent managed to purchase used tubs and toilets from a hotel in Washington. Each director paid for the construction of her own cabin; some of them shared cabins and shared the expense. Because the cabins were all

Figure 95. Directors' cabins, Stratford Hall, Stratford, Virginia. Built in the 1930s to accommodate Stratford's directors, who represented various states, these log cabins provided short-term overnight lodging. (Photograph by the author, 2014)

privately owned, they were all custom-designed, complicating the process. Frank Cheatham, the superintendent's son, provided the designs, working with each owner to create eighteen cabins by 1940.[30]

The cabins were located out of sight of the main house and formed a grouping in the woods (fig. 95). The logs were not notched at the corners, but toenailed into vertical posts. Exposed logs and stone fireplaces added to the rustic nature of the interiors. The smallest cabin measured 14 by 16 feet, with a lean-to bathroom; the largest was a quadruple, initially shared by four directors until acquired, room by room, by one of them. A "Commons," a larger cabin with a recessed porch, stood at one end of the cluster, providing a space for socializing as well as breakfast. In 1936 the foundation built a dining room, also of log. One consideration for that building was that there be two small dining rooms, labeled "colored" and "white," for the directors' chauffeurs.[31]

The intersection of race, class, and gender at these buildings is undeniable. The directors were all white, female, and upper class. For them, participation as a director at Stratford Hall offered a few weekends a year away from their duties at home, and sleeping in log cabins added to the enjoyment. Jessie Ball DuPont, the wife of Alfred I. DuPont of Delaware, expressed great enthusiasm for her cabin in her correspondence to the superintendent. Before she had seen the plans she wrote, "and naturally as I am going to live in a 'dog-trot' cabin I am very much interested in it. In fact I don't think I have ever been more excited over any possession of mine before." She arranged to share a cabin with two other directors, she taking half and the other two sharing the other half, with a wide hallway in between. After she received the drawings, she wrote, "Am glad that my cabin-mates decided to have the bath in the portion of the cabin where the dog was to trot." And as she issued the final payment, she called the cabin "The greatest bargain I ever got—that lovely half of a cabin for just exactly $280.00. Have already had that much fun out of it."

The navigation of race involved the 1930s—keeping African American and white chauffeurs separated, for instance—as well as the past. The cabins were located near, or perhaps atop, a graveyard for slaves. A monument erected there in 1953, to honor "those Negroes who served Stratford so faithfully," was reinterpreted by another sign erected a few decades later. The resemblance of the cabins to slave quarters, separated from the main house and clustered together, was not accidental. As one director wrote, while pleading for a stone fireplace rather than brick, "The fundamental idea of all this cabin construction of course is to have the whole group look as much like the 'quarters' on an old Southern plantation as possible, and there were no brick fireplaces and chimneys, I believe, in the negro cabins in the old days." That white upper-class women would inhabit these log cabins designed to resemble slave quarters was not deemed inappropriate or even ironic, suggesting the complexities of race in the 1930s.[32]

Log cabins had more connotations than slave quarters, though. Just west of Stratford Hall on the Potomac River at Westmoreland State Park, Civilian Conservation Corps workers were building log cabins, contemporaneous with—and not all that different from—the directors' cabins at Stratford Hall, for public use.[33] By the 1930s all sorts of patrons availed themselves of overnight lodging, whether in camps, motels, second homes, or parks. Whether a camp in the Adirondacks or a retreat in the Rocky Mountains, a dude ranch in Wyoming or a YWCA camp in Virginia, a motel in North Carolina or South Dakota, or small buildings arranged around lodges in Utah or New Jersey, the log cabin proved to be the perfect home for the vacationer. Whether designed to resemble slave quarters or pioneers' homes, log cabins became housing appropriate for anybody, especially if they were on vacation.

7

PARKS AND FORESTS

The Log Cabin as a Public Amenity

Touring Americans needed destinations, and parks served the purpose, providing experiences suitable for excursions, whether a day trip to a state park or a month-long tour of national parks in the West. The exoticism of the destination—a place that looked very different from the tourist's urban or suburban home—was evident in the natural surroundings and reinforced by buildings that reflected those environs. Over the first four decades of the twentieth century, parks promoted a form of public architecture that emphasized compatibility with surroundings, and in forested areas that often meant log construction. The coherence of these woodsy designs, along with those that showcased native stonework, led to a new understanding of rustic architecture.[1] Depending on its setting, however, and evolving over the few decades it was popular, rustic design in the parks was more protean than might first appear.

In the 1920s and 1930s, as professional designers took charge of the architecture in the parks, the designs became simplified, reflecting both a national trend toward more streamlined styles as well as the realities of an unskilled workforce. Artifice, such as employing log slabs on a wood frame to simulate log construction, gave way to the use of other materials, such as concrete and corrugated metal, to achieve a rustic, but not imitative, effect. Rustic architecture found its greatest expression in large structures such as lodges and public buildings, but small cabins also appeared, equally embodying the ideal of harmonizing with the landscape. The national design program provided fewer occasions for individualistic flourishes of craftsmanship, but it effectively reintroduced the log cabin to Americans, producing thousands of publicly available log cabins across the country.

The rustic buildings produced by government agencies differed from the log structures built by private interests at about the same time. The impact of the government design program led by the National Park Service (NPS) was far-reaching, stretching across the country and into Alaska. While neither standardized nor completely centralized, the NPS design guidance was coherent and consistent, producing a uniform design ethos. Further, the government has preserved the rustic buildings in parks and forests, unlike roadside commercial buildings or vacation lodgings, so they survive in greater numbers. And by their very nature government buildings are public, available for Americans to visit and appreciate, so they are more prominent in the public memory. Beyond the buildings the NPS designed for its own use, it had even greater influence through its supervision of those in state parks. The rustic designs of the U.S. Forest Service provide a contrast to the parks in both intent and execution that helps clarify the nature of rustic log architecture.

NATIONAL PARKS

Old Faithful Inn in Yellowstone National Park inaugurated rustic architecture in the parks (fig. 96). The government created Yellowstone, at the junction of Wyoming, Montana, and Idaho, as the first national park in 1872; its early buildings, constructed by private companies, displayed styles popular nationwide. But in 1903 Harry Child, with funding from the Northern Pacific Railroad, began construction of Old Faithful Inn in a style reminiscent of Adirondack lodges. The architect, Robert Reamer, had no known affiliation with the Adirondacks, but he captured the same spirit with a stone, log, and shingle exterior, steep gable roof with dormers, porches decorated with logs and branches, massive stone fireplace, and quirky rustic details. Like the Adirondack lodges, Old Faithful Inn was large, even before its two major additions stretched it to seven hundred feet across. Its soaring lobby, seventy-seven feet high, ringed with balconies, was breathtaking (fig. 97). Only the first story was constructed of load-bearing logs; the upper stories, which cantilevered out over the first, were wood framed and clad in wood shingles. The

Figure 96. Old Faithful Inn, Yellowstone National Park, Wyoming. The steep roof, multiple dormers, and free use of logs of this building, constructed 1903, inaugurated a new Rustic Style for the parks. (Jet Lowe, photographer, 1989, Historic American Engineering Record, Library of Congress)

half logs covering the walls and ceiling of the lobby, as well as the branch ornament throughout, contributed to its impact as the ultimate in log buildings.[2]

As they had with Old Faithful Inn, railroad companies and other concessioners undertook most of the significant construction in other parks in the first decade or two of the twentieth century. As commercial entrepreneurs, they understood the importance of enticing visitors through promoting images that evoked a place. A restaurant concessioner for the Santa Fe Railway, the Fred Harvey Company, created a Spanish Colonial image for the American Southwest, helping to define how different that region was—and thus how deserving of a visit from the well-traveled tourist. Similarly, concessioners in national parks aimed to attract tourists by defining their places, and native log construction was often the means.

The National Park Service drew on the examples set by concessioners, but with a difference. By the time the NPS was established in 1916, increased use of the

Figure 97. Interior, Old Faithful Inn, Yellowstone National Park, Wyoming. Old Faithful's dramatic interior features logs as ornament as well as ceiling cladding. (Jet Lowe, photographer, 1989, Historic American Engineering Record, Library of Congress)

automobile meant that the number of park visitors was dramatically increasing. The NPS did not need buildings that would attract visitors; it needed buildings to service them and its own personnel. Parks required facilities for visitor contact, administration, maintenance, and employee housing. The first director of the NPS, Stephen Mather, decreed in a 1918 statement of policy, "In the construction of roads, trails, buildings, and other improvements, particular attention must be devoted always to the harmonizing of these improvements with the landscape." With this statement, he discouraged showy, dramatic buildings such as Old Faithful Inn but encouraged the use of local materials. The concept of harmony, though, changed over time. Mather funded one building personally—the Rangers' Club at Yosemite National Park—and it can be assumed that he approved of its appearance (fig. 98). Designed in 1920 by Henry Sumner, the Rangers' Club had a wood frame with shingle and board-and-batten siding and several chalet-type features, including a steep gable roof with dormers and balconies with jigsawn railings.[3] Over the next decade, Mather's accomplished staff led the NPS away from chalets to a more subtle understanding of rustic architecture.

The most influential NPS designer was Thomas Vint, who helped frame the development of rustic architecture in the parks over the course of a thirty-nine-year career. Beginning in 1922 as a landscape architect at Yosemite, Vint became head of the Landscape Division in the San Francisco office in 1927 and then moved to Washington to lead the Branch of Plans and Designs in 1934. He trained his staff to design buildings that were deliberately unobtrusive as well as harmonious with their surroundings. True harmony with a natural setting, he felt, meant that professionals should design each building for its specific site.[4] Further, he pro-

Figure 98. Rangers' Club, Yosemite National Park, California. The steep roofs and shed dormers gave this 1920 building a chalet appearance that would soon be deemed inappropriate for park buildings. (Courtesy of the Yosemite National Park Archives, Museum, and Library)

moted master plans for parks, which contained studies of existing conditions along with long-term plans for development. When construction funding became available in the 1930s, Vint was poised with a well-trained staff to supervise the work and had master plans in place to identify construction needs.

The nation's worst economic depression resulted in unprecedented resources flowing toward the parks. Soon after Franklin D. Roosevelt's inauguration in 1933, the Emergency Conservation Works Act provided for a Civilian Conservation Corps (CCC) of young men aged eighteen to twenty-five to perform unskilled labor. Housed and organized by the War Department, CCC employees worked for the NPS and the U.S. Forest Service. Although much of the CCC work consisted of tree planting and road building, the agencies soon began to use the recruits to help with construction of buildings. When led by experienced and accomplished craftsmen, the CCC workers were capable of producing remarkable rustic log buildings. Often, though, log buildings became simpler and more regularized to accommodate the learning curve of these unskilled workers. One year after the program was inaugurated, national parks had 67 CCC camps of about two hundred men each. By the end of the summer of 1934, there were 102 camps. Other New Deal programs, such as the Public Works Administration (PWA), brought an infusion of funding to the parks; in its first year, 1935, the PWA funded more than 150 projects in national parks. The Works Progress Administration (WPA) funded additional labor.[5] The national parks benefited from all these resources, building hundreds of new structures for visitors and administration.

In the construction boom of the 1930s, the NPS endeavored to articulate, model, and lead the development of a rustic aesthetic in its own parks as well as in other areas. One of the farthest-reaching efforts was a publication titled *Park Structures and Facilities* issued by the NPS in 1935. Albert Good, an architect in the State Park Division of the NPS, compiled and edited this volume, the product of a committee of NPS designers from across the country. The need for the publication was twofold. First, the NPS was breaking new ground in the field of appropriate architecture for natural landscape areas; as NPS director Arno B. Cammerer described it, "Stimulated by the problems this work has presented, competent architects have produced designs—and seen them converted into reality—that denote a real advance in this somewhat specialized field."[6] Secondly, the work of the NPS architects and landscape architects was increasing at a rate they could no longer adequately supervise. NPS staff not only worked on a backlog of facilities in their own parks, but they also supervised construction in state parks, even creating a specific division for that purpose. Through this publication NPS architects endeavored to influence those designs.

The book consisted of a short introduction, termed "Apologia," followed by numerous examples of park structures organized by function. Photographs, plans, and elevations illustrated the examples, and sometimes-critical text discussed them (see fig. 74). The NPS published *Park Structures and Facilities* internally in a small run of 2,250 copies. Three years later the Government Printing Office reissued it in an expanded edition, titled *Park and Recreation Structures.* It had grown from one volume to three, incorporating more examples from recent New Deal–funded construction.

Although Good took issue with the term "rustic," hoping "that a more apt and expressive designation for the style may evolve," he laid out the guiding principles in his "Apologia "Successfully handled, it is a style which, through the use of native materials in proper scale, and through the avoidance of rigid, straight lines, and over-sophistication, gives the feeling of having been executed by pioneer craftsmen with limited hand tools. It thus achieves sympathy with natural surroundings and with the past."[7] He went on to discuss these elements. He argued that a large scale might be required in dramatic, rugged surroundings. He noted that the natural features of the park, not the buildings, should be emphasized, so that architecture would be subordinate to the environment. He advised the use of screening, muted colors, horizontal lines, and low roofs to minimize the impact of the buildings.

To achieve "that sought-for 'primitive' character in park structures," Good drew attention to the quality of native materials, not just the fact that they might be native. "Native logs fashioned to the rigid counterpart of telephone poles or commercial timber, have sacrificed all the virtue of being native. . . . Logs desirable in the park technician's viewpoint are pleasingly knotted." He acknowledged that leaving the bark on logs only brought more problems later, as the bark fell off, so he advised peeled logs. Wood shingles or shakes should be an inch thick and laid in "properly irregular, wavering, 'freehand' lines. The straight edge as a precision tool has little or no place in the park artisan's equipment." This designed informality was tricky to negotiate and could devolve into cuteness. But Good abhorred "twig" architecture, as he termed it—the flourishes found in buildings like Old Faithful Inn.[8]

Good's "Apologia" also openly discussed an item on which his committee could not agree: whether native materials should be used honestly. Should workers construct buildings of logs using pre-industrial methods, or was it acceptable to employ wood frames clad with log slabs, which achieved the same appearance? In considering this problem, he also raised the issue that the historic method consumed more logs, which was counter to the conservation goals of the parks. In the 1938 edition of the manual, Good's own position became clearer. He advocated a middle course, urging that some significant buildings be constructed according to the old methods to "reproduce faithfully pioneer log construction to create, and so preserve for study, the fast disappearing construction methods of the frontier." Other buildings, those that were "minor and oft-repeated" would be more efficient if built with newer, cheaper construction methods.[9]

Good's expression of rustic architecture combined sympathy for the natural setting with an interest in the past. Significantly, most of these designs were not for historical parks, which might have an interest in promoting historic architecture, but for parks designated for their awe-inspiring natural beauty. His equation of "rustic" with "pioneer" pointed to inspiration from the past. His description of a lookout tower in Muskegon State Park, Michigan, which was built in the form of a blockhouse, further shows his hand: "A graceful salute to the days of the Frontier! For the pleasantly dishonest authenticity of this new-old blockhouse we are indebted to the salvaged timbers of a wrecked lake vessel. This lookout inspires recall of vanished men and vanquished wilderness—a shrine for the Unknown Pioneer." Nor was Good alone in this evocation of the past. Herbert Maier, a National Park Service designer who served on the committee that reviewed *Park Structures,* noted in a 1935 speech that the use of native materials was consistent with the habits of frontiersmen: "Whether he set up his abode on the forest, or sod or adobe covered plains, or in a rock-strewn country, he was forced to adopt the natural materials immediately at hand, and when the structure was completed it consequently echoed the identical materials and color from its surroundings."[10] To NPS designers, these buildings of native materials were more than just opportune; they also carried with them associations of a romanticized past. Invocations of pioneers bravely confronting primitive conditions revealed a view of the past that cast a rosy glow on a complex story of conquest and settlement.

Good's articulation of rustic design was not original; he drew on more than a decade of experience his colleagues had accumulated.[11] Mount Rainier National Park in Washington offers an illustration of the evolution of NPS design. The

Figure 99. Interior, Paradise Inn, Mount Rainier National Park, Washington. Built in 1917 by a concessioner, the Paradise Inn flaunted logs in its elaborate trusses. (Photograph by the author, 2014)

Rainier National Park Company—a private organization created at the urging of Stephen Mather to provide visitor facilities at the park—built the Paradise Inn in 1917. Located in an area of especially high snowfall, the hotel had steep gable roofs with dormer windows. Heath, Gove, and Bell, architects from Tacoma, Washington, designed the building with an exposed log frame and wood-shingle siding. Inside, the network of weathered, silvery cedar logs forming the frame and trusses in the 50 by 112–foot lobby recall a forest (fig. 99). Stone fireplaces and chimneys at either end extend 40 feet to the ceiling. Furniture fashioned of logs, including a piano and a 14-foot tall grandfather clock, adds to the enchantment.[12]

A decade later, the NPS built different buildings for itself. By then, Thomas Vint was the chief landscape architect of the NPS; he assigned landscape architect

Figure 100. Longmire Community Building, Mount Rainier National Park, Washington. This National Park Service–designed building appeared to be log construction, but it was instead a wood frame with half-logs attached. (Jack Boucher, photographer, 1996, Historic American Buildings Survey, Library of Congress)

Ernest A. Davidson to Mount Rainier. For the area in Mount Rainier called Longmire, they designed a community building completed in 1927 (fig. 100). Vint was proud enough of this design to include it in a 1932 portfolio of drawings that he assembled to provide models for his staff. The community building is a large, one-story, side-gabled building with paired vertical logs at the corners and between the wide windows. Its main room, 61 by 31 feet, has a stone fireplace at one end and a stage in a projecting bay in the other. The space is open to the ceiling; log scissor trusses draw the eye upward (fig. 101). A wing to the rear provided public bathrooms and private living quarters. Eight years after construction, the community building received criticism in *Park Structures and Facilities:* "A park structure of importance that after pointing the way for many later buildings, has been far outrun in achievement of the subtleties of design and execution making for true park structural character. The thinness of the roof shingles and the masonry of the

Figure 101. Section, Longmire Community Building, Mount Rainier National Park, Washington. An open interior with scissor trusses, a dramatic stone fireplace, and exposed walls added to the rustic nature of the building. (Mount Rainier National Park Archives, 1927)

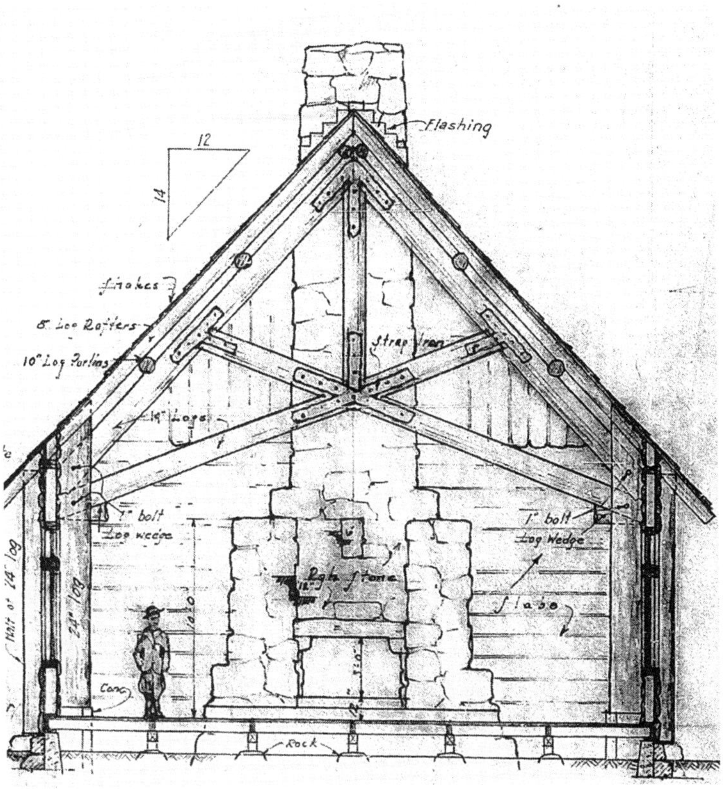

chimneys are unfortunate. Comparison of the almost mechanical stiffness of the rafter ends with the handcrafted quality of the 'whittled' rafter ends of other subjects more recently built, will indicate one such advance in structural technique." Although the community building displays a log exterior and interior, this material is a veneer—log slabs over wood frame.[13]

A few years later, on the opposite side of the park at Yakima Park, now known as Sunrise, the NPS built one of the strangest administrative groupings. The need was for community, administration, and residential buildings, and log was the obvious material. Here the NPS encouraged sensitivity not only to the natural surroundings but also to the cultural heritage, so Davidson and architect A. Paul Brown looked to the past. As Davidson described it:

> It was desired to make our construction there as well suited to its landscape environment as possible, and more than that, we wished to build into the structures as much of local or historical interest as might be secured without sacrificing other values. Yakima Park was known as a summer rendezvous of Yakima and other Indian tribes. Since their "architecture" offered no possibility of adaption, the next step was taken to the time when white pioneers of the locality erected buildings for protection against Indians or other enemies. The Historical Museum at Tacoma was searched for pictures of old structures, with a log blockhouse type in mind, which seemed quite adaptable.[14]

Looking to the area's Native American heritage, Davidson instead designed buildings explicitly hostile to them—defensive structures for white settlers.

The first building, completed in 1930, was in the form of a blockhouse (fig. 102). The thirty-two-foot square hip-roofed building, with the second floor overhanging the first, had a wood frame clad with log siding saddle-notched at the corners. The logs projecting irregularly beyond the notches, the rough finish of the ends of the logs supporting the second story, and the stepped stone foundation contrasted with the regularity of the logs and symmetry of the design. This unusual building received praise in *Park Structures and Facilities:* "Even without the benefit of the magnificent background afforded by Mt. Rainier this log building would be an outstanding contribution to park architecture. Obviously, but not too self-consciously, inspired by the early block-house, here is a building representative of logical and legitimate adaptation of a traditional form. The log work is neither too precise nor too laboriously rustic." The building served as the administrative and interpretive building, with living quarters upstairs, until two adjacent buildings were completed in 1943 (fig. 103). One of these was a blockhouse similar in appearance and construction to the first. The community building between them had a log frame with a Pratt truss supporting the roof. Again, workers added a saddle-notched log wall to the exterior of the frame, visible on the interior. Behind this building, a stockade fence, built to screen the utilitarian areas, complemented the fort theme.[15]

The NPS also built smaller, residential buildings for its staff, and log cabins suited this purpose perfectly. As Good's *Park Structures and Facilities* noted, "Of all park structures, those cabins which echo the pioneer theme in their outward appearance, whether constructed of logs, shakes, or native stone, tend to jar us least

Figure 102. Yakima (now Sunrise) Administration Building, Mount Rainier National Park, Washington. Landscape architect Ernest Davidson intended the 1930 blockhouse design to relate to the area's history. (Good, *Park and Recreation Structures* [1938], 1:64)

with any feeling that they are unwelcome." But to Good, the placement of these cabins in groups in residential areas detracted from the pioneer feel: "The fact that park cabins are usually erected in colonies or groups (frontier cabins as a rule were not) destroys somewhat the feeling of almost complete fitness that is produced by a single primitive cabin."[16] Parks also needed remote cabins for rangers on patrol,

Figure 103. Yakima (now Sunrise) Administration and Community Buildings, Mount Rainier National Park, Washington. Another blockhouse and a community building completed the complex in 1943. (John Stamets, photographer, undated, Historic American Buildings Survey, Library of Congress)

and these provided an opportunity to build the best representation of a pioneer cabin. At Mount Rainier, the St. Andrews Patrol Cabin, constructed in 1922 on the Wonderland Trail circling the mountain, serves as a good example (fig. 104). The one-room, 14 by 19–foot cabin has a side-gable roof that extends to cover the porch across the front. Particularly rustic aspects are the pointed ends of the round, saddle-notched logs and elaborate, hammer-finished ironwork on the front door. Even for a remote cabin, the rustic aesthetic prevailed in the early days of the NPS.

An evolution in NPS structures is also evident at Alaska's Denali National Park, established as Mount McKinley National Park in 1917. When construction began in 1922, the park had no budget, so park personnel fashioned cabins out of materials at hand, which included lumber and logs from an abandoned Alaska Road Commission construction site. When Harry Karstens, the superintendent, wanted

Figure 104. St. Andrews Patrol Cabin, Mount Rainier National Park, Washington. Built in 1922, this small cabin asserts its rustic nature through the finished ends of the logs and other details. (Photograph by the author, 2014)

to move the headquarters site two years later, he proposed building the facilities of log, with "an eye to their permanency and attractiveness, and also for warmth and comfort." The one surviving building of this period is a modest 20½ by 19½–foot cabin, built of horizontal logs double-notched at the corners, which served as an office (fig. 105).[17] Other buildings at headquarters were also log, or wood frame from salvaged materials. Generally, they were no different from other buildings in remote Alaska locations, reflecting local building traditions, uninfluenced by NPS landscape architects in distant offices.

Similarly, in 1927 rangers constructed a patrol cabin on the Toklat River about fifty miles from headquarters, using horizontal logs saddle-notched at the corners and chinked with moss (fig. 106). Small logs laid on purlins perpendicular to the ridge, then covered with tarpaper and moss, formed the low gable roof. The roof extended about five feet past the front wall to cover the entrance area; vertical

Figure 105. Office building, Denali National Park, Alaska. Built in 1926, this is the oldest building at park headquarters. (Jet Lowe, photographer, 1985, Historic American Buildings Survey, Library of Congress)

logs supported this porch roof. Superintendent Karstens explained the building of this series of patrol cabins: "In this construction it was necessary for the rangers to whip-saw lumber from logs with a reconditioned crosscut saw, for doors, window frames, tables and shelves and in several cases, floors. Most of the cabins having no floors in them. All construction is necessarily crude and with no conveniences as funds were lacking."[18] At the Toklat River site, a stove, not a picturesque but inefficient stone fireplace, heated the cabin. Rangers also built a cache for storage of food and doghouses to shelter sled dogs, all constructed of round saddle-notched logs.

The next year, the San Francisco office began to get involved when Harry Karstens met with Thomas Vint there. Subsequently Vint provided drawings for three new buildings as well as a site plan for headquarters. Given his insistence on rustic buildings being appropriate for their specific setting, this is surprising, because Vint did not visit McKinley until the following year. But from 1928 on, the San Francisco office designed McKinley's headquarters buildings in a uniformly rustic style, to the extent that the acting director of the NPS, Arno B. Cammerer, turned down the offer of a surplus building from the Alaska Railroad because it

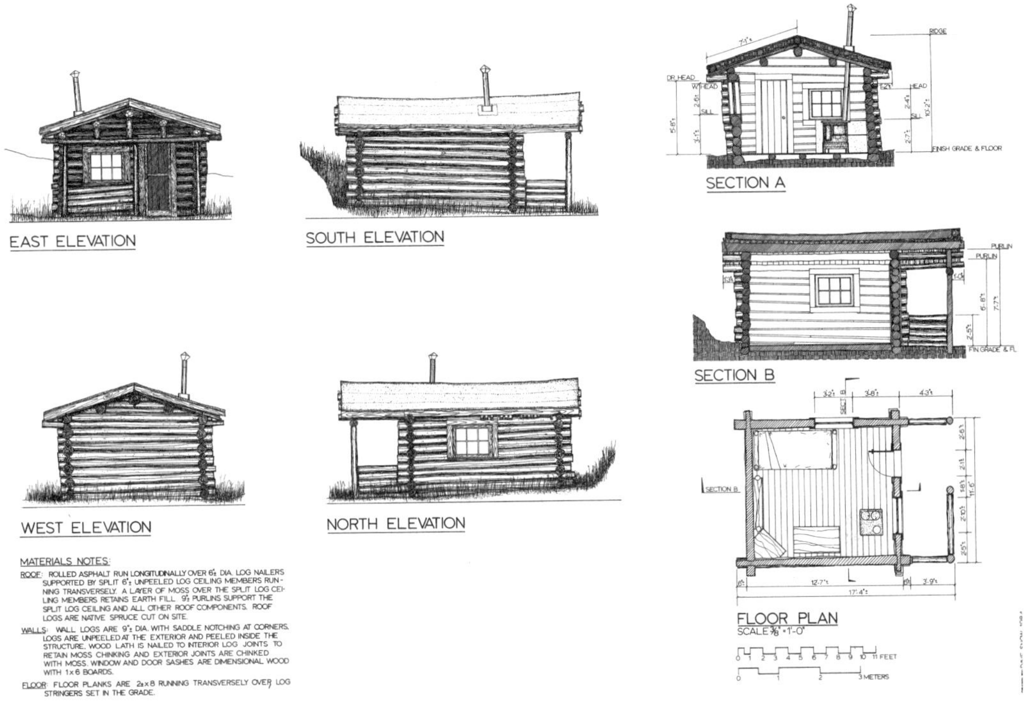

Figure 106. Toklat River Patrol Cabin, Denali National Park, Alaska. This 1927 cabin typified Alaskan log construction, with a sod roof, sill logs laid directly on the ground, and the roof extended over the gable front. (Dave Snow, delineator, 1984, Historic American Buildings Survey, Library of Congress)

"might not fit in." Cammerer urged that construction of park buildings be "in harmony with the park location and following our own designs." The three buildings Vint designed in 1928—ranger's quarters, warehouse, and barn—had round logs, saddle-notched at the corners, and tarpapered roofs. At the side-gabled ranger's cabin, pairs of vertical logs supported a shed roof over the entryway. The barn's fat logs were pointed at the ends, while the dramatic taper of the logs of the warehouse created a pattern at the corners (fig. 107). These first three buildings were subtly rustic log structures, characteristic of the area.[19]

The headquarters buildings received some upgrades in the early 1930s, gaining corrugated steel roofs instead of tarpaper and concrete chinking instead of moss. The superintendent thought "the buildings now present a much better appearance

Figure 107. Warehouse, Denali National Park, Alaska. The steep taper of the logs creates a pattern at the corners of this building designed in 1928 by the San Francisco office of the National Park Service. (Jet Lowe, photographer, 1985, Historic American Buildings Survey, National Park Service)

besides providing added warmth." But regional landscape architect Ernest Davidson, who visited the park in 1935, brought the most drastic changes. Because the superintendent advised him that he was having trouble obtaining logs, Davidson recommended "hewn-type timbers for trim, with rough lumber siding of special t & g [tongue-and-groove] or shiplap style . . . or with siding of jumbo shake-shingles." So when CCC workers arrived in the summers of 1938 and 1939, they constructed wood-frame buildings with clapboards and board-and-batten siding. They also built a structure of concrete to house the machine shop and garage, while they gave a new residence a log veneer (fig. 108).[20] The park had moved from buildings designed by rangers and constructed out of materials at hand—naturally rustic—to professionally designed buildings, constructed of a wider range of materials—the Park Service's rustic architecture.

STATE PARKS

The greatest impact of NPS designers in promulgating a rustic architecture appropriate for parks was not in national parks, however, but in state parks. Because

Figure 108. Employees' residence, Denali National Park, Alaska. Civilian Conservation Corps workers gave this 1940 residence a log veneer with battered corners. (Jet Lowe, photographer, Historic American Buildings Survey, National Park Service)

the NPS administered the work of the federal government in parks, it governed the appearance of federally funded state park buildings constructed in this period. The NPS aesthetic and organization permeated the state parks, resulting in log buildings and other rustic constructions that strongly resembled those in national parks.

The state park movement was relatively recent. Although California had established Yosemite as a state park in 1864, before it became a national park, few state parks had followed, and by 1920 only fifteen states had their own parks. Stephen Mather, then director of the NPS, recognized their potential, though, reasoning that they could provide an outlet for hordes of automobile-empowered visitors that might otherwise overwhelm the delicate balance of nature and accessibility in national parks. State parks could also be located closer to metropolitan areas and serve large urban populations, unlike the national parks of the West. As places of secondary natural interest, state parks were also appropriate for more intensive recreational use than national parks. Mather called a meeting of state park officials in Des Moines, Iowa, in 1921, resulting in the formation of the National Conference of State Parks. Over the next decade, new parks were created in twenty states.[21]

The NPS had authority to administer federal funds to state, county, and municipal parks, and CCC work was included in that mandate. The NPS maintained tight control over these responsibilities, requiring master plans for state parks, establishing a hierarchy of construction supervisors, and promulgating the NPS's rustic aesthetic. The impact was enormous: the NPS administered CCC work in 655 parks and related areas, more than 70 percent of which was in nonfederal areas. By the end of 1934, along with the 102 CCC camps in national parks, there were 268 in state parks; a year later, there were 475 state park CCC camps.[22] The NPS set up a State Park Division to oversee this work and published a handbook, *Park Structures and Facilities,* in 1935 to help guide the plans. Both NPS personnel and this publication drew heavily on recent experience with NPS rustic architecture.

One of the states that had already established parks by the time of Mather's interest was Minnesota. The state administered twenty-three parks and monuments by 1925 and was poised to take advantage of the NPS's interest in state parks. There was also a personal connection: Conrad Wirth, who headed the NPS's CCC program, was the son of Minneapolis parks administrator Theodore Wirth. Minnesota state parks accommodated three CCC camps; by the end of the New Deal, twenty-nine Minnesota parks, including some newly formed ones, received federal assistance, much of it from the Works Progress Administration. The NPS supervised all of this work.[23]

Established in 1891, Itasca State Park, which included the headwaters of the Mississippi River in northern Minnesota, reflects the development experienced by many state and national parks. The state funded construction of the first major building in the park, Douglas Lodge, which opened in 1905 (fig. 109). The two-story log lodge measured 80 by 40 feet, with a rear wing housing the kitchen. A stickwork balcony stretched across the front, and a stone chimney decorated the gable end. The lodge contained a dining room, kitchen, and living room on the first floor and guestrooms on the second floor. The exposed log interior and stone fireplace in the living room enhanced the rustic charm. Over the next twenty years, park officials added more than a dozen log structures to the park, including a two-story clubhouse with a mansard roof and bell-shaped dormer windows in 1911; a headquarters building, extending 128 by 45 feet in an I-plan, constructed in 1923; and six cabins lining the lakeshore near Douglas Lodge (fig. 110). These cabins, most of which have a living room, bathroom, stone fireplace, three bedrooms, and porches on the lake side, have round logs saddle-notched at the corners. Similar to

Figure 109. Douglas Lodge, Itasca State Park, Minnesota. Built in 1905, the lodge inaugurated the rustic aesthetic in this park. (Photograph by the author, 2014)

Figure 110. Cabin 8, Itasca State Park, Minnesota. Park officials added six lakeside cabins in the 1920s. (Photograph by the author, 2014)

some of the other log buildings from the 1920s, the log ends are highly finished, coming to a blunted point. Two buildings that were not constructed of log—a motel and a dormitory—had siding that resembled logs.[24]

With the establishment of a CCC camp at Itasca in the summer of 1933, the park embarked on an extensive building program, constructing more than thirty new buildings, most of them log, within the next decade. The first structure built by the CCC was a whimsical log cabin of oversized logs—so large in diameter that only four courses were necessary to form the walls (fig. 111). The building received this comment in *Park Structures and Facilities:*

> Only the sworn statement of one who is well informed, to the effect that this cabin was built from wind-falls and not cut timber, permits conservationists to show this cabin here. Almost humorous in its scale, it is far from that as a reminder of magnificent forests all but extinct. As a relic of the days when trees were trees, this cabin can inspire us to firm resolution to permit them to

Figure 111. Old Timer's Cabin, Itasca State Park, Minnesota. Civilian Conservation Corps workers built this whimsical cabin of old-growth timber in 1934. (Jet Lowe, photographer, 1990, Historic American Buildings Survey, Library of Congress)

be so again in the long term future. Somewhere between the scale of this log work and the spindling scale of the majority of present day log structures is the happy and satisfying medium that is too infrequently seen. The random informality of the axe-hewn log ends contributes greatly to the naïve charm of this little building.[25]

Another exaggerated building was the pump house, built in 1937–38, in which oversized boulders comprised the lower half of the walls and oversized logs the upper half. A low hip roof with wide eaves crowned the small, eleven-foot square building.

Most of the other buildings intended for public use exhibited a more straightforward log construction, resembling the cabins built in the 1920s, using round logs with saddle-notched corners, set on a stone foundation. The visibly tapered logs, irregular projections beyond the notches, and roughly finished ends produce an unpolished look characteristic of rustic designs. Unlike at some national parks, the CCC work at Itasca did not rely on simulated log siding. The park had a few fanciful log buildings, but mostly its architecture evolved into sober, unobtrusive designs.

The last CCC-built structure at Itasca suggested a new direction for log buildings. Members of the Veterans Conservation Corps, composed of World War I veterans, constructed the Forest Inn in 1939–41 to house a soda fountain, store, and recreation room (fig. 112). The use of ashlar stone, both in the walls up to the windowsills and in the large pavilion announcing the entrance, adds straight lines and right angles to the one-story building, which otherwise has rustic qualities in its saddle-notched logs and exposed log rafter ends. While modernism influenced this building's design, its use of local materials still places it in the rustic tradition. The park's architecture clearly reflected the national aesthetic of harmonious, rustic designs, well built of local materials.

In contrast to Itasca State Park's long history, Pine Mountain State Park in southwest Georgia was a creation of the New Deal. The healing waters of Warm Springs, Georgia, attracted President Franklin D. Roosevelt as early as 1924, and he made frequent journeys during his presidency. Nearby, beginning in 1933, state officials created Pine Mountain State Park (now Franklin Delano Roosevelt State Park, Western Half) with the help of the NPS and the CCC. Located on a forested ridge, the park offered woodsy surroundings and cool temperatures. Along the

Figure 112. Forest Inn, Itasca State Park, Minnesota. Built by the Veterans Conservation Corps in 1939–41, the Forest Inn combines rustic features, such as the bulging notching, with the straight lines of modern architecture. (Photograph by the author, 2014)

ridge, the NPS planned a seven-mile parkway with a stone tavern and four stone cabins, presenting views as well as lodging for tourists. Lower down the slope, a newly created lake provided a focus for seven log cabins. CCC workers built these log buildings, painted them dark brown, and chinked them with concrete; massive stone chimneys and fireplaces augmented the rustic feel. Unlike the "overnight" cabins on the ridge, these were "vacation" cabins, intended for longer stays and equipped with small kitchens. The cabins were set back from the lake a respectful distance, so as not to impose on the view from the opposite shore. Pine Mountain was one of nine parks that Georgia gained in this decade, not having had state parks before.[26] Once again, the NPS supervised construction, bringing the rustic aesthetic to this new state park.

The State of Virginia opened six new state parks in June 1936, including Westmoreland State Park, on the Potomac River between Stratford Hall and George Washington Birthplace National Monument.[27] Between 1934 and 1936, CCC workers built ten log cabins in a variety of plans (figs. 113 and 114). Sizes ranged from one to three rooms, plus kitchen and bathroom. Workers built six of the

Figure 113. Plan, Cabin 6, Westmoreland State Park, Virginia. The state of Virginia created six new parks in 1936. At Westmoreland, Civilian Conservation Corps workers built ten log cabins. (Good, *Park and Recreation Structures* [1938], 3:35)

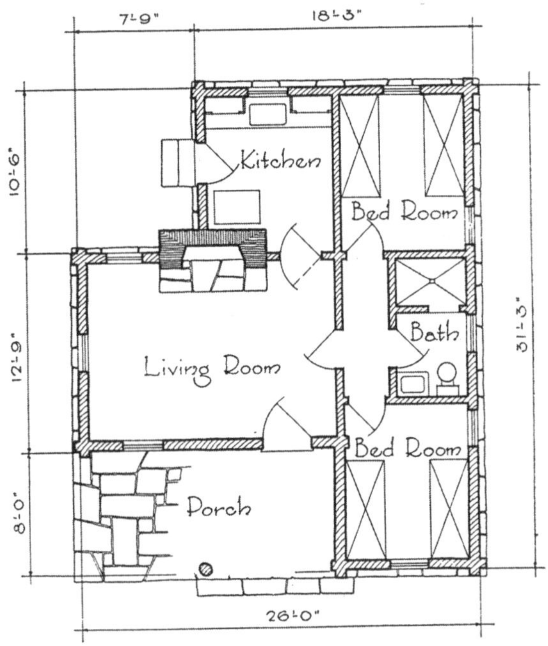

Figure 114. Cabin 6, Westmoreland State Park, Virginia. Albert Good called the cabins at Westmoreland "almost idyllic in spirit and setting." (Photograph by the author, 2014)

cabins with round horizontal logs, saddle-notched at the corners with rough ends, and four with vertical logs. Carved doorknobs, hammer-finished ironwork on the doors, and rough stone fireplaces and chimneys added to the rustic feel. Good complimented the "quality of the log work" and the "texture of the shingled roof" and called the cabins "almost idyllic in spirit and setting."[28] By 1941, though, the park interpreted rustic architecture differently. Two cabins added then, at the very end of the CCC work, were wood frame with board and batten siding, reflecting a more expeditious approach.

NATIONAL FORESTS

The U.S. Forest Service provides an interesting contrast to the National Park Service. Also administering large forested areas, and also a beneficiary of the Civilian Conservation Corps' labor, the Forest Service took a different approach to its buildings. This was due in part to the agencies' different functions; the NPS was always focused on accommodating the public, while the Forest Service came to its recreation role more slowly. In addition, national forests furnished lumber, so the U.S. Forest Service thought sawn lumber was a suitable expression of the agency, whereas national parks preserved trees, so log construction was a more apt reflection of the parks.

Like the NPS, in the early twentieth century when Forest Service personnel were just establishing their presence and constructing their own buildings in remote areas, they tended to build log cabins. Cut Foot Ranger Station in Chippewa National Forest, Minnesota, serves as an example (fig. 115). Rangers built this one-room, side-gabled building with round logs, V-notched at the corners, possibly as early as 1904, as the first ranger station in the forest. Ranger Horace Lydick, who occupied the cabin in 1908–9, noted that the floor was so rough that he planed it by hand in the evenings. A stove heated the cabin, which did not have running water. Typical of log cabins built locally, it reflected no influence from Forest Service designers. As Forest Service design professionalized in the 1910s and 1920s, though, wood-frame bungalows rather than log cabins characterized its administrative areas.[29]

By the time the Forest Service undertook construction with CCC crews, designers within the agency promoted rustic architecture that emphasized harmony with surroundings but often achieved it through wood-frame buildings. The

Figure 115. Cut Foot Ranger Station, Chippewa National Forest, Minnesota. Dating from early in the national forest's history, probably around 1904, this cabin was built by rangers for their own use. The building subsequently became a garage, with wide doors in the end; it has been restored as a cabin. (Photograph by the author, 2014)

Pacific Northwest Region, for instance, which constructed more buildings than any other Forest Service region in the 1930s, built all of its administrative buildings of wood frame. By contrast, C. P. Fickes, an engineer in the region that encompassed Montana, North Dakota, and part of Idaho, advocated log construction. In a six-hundred-page handbook issued in 1935, he asserted, "Most Forest Service buildings will be of log construction." He acknowledged the perception that they cost more, but noted, "Good axemen with considerable mechanical skill can construct log buildings of good appearance almost as cheaply as frame buildings can be erected. The material cost is much less for log buildings, but the labor cost is commensurately higher." He acknowledged, however, that logs were not suitable for year-round dwellings because they were difficult to keep clean. Fickes included plans and elevations of extant examples. Of the eleven ranger residences, three were log; of the three cabins (which were one or two rooms, without bathrooms), two were log. Fickes's advice tended toward the practical, and in 1945 the Forest Service issued the publication *Building with Logs,* in which he expanded his technical guidance and geared it toward the general public. Unlike NPS experts, Fickes advocated the use of "chinkless" log construction, which he attributed to an "old idea" practiced in Scandinavian countries. If chinking had to be used, he recommended covering it with long thin poles. But Fickes also succumbed to the romance of log buildings, preferring saddle-notching to dovetailing because the latter "detracts from the 'loggy' appearance desirable in log structures."[30]

The Forest Service's consulting architect, W. Ellis Groben, also preferred log buildings. In 1940 he wrote a paper about the future of Forest Service architecture in which he excoriated the custom of employing "urban" styles in remote areas and argued that the Forest Service buildings should have an identifiable character. But a universal style would not be appropriate, he felt, because he also advocated sensitivity to local surroundings. Logs provided a solution, not only for aesthetic reasons, but also because of their long history as a building material. "Log buildings, primitive in character and associated with the early history of our country, bespeak the forests themselves. In certain sections of several northern Regions, low, one-story structures, built entirely of logs or a combination of logs and stone, have been customary for generations." He praised the Forest Service for continuing to build of log despite its cost: "In continuing to erect them [log buildings], it performs a highly laudable undertaking in perpetuating the art and traditions of log work in this country, despite the fact that the craftsmanship required to cut and fit the logs involves greater expense than that of other forms of wood construction."[31] While the Forest Service's promotion of log construction for its own buildings, where appropriate, was less wholehearted than the NPS's, the Forest Service nonetheless saw virtues in log construction that overrode its impracticality.

One Forest Service administrative building constructed in this period was a tour de force of log craftsmanship. The Supervisor's Office Building for the Chippewa National Forest in northern Minnesota is a two-and-a-half-story log building in

Figure 116. Supervisor's Office Building, Chippewa National Forest, Minnesota. It is unusual to find a two-and-a-half-story building of logs, but Civilian Conservation Corps and Works Progress Administration laborers achieved it in this building in 1936. The lookout tower stood behind the building. (Leland J. Prater, photographer, 1938, courtesy National Archives, photo no. 95-GP-5318-372596)

an H-shaped plan, measuring 70 by 50 feet (fig. 116). Supervised by builder Isaac Boekenoogen, CCC and WPA laborers used red pine logs, left in the round and grooved lengthwise, to produce the close fit associated with Scandinavian builders. The interior partition walls, also of log, divide the floors into three rooms on a side, with the large central area left mostly open, and add to the complexity of the log construction. Nels Bergley supervised construction of the dramatic stone fireplace and chimney, which rose 32 feet through the center of the building. Bergley had the stones split and book-matched, so that the design is symmetrical. Irregular, frost-cracked maple branches served for the newel post and balustrade, while the stairs were thick planks, left in the round on the sides (plate 16). This spectacular building, completed in 1936 at a cost of $225,000, displays the kind of rustic boldness that appeared only rarely in the Forest Service—or even the NPS—in this period.[32]

Forest Service recreational structures geared for the public were more likely to employ logs in fanciful, evocative ways. Although not log construction, Timberline Lodge, located at the six-thousand-foot elevation in Mount Hood National Forest, Oregon, was the Forest Service's most extreme expression of the rustic style. Designed by architect Gilbert Stanley Underwood and constructed in 1936–37 by WPA workers, Timberline was wood frame, covered with shingles, with a steep hipped roof and a prominent stone first floor. Inside, heavy timber provided the structure, in the form of giant hand-hewn columns and smaller trusses, and smaller logs for the ornament—newel posts, railings, and furniture.[33] In contrast to the NPS, the Forest Service's most exuberant expression of the Rustic Style occurred near the end of the style's popularity, not the beginning.

With design guidance provided at the regional level, not national, the Forest Service rejected the more centralized approach undertaken by the NPS. Similar to the NPS experience, Forest Service personnel built log cabins as the first structures in a forest, following local custom. But as design became professionalized, some northern regions spurned log buildings entirely, while others encouraged them. Where available, skilled craftsmen produced some truly outstanding examples of rustic architecture. In comparing Forest Service rustic buildings to those of the NPS, and NPS buildings to each other, it becomes evident that ideas of compatibility and harmony varied widely and changed over time. At times, for the Forest Service it may have been wood-frame bungalows, and for the NPS poured concrete, but for the most part government agencies furthered the appreciation of log cabins as appropriate both aesthetically and culturally.

With the onset of World War II, the country's greatest investment in its parks came to an end. Work programs such as the CCC and WPA ended, Americans stopped traveling as much in the face of gas and tire rationing, and funding and materials for construction became scarce. By the time construction started again in the late 1940s and 1950s, the aesthetic had changed, and rustic architecture was out of fashion. The new preference was for modernism; simple, unadorned structures were viewed as harmonious, just as log buildings had been a generation earlier. In 1956 the NPS began a construction program called Mission 66, which codified the new modernist buildings as the face of the parks.[34]

Critics derided rustic architecture for being romantic and nostalgic. What a previous generation had seen as sensitivity to cultural, as well as natural, context, postwar designers thought was sentimentality. As landscape architect George Nason wrote in a 1940 NPS publication, "Rude buildings are an affectation. They can only be produced by an effort so deliberate and self-conscious that they lay the designer open to the charge of sophistication. They are not a protest against overelaboration but an elaborate protest against progress in architecture." Nason's attack continued: "There is nothing so quarrelsome with a friendly park as a building outruding the rudeness of the pioneer: cartoons of his dignified deprivations. . . . The little uncouth cabin of our ancestor has the dignity of the best that was in the ability and the financial resources of the man. The glorified pioneer structures of today, some 100 and 200 feet in length with an exaggeration of every uncouthness produced at colossal expense, are a species of tawdry circus showmanship, not examples of simple honesty. They are designed to awe rather than usefully charm." Other architects disdained the rustic buildings' "Hansel-and-Gretel feeling."[35] The critics were right at least in one respect: romanticism did characterize NPS designers' use of the rustic.

Another issue behind the shift to modernism in the parks was that of cost. The simplicity of modernist buildings' design meant that their construction and maintenance were simpler as well. Factory-made materials and repetitive elements also reduced costs. The New Deal park buildings were undeniably labor-intensive, although it is clear that by the 1930s the NPS had taken cost-saving steps such as simulating log and stone construction.[36] The NPS had constructed the most labor-intensive park buildings in the 1920s, if not earlier, when elaborate chalet-like buildings aimed to awe the visitor. By the 1930s a more sober rustic architecture had taken hold, with more unobtrusive designs, but the rustic's reputation as being costly persisted. The trend toward designs that required less labor and cheaper materials would contribute to the abandonment of the rustic aesthetic.

The rustic movement that resulted in the construction of so many log buildings in national and state parks began in the first two decades of the twentieth century, attained a professional maturity in the 1920s, thrived in the 1930s, and was over by the 1940s. The NPS did not invent rustic architecture but did popularize it, carrying it to almost every state in places that the public was encouraged to enjoy. The

NPS's promotion of rustic designs was not a reflection of cheap labor provided by the CCC—rustic architecture had established itself in parks a decade before federal funds and labor started flowing—but it was, rather, a natural result of a focus on unique places. Nor was the NPS's idea of rustic architecture monolithic—the concept of "harmony" ranged from chalets to simple round-log cabins to materials that simulated log construction. But the NPS's use of the rustic represented the last great flourish of log building. Log cabins would continue to be built, but usually in isolated instances by dedicated individuals.

EPILOGUE

The Log Cabin Today

In July 2004, Mark and Carol Plichta began construction on a new log house (fig. 117). Located on the shores of Lake Superior, the house welcomes the outdoors, with a porch across the front and a deck across the back, facing the water. The one-and-a-half-story house has cross gables with large windows in all of the gables. The open interior has high ceilings in the living room and kitchen (fig. 118). The house is open, airy, and light, and about as unlike a small, dark log cabin as it is possible to be.

The construction of the house also reflects the distance that log building has traveled over the centuries. Like many log house builders before them, the Plichtas did most of the construction themselves, contracting out only the concrete foundation, electricity, and plumbing. But unlike log house builders of earlier centuries, the Plichtas turned to a log house company to provide plans, supply the logs, advise on construction, and furnish everything that was needed. This is the new face of log construction: companies that sell plans and milled logs to fit.

Hiawatha Log Homes, in Munising, Michigan, provided the Plichtas' log house. Founded in 1983, Hiawatha offers a variety of floor plans, all of which can be modified to the owner's desire; precision-milled, kiln-dried logs, precut and numbered for the owner's house; and options to provide just the logs, build the shell of the house, or build the whole house. Hiawatha also offers a choice of log forms, either one it calls a "Swedish Cope," which is scribed the length of the log for a tight fit, or

Figure 117. Plichta house, Little Traverse Bay, Michigan. Built by the Plichtas in 2004–7, this new log house has precision-milled logs, precut to fit. (Photograph by the author, 2014)

tongue-and-grooved. Besides whole round logs, the company also sells half logs, so that stud framing and insulation can be added to the interior. The precision milling produces logs with a consistent diameter and no taper, as well as notches that are interchangeable, not fitted. Hiawatha's primary market is retirees, often teachers and doctors, who own a plot of land.[1]

The Plichtas selected the "Norway" plan, then altered it to suit their needs, enlarging it to 1,600 square feet on the first floor and 500 square feet in the loft (fig. 119). Helped by a brother who was a licensed contractor, as well as other family members, the Plichtas put up the log walls in three days but took three years to complete the house. They selected the full round red pine logs with the Swedish cope, but above the eleventh course, in the gables, the wall changes to a stud frame with half logs on the exterior and interior. Where whole logs are used, rubber strips between the logs seal them, then a screw placed every sixteen inches, as well as

Figure 118. Interior, Plichta house, Little Traverse Bay, Michigan. Unlike in log cabins of the past, the interior is light and airy. (Photograph by the author, 2014)

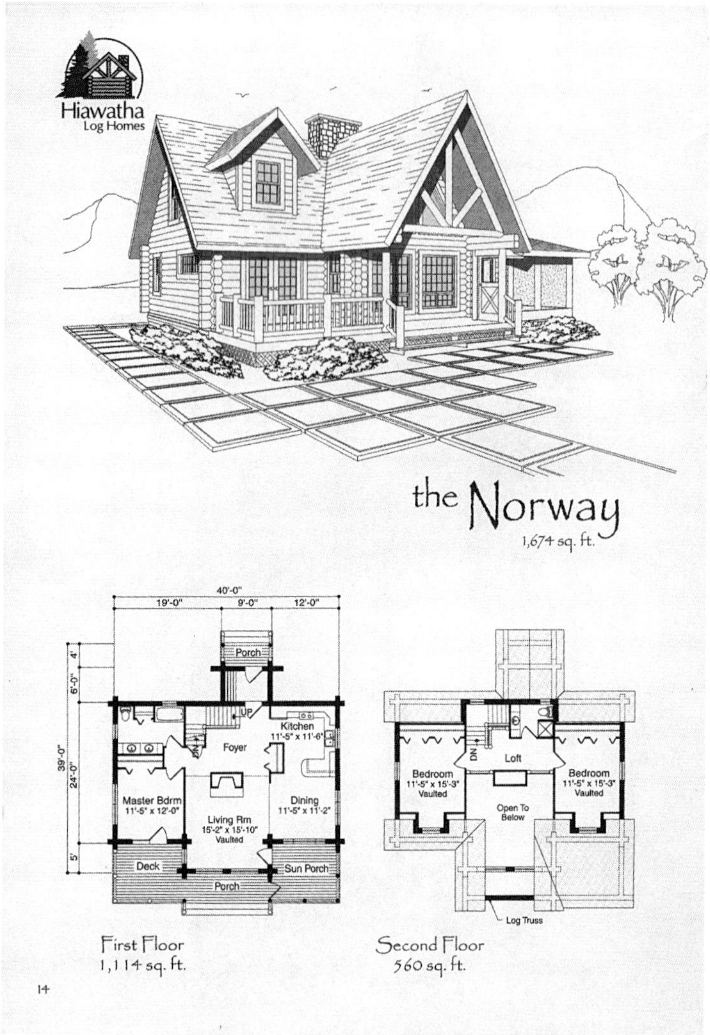

Figure 119. The "Norway" plans and perspective. The Plichtas selected this design from Hiawatha Log Homes of Munising, Michigan. The company provided the logs, and the Plichtas adapted the design to their liking. ("Floor Plans and Details," booklet, Hiawatha Log Homes)

saddle notching at the corners, hold them in place. Faced with a short construction season in this northern climate, and still employed full-time elsewhere, the Plichtas finished the main part of the house and built a garage during the first summer; finished the outside of the house, windows, and stairs the second summer; and completed the inside the third summer. Finally, in October 2007, the house was ready for occupancy. A few years later, Mark Plichta retired from his job as a professor, they sold their house in town, and this became their full-time residence.

Pleased with their new house, the Plichtas cited several reasons for choosing log, which they acknowledge costs 25 or 30 percent more than its equivalent in wood frame. They thought it would be a challenge to build—an "adventure"—and they liked producing something different. They also thought that a log house would be appropriate for its environment, set as it is in a woodsy area overlooking Lake Superior. Further, they like the cozy, solid feeling that a log house imparts.[2] The appeal of a log house is clear here: adventurous, compatible with its surroundings, and home-like.

Hiawatha is by no means the only provider of log houses (which are invariably called "homes"). Many other companies, usually based in areas with ample forests, offer a similar array of services. The plans are typical of today's houses, with great rooms, fireplaces, and numerous bathrooms and closets. Given that they are often intended for vacation areas, the designs feature porches and large windows. While round logs with saddle notching are most common, companies also provide dovetailed, mortise-and-tenon, or butt-jointed corners as well as partially rounded logs. Some companies offer wood-frame construction that looks like log on the outside, while others offer logs that look like clapboards, in order to meet design requirements in subdivisions that prohibit log houses. Other companies retain the handcrafting, keeping the taper in the log. In these cases, the company assembles the building to fit at the factory and then labels, disassembles, moves, and reassembles it at the building site. The National Association of Home Builders Log Homes Council claims that more Americans are living in log houses today than at any time in history. While firm numbers are hard to obtain, it appears that more than twenty-six thousand log homes are built each year.[3]

The factory-milled log house is, on the one hand, far away from the iconic log cabin. It is not handcrafted or built from logs on-site; it is usually large, with bathrooms and porches and expansive windows; and it is a product of the market economy.[4] But on the other hand, it is very much a part of the log cabin's history. Like the Plichtas, other homeowners choose log construction because of its appropriateness for the setting, for its closeness to nature, and for its solidity. They also choose it for its long history and its associations with the past. While today's expansive log home may not resemble the classic log cabin of the early nineteenth century, it is certainly inspired by it. The current log house reflects a rising standard of living, with more space, more amenities, and a different attitude toward the outdoors, one that sees it as a place of recreation, not work.[5]

Other log cabin enthusiasts devote their efforts to existing, historical log cabins. Restoration of old log buildings—sometimes abandoned outbuildings, sometimes covered up farmhouses—appeals to some homeowners. After a resurgence of log cabin building in the 1960s and 1970s by back-to-the-land adherents, interest shifted to rescuing abandoned log buildings. Charles McRaven notes that the first edition of his book, published in 1978 as *Building the Hewn-Log House,* focused on new construction, while his third edition, titled *The Classic Hewn-Log House: A Step-By-Step Guide to Building and Restoring* and published more than twenty-five years later, concentrates on restoration and rebuilding. In general, craftsmen find abandoned log buildings; dismantle, move, reerect, and re-chink them; and then either add new construction to convert them to residences or make them into outbuildings with new functions.[6]

Historic log buildings are also available to the public through museums. Several log cabins exhibited to the public, such as those associated with Abraham Lincoln and Booker T. Washington, or sites such as Valley Forge, have served as resources for this book. Other museums display log cabins not for any association with famous people or events, but for their innate interest. Old World Wisconsin is one of the best examples of this type. Opened in 1976, the open-air museum displays sixty-nine historic buildings collected from across the state in order to represent the various ethnic groups that settled Wisconsin in the nineteenth century. Several of the buildings are log, arranged in farmsteads to evoke their original purposes (fig. 120). The establishment of the museum reflects not only the growing awareness of social and ethnic history in the 1970s, but also the interest in handcraft and self-sufficiency expressed in the back-to-the-land movement at that time.[7]

The log cabin today is available in many forms: in its original use, such as farmhouses and recreation buildings; in an adapted use, such as old barns moved to new sites and converted into residences; in an exhibited use, such as open-air museums and historic sites devoted to important people and events; and as brand new, expanded to accommodate modern uses and constructed using new technology. Log cabins exist in harmonious settings across the United States, serving as shelter and cultural markers.

The role of the log cabin as an American icon has seen many variations, bound

Figure 120. Schottler House, Old World Wisconsin, Eagle, Wisconsin. Built in 1847, with its lean-to added in about 1855, this log house represents German craftsmanship. The same family owned it for more than a century, until it was dismantled and moved to the outdoor museum. (Photograph by the author, 2011)

up as it is in nostalgia and romance. Each viewer, user, or creator finds in a log cabin a different reason to interact with it. For some, it is the sheer beauty of a building that arises out of its surroundings and melts back into them. For others, it is the challenge of working with one's hands in a way that many have before, producing a timeless shelter. For yet others, it is the linkage to an American past in which individuals made their own way, using the resources of the land. In the past, the attraction of log cabins might have been one of necessity or lack of other options. It might have been a test of one's fortitude or a display of one's accomplishments. It might have been a symbol of one's cultural heritage or a sign that one had adapted to a new land.

This very malleability of the log cabin—the multiple meanings contained in a simple building—is the strength of the log cabin as an American icon. It encompasses different beliefs about the resiliency of Americans, about their individuality, and about their relationship to the land. Some have seen, and continue to see, the log cabin as a dark, leaky hovel, while others see it as a charming cottage; some see it as a sign of abject poverty, others as a political advantage; some see it as a means of conquering a land through settlement, others as evidence of self-reliance. It is all these qualities and more, added together, as contradictory as they are, that begin to describe an American culture that sees itself in a log cabin.

HISTORIOGRAPHICAL NOTE

The historiography of the log cabin has concentrated on its origins in America. This fundamental issue, which has occupied historians, geographers, and folklorists for several generations, has tended to focus on whether English colonists were the first to build in log. If not them, then was it the Swedes in Delaware? And if it was the Swedes, then were they responsible for its eighteenth-century dominance, or did the Germans reintroduce it with far greater impact?

In the 1920s, two scholars cast doubt on the likelihood of English colonists having been the first to build log cabins. The first to debunk this myth was architect Fiske Kimball in *Domestic Architecture of the American Colonies and of the Early Republic,* published in 1922, just a year after Plymouth's tercentenary celebrations. Kimball identified the Swedes as the most likely originators. A few years later, lawyer and archeologist Henry Chapman Mercer delivered a series of lectures, subsequently published as articles, which reflected his close attention to the historical record. He recognized that the English built horizontal-log blockhouses in New England, but he dismissed them as a model for houses.[1] The first log dwellings, he posited, were built by the Swedes.

This new scholarship was slow to spread, though, and Harold Shurtleff became frustrated by the persistence, in historical memory as well as at historic sites, of the primacy of British log cabins. Shurtleff, an architect, headed the Research Department at Colonial Williamsburg. His *The Log Cabin Myth* explores the written record of colonial America, up and down the East Coast. Like Kimball and Mercer, Shurtleff eliminated colonial settlements as sources for the log cabin until he reached New Sweden, for which he relied heavily on *The Swedish Settlements on the Delaware,* published by Amandus Johnson in 1911. Citing the tradition of log building in Sweden and Finland, a handful of contemporary descriptions of buildings in New Sweden, and some descriptions dating from after the period of Swedish rule, Shurtleff argued that the Swedes who settled in Delaware introduced the log cabin to America.[2]

The next to pick up the Swedish banner was Clinton Alfred Weslager, an amateur historian and archeologist who spent most of his career working in sales for the DuPont Company in Delaware. Weslager's 1969 book, *The Log Cabin in America: From Pioneer Days to the Present,* discussed the historical record, as had Shurtleff, but also added a fieldwork component. Weslager identified a number of log buildings in the Delaware valley that appeared to be Swedish, or derived from Swedish tradition. Determining construction dates for these buildings was all but impossible, as Weslager acknowledged; the lack of specific contemporary descriptions of Swedish houses meant that there were no diagnostic characteristics. Weslager noted that the Swedes built with both round and hewn logs, with various forms of notching, and in a range of permanence, from makeshift to highly finished. The only characteristic he could identify as Swedish was a corner fireplace, and even that was not universal. Weslager also pointed out that at least half of the Swedes in the colony were descendants of Finns who had migrated to Sweden in the late sixteenth century, but the Finnish building techniques were no more distinctive than the Swedish. Weslager explored twenty log dwellings in Pennsylvania, New Jersey, and Delaware that he thought had Swedish connections. The buildings' characteristics ranged from hewn logs with dovetailed corners to round logs with ends that extended past the notching, fireplaces in corners and in the center of the gable end, and both one and two stories. Weslager was unable to determine a definitive construction date for any of them. At the site of one cabin, now on display at the Delaware Agricultural Museum in Dover, he undertook an archeological dig that pointed to a 1750 construction date. Still, he held that "the builder had been influenced by older Swedish and Finnish cabins then still in existence" in the area.[3]

Geographers have been extremely influential in the study of the log cabin. In his 1965 landmark article, "Folk Housing: Key to Diffusion," Fred B. Kniffen, a geographer from Louisiana State University, posited that folk housing, such as the

I-house and log buildings, identified cultural complexes and that movement and influence could be readily charted from their distribution. Kniffen dismissed the Swedes as being influential (they were "lost in a sea of alien culture," as he described it) and credited Germans in Pennsylvania with reintroducing log construction that the Scotch-Irish then spread west and southwest. The next year Kniffen coauthored an article with folklorist Henry Glassie that examined wood construction more generally. In their discussion of horizontal log construction, the authors concentrated on the distribution of types of corner notching, charting the spread of the half dovetail and V-notch from their Pennsylvania German hearth to points south and southwest.[4]

In 1985 geographer Terry G. Jordan's book, *American Log Buildings: An Old-World Heritage,* revived the Swedes-in-Delaware theory. Jordan undertook extensive fieldwork in northern Europe looking for precedents, complemented by fieldwork in the United States, and concluded that Swedes, and particularly the Finns among their number, had the preponderant influence on mid-Atlantic log construction. In 1989 Jordan coauthored a book with geographer Matti Kaups, *The American Backwoods Frontier: An Ethnic and Ecological Interpretation,* which looked more broadly at the frontier experience, including aspects such as farming techniques as well as construction methods. Their conclusion was an even more emphatic endorsement of the Finns as progenitors, explaining the Finns' influence in part by their ability to assimilate into the larger culture.[5]

Historian Patricia Irvin Cooper argued for two places of origin. Her studies of the coastal plains of Georgia and North Carolina led her to conclude that while one hearth, the German one in Pennsylvania, might have contributed to the settlement of the upland south, another hearth, the Swede-Finn one in Delaware, added to the diffusion of its architecture along the coast. Historian Carl Lounsbury likewise found that Swedish influence accounted for the appearance of log construction among Anglo-American colonists in the Chesapeake Bay region as early as the 1660s.[6]

The English did not bring log construction to the colonies, but historians such as Lounsbury have found instances of early adoption. Although some scholars of log cabins dismissed the New England "garrison houses"—houses built of horizontal squared logs—as being military in character and irrelevant to the larger log cabin story, others rejected that distinction. Richard Candee identified dozens of log houses built before 1750 in Maine and New Hampshire that were not primarily defensive in character, but that were nonetheless built of thick planks laid horizontally, notched at the corners.[7]

This extensive scholarly dispute will probably never be definitively settled. The written record is not specific enough to solve it, and the built examples that survive cannot be documented with enough certainty to draw conclusions. And the argument concerns just one aspect: the introduction of the log cabin to the East Coast of the United States during the colonial period. Also to be considered are the French influence in the Mississippi Valley, Russian influence in the Northwest, Mexican influence in the Southwest, and Scandinavian influence in the Upper Midwest. Furthermore, some scholars discard building material as a reflection of cultural influence entirely, finding that floor plans are a better determinant of cultural persistence. People cleave to their traditional forms even as they use alternate materials, depending on circumstances.[8]

The nature of the historical debate is interesting in itself. The East Coast orientation, the focus on origins, and the argument over different ethnic groups say as much, perhaps, about the scholars and the times in which they operate as they do about log cabins. As one example, Terry G. Jordan, John T. Kilpinen, and Charles F. Gritzner's book, *The Mountain West: Interpreting the Folk Landscape*, which includes important chapters on log dwellings, log outbuildings, and log carpentry traditions, delights in its own bias toward field research. "Dirty boots and wet socks go with cultural geography, and we know more about sunburn and sore feet than we do of hemorrhoids," they proclaim in a dig at library-based research, and "we distrust data gathered in any other manner."[9] Log cabins tend to elicit this kind of enthusiasm from scholars partial to the fundamentally outdoorsy nature of this basic building type. These sentiments are shared by builders, occupants, and preservationists, not only scholars, as this book has shown. The historiography of the log cabin's origins reveals that the log cabin was brought to America by several cultural groups and that it was readily taken up, as convenient, by others.

ESSAY ON SOURCES

Because each of the chapters in this book draws on a discrete set of sources, cited fully in the endnotes, a consolidated bibliography did not seem helpful. Instead, a broad discussion of the kinds of sources shows the range of possibilities beyond published, secondary sources. As a work that synthesizes geographically specific fieldwork and analysis undertaken by others, this book owes a particular debt to these unpublished sources.

The Historiographical Note discusses some scholars of log cabins in terms of their interest in the origin of the log cabin in America. These scholars' publications—Fred Kniffen's "Folk Housing: Key to Diffusion," first published in the *Annals of the American Association of Geographers* in December 1965, reprinted in *Common Places: Readings in American Vernacular Architecture,* edited by Dell Upton and John Michael Vlach (Athens: University of Georgia Press, 1986), 3–26; Henry Glassie's *Pattern in the Material Folk Culture of the Eastern United States* (Philadelphia: University of Pennsylvania Press, 1968); and Terry G. Jordan's *American Log Buildings: An Old World Heritage* (Chapel Hill: University of North Carolina Press, 1985), among others—also sparked an interest in finding and studying log cabins in the field. The National Historic Preservation Act of 1966 provided the means for field survey by authorizing federal funding through the states, state historic preservation offices undertook and supervised the survey work, and the scholarly environment encouraged attention to the details of log cabins. The

National Register of Historic Places serves as the repository for many of the results of these surveys, in the form of nominations for listing.

The National Register is under the aegis of the National Park Service, in which other divisions also study buildings. The Historic American Buildings Survey, established in 1933, documents the nation's built heritage and, over time, has recorded many log cabins on the verge of disappearing. HABS and the National Register are concerned with buildings both inside and outside the national parks, while other divisions of the National Park Service document buildings that stand within its own parks through a range of official documents. Historic structure reports, historic resource studies, cultural landscape reports, and administrative histories all proved extremely useful to this project. Better yet, most of the National Park Service's reports and documentation are available online, which is truly a boon for the researcher of unpublished material.

Archives across the country provided access to unpublished materials other than those of the National Park Service. Archivists and curators made reports, correspondence, diaries, and photographs available at places such as Old World Wisconsin in Eagle, Wisconsin; Stratford Hall in Stratford, Virginia; the Hermitage, in Hermitage, Tennessee; and three institutions in Plymouth, Massachusetts: Pilgrim Hall, Plymouth Antiquarian Society, and Plimoth Plantation Library. Another type of unpublished material is the guidebooks produced for the annual meetings of the Vernacular Architecture Forum—specifically, Leland Roth, *Building at the End of the Oregon Trail* (1997); *Cotton Mills, Planned Communities, and the New Deal: Vernacular Architecture and Landscapes of the New South,* edited by Debbie Curtis Toole (1999); Arnold R. Alanen, *A Field Guide to the Architecture and Landscapes of Northern Minnesota* (2000); *Architecture and Landscape of the Pennsylvania Germans, 1720–1920,* edited by Nancy van Dolsen (2004); and *Down Jersey: From Bayshore to Seashore,* edited by Robert W. Craig (2014)—although the opportunity provided by those meetings to visit the buildings was even more valuable.

Another result of the surge of fieldwork was focused publications that examined log cabins in a region or state. Particularly valuable were Jennifer Eastman Attebery, *Building with Logs: Western Log Construction in Context* (Moscow: University of Idaho, 1998); Donald A. Hutslar, *The Architecture of Migration: Log Construction in the Ohio Country, 1750–1850* (Athens: Ohio University Press, 1986); Charles E. Martin, *Hollybush: Folk Building and Social Change in an Appalachian Community*

(Knoxville: University of Tennessee Press, 1984); Warren E. Roberts, *Log Buildings of Southern Indiana* (Bloomington: Trickster Press, 1984); and Michael Ann Williams, *Homeplace: The Social Use and Meaning of the Folk Dwelling in Southwestern North Carolina* (Athens: University of Georgia Press, 1991). An important book that synthesized years of fieldwork was *The Chesapeake House: Architectural Investigation by Colonial Williamsburg,* edited by Cary Carson and Carl R. Lounsbury (Chapel Hill: University of North Carolina Press, 2013), which was published during the preparation of my book. Chapters on slave housing by Edward A. Chappell and on wood construction by Willie Graham were particularly valuable.

Other published work formed the basis of some of my analysis, including memoirs and diaries such as Caroline Kirkland writing as Mrs. Mary Clavers, *A New Home: Who'll Follow? or, Glimpses of Western Life* (New York: C. S. Francis 1839); Sam Keith writing from the journals of Richard Proenneke, *One Man's Wilderness: An Alaskan Odyssey* (Anchorage: Alaska Northwest Books, 1999); and Theodore Roosevelt, *Hunting Trips of a Ranchman: Sketches of Sport on the Northern Plains* (New York: G. P. Putnam's Sons, 1885). Novels also shed light on log cabin experiences and attitudes, such as Harriet Beecher Stowe, *Uncle Tom's Cabin* (New York: Signet Classics, 2008); John Pendleton Kennedy, *Swallow Barn, or A Sojourn in the Old Dominion* (New York: George P. Putnam, 1852); Lucy Furman, *The Glass Window: A Story of the Quare Women* (Boston: Little, Brown, 1925); and Laura Ingalls Wilder, *Little House in the Big Woods* (1932; rev. ed., New York: HarperCollins, 2004) and *Little House on the Prairie* (1935; rev. ed., New York: HarperCollins, 1971). All of these memoirists and novelists used the log cabin didactically, which did not lessen their usefulness.

People are always a good source, and perceptive comments, offered even incidentally, came from too many friends and colleagues to note here. Douglass Reed in Pennsylvania and Alan Pape in Wisconsin both took the time to explain aspects of log construction and reconstruction. The Log and Timber Home Show in a convention hall near Dulles Airport, outside of Washington, DC, gave a sense of the current market. Gary Bufe of Hiawatha Log Homes in Munising, Michigan, gave a tour of his log cabin manufacturing facility, and Mark and Carol Plichta of Little Traverse Bay, Michigan, generously offered their log house as a sample Hiawatha product.

Finally, and most importantly, the buildings themselves served as an important source. Visiting dozens, if not hundreds, of log cabins, many of which were open to the public, revealed the range of buildings, variations in size and construction, changes over time, and quirky details. Further, the interest in preserving and interpreting log cabins, the enthusiasm demonstrated by their protectors and visitors, and the commitment shown by their stewards provided another dimension to this book by demonstrating that log cabins have many lives past their initial construction and inhabitation, into the present day.

NOTES

INTRODUCTION

1. For his reminiscence of this adventure, see William Dean Howells, *My Year in a Log Cabin* (New York: Harper & Brothers, 1893).

2. Alison K. Hoagland, *Buildings of Alaska* (New York: Oxford University Press, 1993), 249–50. William E. Brown, *Gaunt Beauty—Tenuous Life: Historic Resources Study, Gates of the Arctic National Park and Preserve* (Washington, D.C.: National Park Service, 1988), 1: 307, 336–52, 499–500; 2: 94.

3. Harold R. Shurtleff, *The Log Cabin Myth: A Study of the Early Dwellings of the English Colonists in North America* (Cambridge: Harvard University Press, 1939). See the Historiographical Note in this volume.

4. Wickersham, 25 August 1900, James Wickersham correspondence, University of Alaska–Fairbanks Archives.

1. "THE TRUE RUSTIC ORDER"

1. Orsamus Turner, *Pioneer History of the Holland Purchase* (Buffalo: Jewett, Thomas, 1849), 563.

2. Ibid., 565, 566.

3. See Donald A. Hutslar, *The Architecture of Migration: Log Construction in the Ohio Country, 1750–1850* (Athens: Ohio University Press, 1986).

4. Some stovewood houses date to the mid-nineteenth century, but the method experienced a resurgence in the 1920s and 1930s with the use of portable power saws. Richard W. E. Perrin, "Wisconsin 'Stovewood' Walls: Ingenious Forms of Early Log Construction," *Wisconsin Maga-*

zine of History 46, no. 3 (Spring 1963): 215–19. Robert Stratton, "Stovewood Barns," *Michigan History* 74, no. 1 (January/February 1990): 40–44. William H. Tishler, "Stovewood Construction in the Upper Midwest and Canada: A Regional Vernacular Architectural Tradition," *Perspectives in Vernacular Architecture I,* ed. Camille Wells (Annapolis, Md.: Vernacular Architecture Forum, 1982): 125–36.

5. Thaddeus Mason Harris, *The Journal of a Tour into the Territory Northwest of the Alleghany Mountains* (Boston: Manning and Loring, 1805), 15.

6. Charles E. Martin, *Hollybush: Folk Building and Social Change in an Appalachian Community* (Knoxville: University of Tennessee Press, 1984), 17.

7. Mac E. Barrick, "The Log House as Cultural Symbol," *Material Culture* 18, no. 1 (1986): 11, 13.

8. Hutslar, *Architecture of Migration,* 309. Warren E. Roberts, *Log Buildings of Southern Indiana* (Bloomington: Trickster Press, 1984), 5, 61. J. M. Peck, *A New Guide for Emigrants to the West, Containing Sketches...* (Boston: Gould, Kendall, and Lincoln, 1836), 118. Douglass Reed, interview by author, June 9, 2014. Henry Irven Gaines, *Kings Maelum* (New York: Vantage Press, 1972), 63.

9. Warren E. Roberts, "The Tools Used in Building Log Houses in Indiana," in *Common Places: Readings in American Vernacular Architecture,* ed. Dell Upton and John Michael Vlach (Athens: University of Georgia Press, 1986), 182–203. Quote from Terry G. Jordan, *Texas Log Buildings: A Folk Architecture* (Austin: University of Texas Press, 1978), 12. For a detailed description of the construction process, see Martin, *Hollybush,* 17–26.

10. "Hutting tools furnished for one regiment, December 1779," cited in Eric Olsen, "Huts," research paper from Morristown National Historic Site, n.d., 7. Peck, *New Guide for Emigrants,* 119. Bruce D. Bomberger, "The Preservation and Repair of Historic Log Buildings" (Washington, D.C.: National Park Service, Preservation Assistance Preservation Briefs, 1991), 6.

11. Bomberger, "Preservation and Repair," 5–6. Hewn logs cost twice as much as round, although any log construction was cheaper than frame. Brian Coffey, "From Shanty to House: Log Construction in Nineteenth-Century Ontario," *Material Culture* 16, no. 2 (1984): 69. Plank construction defined by Carl R. Lounsbury, *An Illustrated Glossary of Early Southern Architecture and Landscape* (New York: Oxford University Press, 1994), 278–79. In Ontario, however, Coffey defined plank houses as houses in which the planks were laid with the thicker sides flat for an even more secure structure (68). Another form of construction, in which planks are set vertically, without a frame, is also called plank construction or, in some places, boxed. Michael Ann Williams, *Homeplace: The Social Use and Meaning of the Folk Dwelling in Southwestern North Carolina* (Athens: University of Georgia Press, 1991), 31–32. Catherine W. Bishir, Michael T. Southern, and Jennifer F. Martin, *A Guide to the Historic Architecture of Western North Carolina* (Chapel Hill: University of North Carolina Press, 1999), 70.

12. Robert Carlton [Baynard Rush Hall], *The New Purchase; or, Seven and a Half Years in the Far West* (1843; repr., Princeton: Princeton University Press, 1916), 93.

13. See chapter 2 for a short description of Lincoln Logs. The arguments concerning notch selection are summarized by Hutslar, *Architecture of Migration,* 36–42. See also Barrick, "Log House," 5.

14. Douglass Reed interview. Willie Graham, "Timber Framing," in *The Chesapeake House: Architectural Investigation by Colonial Williamsburg,* ed. Cary Carson and Carl R. Lounsbury (Chapel Hill: University of North Carolina Press, 2013), 224.

15. Hutslar, *Architecture of Migration,* 374. Roberts, *Log Buildings,* 22, 75–85. See Nancy Van Dolsen, "The Brick-Cased Log Houses of Cumberland County, Pennsylvania," *Perspectives in Vernacular Architecture III,* ed. Thomas Carter and Bernard L. Herman (Columbia: University of Missouri Press, 1989), 99–107.

16. Lynne Richards, "Dwelling Places: Log Homes in Oklahoma's Indian Territory, 1850–1909," *Material Culture* 25, no. 2 (1993): 8. John Linley, *The Georgia Catalog: Historic American Buildings Survey, A Guide to the Architecture of the State* (Athens: University of Georgia Press, 1982), 18. Also, George Washington ordered chinking removed at Valley Forge on May 27, 1778, to increase ventilation and, thus, sanitation. Jacqueline Thibaut, *In the True Rustic Order: Material Aspects of the Valley Forge Encampment, 1777–1778,* vol. 3 of *Valley Forge Historical Research Report* (King of Prussia, Pa.: Valley Forge National Historical Park, 1979), 33.

17. Frederick Law Olmsted, *Journey in Seaboard Slave State, with Remarks on Their Economy* (New York: Dix and Edwards, 1856), 385–86. Jonathan Cross, cited in S. Allen Chambers Jr. *Buildings of West Virginia* (New York: Oxford University Press, 2004), 18. Edward C. Carter II, John C. Van Horne, and Charles E. Brownell, eds., *Latrobe's View of America, 1795–1820* (New Haven: Yale University Press, 1985), 270.

18. Jordan, *Texas Log Buildings,* 83. Lounsbury, *Illustrated Glossary,* 297.

19. John S. Williams, "Our Cabin; or, Life in the Woods," *American Pioneer* 2, no. 10 (October 1843): 445.

20. Peck, *New Guide,* 118. Cited in Paula Stoner Reed, "Building with Stone in the Cumberland Valley: A Study of Regional Environmental, Technical, and Cultural Factors in Stone Construction" (Ph.D. diss., George Washington University, 1988), 116. Lounsbury, *Illustrated Glossary,* 56–57. Bishir, Souther, and Martin, *Guide to the Historic Architecture,* 386. Jordan, *Texas Log Buildings,* 84.

21. Peter Kalm, *Peter Kalm's Travels in North America: The English Version of 1770,* ed. Adolph B. Benson (New York: Dover, 1987), 728. Douglass Reed interview. Roberts, *Log Buildings,* 94. Plans of multiroom log houses are discussed in William J. Macintire, *The Pioneer Log House in Kentucky* (Frankfort: Kentucky Heritage Council, 1998), 7–13.

22. Scandinavians employed front-gable entrances in the Delaware valley. Terry G. Jordan and Matti Kaups, *The American Backwoods Frontier: An Ethnic and Ecological Interpretation* (Baltimore: Johns Hopkins University Press, 1989), 196–208. Folklorist Henry Glassie, on the other hand, stated flatly that "the usual American folk house has its door in the side—not in the gable—and is oriented with that door toward a road, lane, or waterway." Henry Glassie, *Pattern in the Material Folk Culture of the Eastern United States* (Philadelphia: University of Pennsylvania Press, 1968), 218.

23. Henry Glassie, "The Types of the Southern Mountain Cabin," in *The Study of American Folklore: An Introduction,* ed. Jan Harold Brunvand, 3rd ed. (New York: W. W. Norton, 1986), 543–52. Roberts, *Log Buildings,* 115–16.

24. Carlton, *New Purchase,* 94–95. Williams, *Homeplace,* 50–61.

25. William D. Moore "From Peru to Alaska" (University of Washington Manuscript Collection, typescript, [1923]), unpaginated.

26. Alison K. Hoagland, *Mine Towns: Buildings for Workers in Michigan's Copper Country* (Minneapolis: University of Minnesota Press, 2010), 3–5. Howells, *My Year,* 4. Martin, *Hollybush,* 28–30.

27. Williams, *Homeplace,* 65–67.

28. Basil Hall, *Travels in North America, in the Years 1827 and 1828* (Edinburgh: Robert Cadell, 1830), 3: 271–72. In an 1815 letter to a prospective overseer, Thomas Jefferson offered him a one-room house with the possibility of expanding it: "Another room with a passage between can quickly be added of hewn logs as is usual in that country, plaistered, with windows, stone chimney, etc." Cited in S. Allen Chambers Jr., *Poplar Forest and Thomas Jefferson* (privately printed, 1993), 88.

29. George Washington, General Orders, December 18, 1777, in Thibault, "Valley Forge," 53.

30. Jonathan Todd, cited in Thibaut, "Valley Forge," 21. Thomas Paine to Benjamin Franklin, cited in Thibaut, "Valley Forge," 6.

31. Washington, General Orders, December 18, 1777, in Thibault, "Valley Forge," 53. Jonathan Todd, 19 January 1778, and John Buss, 2 January 1778, cited in Thibaut, "Valley Forge," 25–26. Thibaut, "Valley Forge," 59.

32. Thibaut, "Valley Forge," 30.

33. Eric Olsen, "Huts," and Thomas Winslow, "Hutting the Troops," Morristown National Historical Park. For a contemporary description of the roof construction, see Joseph Plumb Martin, *Private Yankee Doodle,* ed. George F. Scheer (Little, Brown, 1962; repr., Fort Washington, Pa.: Eastern National, 2012), 168–69.

34. Carole Shammas, "The Housing Stock of the Early United States: Refinement Meets Migration," *William and Mary Quarterly,* 3rd series, 64, no. 3 (July 2007): 579, 556, 570, 566–67. The tax lists of only 62 of the 359 counties survive. Lee Soltow, *Distribution of Wealth and Income in the United States in 1798* (Pittsburgh: University of Pittsburgh Press, 1989), 3, 54. Typical of the recording irregularity was Berkeley Parish, Virginia, located in the Tidewater/Piedmont borderland. Of all houses, valued at either above or below $100, 23 percent were specifically designated as log, another 54 percent received the more generic designation of "wood," while just 5 percent were called frame. In another 18 percent the census taker did not specify a material. There was just one brick house. Ashli White, "The Character of a Landscape: Domestic Architecture and Community in Late Eighteenth-Century Berkeley Parish, Virginia," *Winterthur Portfolio* 34, no. 2/3 (Summer-Autumn 1999): 134.

Other sources point to the dominance of log: In Adams County, in south-central Pennsylvania, 86 percent of the houses listed in 1798 were log, while in Franklin County, the adjacent county to the west, 88 percent were log. P. Reed, "Building with Stone," 166, 151. Franklin County had a heavily German-born population (about 40 percent), but in Lancaster County, to the east, Germans were no more likely to build of log than immigrants from other nations were. In Hempfield Township, for example, where Germans composed 19 percent of the population, two-thirds of them built in log, as did an equal percentage of non-Germans. Gabrielle Lanier, *The Delaware Valley in the Early Republic: Architecture, Landscape, and Regional Identity* (Baltimore: Johns Hopkins University Press, 2005), 182, table 2. In Mifflin County, Pennsylvania, in the Allegheny Mountains, 90 percent of the housing stock was log. Lee Soltow, "Egalitarian America and Its Inegalitarian Housing in the Federal Period," *Social Science History* 9, no. 2 (Spring 1985): 203. In Maryland, more than 70 percent of the dwellings in Baltimore County and more than 80 percent in Carroll County were log, while the percentages were much lower in the eastern counties of Anne Arundel (24 percent) and Prince Georges (21 percent). Carl Lounsbury, "Log Building in the Chesapeake," *Vernacular Architecture* 41 (2010): 78. Liz Gallow, "Observations from the 1798 Tax Record for Anne Arundel, Baltimore, Prince George, and Somerset Counties, Maryland" (Williamsburg, Va.: Colonial Williamsburg Foundation, Architectural Research Department, 2005), unpaginated. Graham, "Timber Framing," 222–23.

35. C. A. Weslager, *The Log Cabin in America: From Pioneer Days to the Present* (New Brunswick: Rutgers University Press, 1969), 150–53. Jordan and Kaups, *American Backwoods Frontier*, 53. W. Barksdale Maynard, *Buildings of Delaware* (Charlottesville: University of Virginia Press, 2008), 5. Henry Mercer, "The Origin of Log Houses in the United States," *Old-Time New England* 18, no. 2 (October 1927): 53. Mercer's articles were published in 1927 but were based on lectures delivered in 1924. Jaspar Dankers and Peter Sluyter, *Journal of a Voyage to New York and a Tour in Several of the American Colonies in 1679–80* (Brooklyn: Long Island Historical Society, 1867), 174. Similarly, in 1683 John Lawson described an Albemarle Sound (eastern North Carolina) storehouse as "a House made of Logs (such as the *Swedes* in *America* very often make, and are very strong)." Cited in Patricia Irvin Cooper, "Cabins and Deerskins: Log Building and the Charles Town Indian Trade," *Tennessee Historical Quarterly* 52, no. 4 (Winter 1994): 275. See Historiographical Note in this volume for more discussion of the log cabin's origins in America.

36. Cary Carson, Norman F. Barka, William M. Kelso, Garry Wheeler Stone, and Dell Upton, "Impermanent Architecture in the Southern American Colonies," *Winterthur Portfolio* 16, nos. 2/3 (Summer/Autumn 1981): 155. Lounsbury, *Illustrated Glossary*, 217–18. Harold R. Shurtleff, *The Log Cabin Myth: A Study of the Early Dwellings of the English Colonists in North America* (Cambridge: Harvard University Press, 1939), 4. Beauchamp Plantagenet [Edmund Plowden], *A Description of the Province of New Albion* (London: James Moxon, 1650), 32. He did not include this description in the first edition, published in 1648. Charles Peterson, "American Notes: Houses for New Albion, 1650," *Journal of the Society of Architectural Historians* 15, no. 3 (October 1956): 2. G. Carroll Lindsay, "American Notes: New Albion (Continued)," *Journal of the Society of Architectural Historians* 17, no. 4 (Winter 1958): 31–35.

37. Hutslar, *Architecture of Migration*, 16. William Byrd, *The Westover Manuscripts: Containing the History of the Dividing Line betwixt Virginia and North Carolina* (Petersburg, Va.: Edmund and Julian C. Ruffin, 1841), 28.

38. Sally McMurry and Nancy Van Dolsen, introduction to *Architecture and Landscape of the Pennsylvania Germans, 1720–1920*, ed. Sally McMurry and Nancy Van Dolsen (Philadelphia: University of Pennsylvania Press, 2011), 2. LaRochefoucauld cited in Gabrielle Lanier, "Landscapes," *Architecture and Landscape*, 13. David Hackett Fischer, *Albion's Seed: Four British*

Folkways in America (New York: Oxford, 1989), 656–57, 660. Kalm, *Peter Kalm's Travels*, 728. Fred B. Kniffen and Henry Glassie, "Building in Wood in the Eastern United States: A Time-Place Perspective," in Upton and Vlach, *Common Places*, 173–75.

The cultural transference is significant here. Just how this preference for log construction was transferred, whether it was close contact or distant observation, has not been documented. McMurry discussed several models of transference in relation to Germans' adoption of American forms. Sally McMurry, "Rural Houses," in McMurry and Van Dolsen, *Architecture and Landscape*, 54. Kniffen and Glassie attribute Scotch-Irish adoption of log construction to "practicality in timber-rich America." Kniffen and Glassie, "Building in Wood," 173. Warren Hofstra documented extensive commercial transactions between Germans and Scotch-Irish in one community in western Virginia, indicating that cross-cultural communication was common. Warren R. Hofstra, "Searching for Peace and Prosperity: Opequon Settlement, Virginia, 1730s–1760s," in *Ulster to America: The Scots-Irish Migration Experience, 1680–1830*, ed. Warren R. Hofstra (Knoxville: University of Tennessee Press, 2012), 112.

39. Joseph Doddridge, *Notes on the Settlement and Indian Wars of the Western Parts of Virginia and Pennsylvania from 1763 to 1783, Inclusive* (Albany, N.Y.: Joel Munsell, 1876), 139.

40. Butler cited in Chambers, *Buildings of West Virginia*, 15. F. A. Michaux, *Travels to the Westward of the Alleghany Mountains, in the States of the Ohio, Kentucky, and Tennessee, in the Year 1802* (London: Richard Phillips, 1805), 17.

41. Brian Coffey and Allen G. Noble, "Residential Building Materials in New York State, 1855–1875," *Material Culture* 21, no. 1 (1989): 6, 13–14.

42. Harold Kalman, *A History of Canadian Architecture* (Toronto: Oxford University Press, 1994), 1: 48–51. Jay D. Edwards, "French," in *America's Architectural Roots: Ethnic Groups That Built America*, ed. Dell Upton (Washington, D.C.: Preservation Press, 1986), 62. Richard W. Hale Jr., "The French Side of the 'Log Cabin Myth,'" *Proceedings of the Massachusetts Historical Society* 72 (October-December 1957–60): 120–22. Mary K. Cullen, "Highlights of Domestic Building in Pre-Confederation Quebec and Ontario as Seen through Travel Literature from 1763 to1860," *Bulletin of the Association for Preservation Technology* 13, no. 1 (1981): 18. Henri Joutel cited in Kalman, *History of Canadian Architecture*, 51. Architect Charles Peterson documented horizontal log construction in French colonial St. Louis, but it was rare. Charles E. Peterson, *Colonial St. Louis: Building a Creole Capital* (Tucson: Patrice Press, 1993), 45, 46.

43. Kalman, *History of Canadian Architecture*, 327–28. Hale, "French Side," 121.

44. Robert C. Bucher, "The Continental Log House," *Pennsylvania Folklife* 12, no. 4 (1962): 14–19. Henry Glassie, "A Central Chimney Continental Log House," *Pennsylvania Folklife* 18, no. 2 (1968–69): 33–39. McMurry, "Rural Houses," 37–40, 50–55.

45. Henry Glassie, "The Appalachian Log Cabin," *Mountain Life and Work* 39 (1963): 5–14. Hofstra, "Searching for Peace," 113. David W. Miller, "Searching for a New World: The Background and Baggage of Scots-Irish Immigrants," in Hofstra, *Ulster to America*, 13. Kniffen and Glassie, "Building in Wood," 175.

46. Eugene M. Wilson, "The Single Pen Log House in the South," *Pioneer America* 2, no. 1 (1970): 21–28.

47. Ernest Ingersoll, *Knocking round the Rockies* (New York: Harper and Brothers, 1882), 79.

48. Richard White, *"It's Your Misfortune and None of My Own": A History of the American West* (Norman: University of Oklahoma Press, 1991), 183–92. D. W. Meinig, *The Shaping of America: A Geographical Perspective on 500 Years of History,* vol. 2: *Continental America, 1800–1867* (New Haven: Yale University Press, 1993), 245. Jon T. Kilpinen, "The Front-Gabled Log Cabin and the Role of the Great Plains in the Formation of the Mountain West's Built Landscape," *Great Plains Quarterly* 15, no. 1 (January 1995): 19–20.

49. Kilpinen, "Front-Gabled Log Cabin," 23–24, 28–29. Jennifer Eastman Attebery, *Building with Logs: Western Log Construction in Context* (Moscow: University of Idaho, 1998), 80.

50. Allen G. Noble, *Wood, Brick, and Stone: The North American Settlement Landscape,* vol. 1: *Houses* (Amherst: University of Massachusetts Press, 1984), 113. Attebery, *Building with Logs,* 23, 76, 108. Terry G. Jordan, Jon T. Kilpinen, and Charles F. Gritzner, *The Mountain West: Interpreting the Folk Landscape* (Baltimore: Johns Hopkins University Press, 1997), 60, 66.

51. William Bartram, *Travels through North and South Carolina, Georgia, East and West Florida* (Savannah: Beehive Press, 1973), 365. Cooper, "Cabins and Deerskins," discusses the diffusion from traders to Indians. Richards, "Dwelling Places," 1–24. The Cherokee who stayed in North Carolina continued to build log cabins into the 1930s. As Michael Ann Williams pointed out, "for this part of southern Appalachia at least, the Cherokee were both the first and among the last to build traditional log dwellings." Email to author, July 11, 2014. Michael Ann Williams, Christie Burns, Meredith Martin, and Sarah Schmitt, "Ravensford Oral History Project: Draft Report" (submitted to Cherokee Central Schools by TRC Environmental Corporation, 2009), 28–29.

52. Charles Frederick Gritzner, "Spanish Log Construction in New Mexico" (Ph.D. diss., Louisiana State University, 1969), 14–15, 51, 70, 69.

53. Ibid., 59–62, 176–84.

54. Ibid., 166–71. John J. Winberry, "The Log House in Mexico," *Annals of the Association of American Geographers* 64, no. 1 (March 1974): 69.

55. One of the ranking officers in the Russian-American Company, which was chartered to colonize Alaska, was Adolph Etholen, a Finn. Although numbers are unreliable, as many as a quarter of Sitka's "Russian" population might have been Finnish. Besides the dramatic Russian Orthodox Cathedral in Sitka, the Russian-American Company also built a Lutheran Church. Maria Jarlsdotter Enckell, "In Search of a People Lost: The Finns in Russian America and Their Descendants" (typescript courtesy of Arnold Alanen, 2010), 7. P. A. Tikhmenev, *A History of the Russian-American Company* (Seattle: University of Washington Press, 1978), 116, 372. Alison K. Hoagland, *Buildings of Alaska* (New York: Oxford University Press, 1993), 187–89.

56. Matti Kaups, "Finnish Log Houses in the Upper Middle West: 1890–1920," *Journal of Cultural Geography* 3 (1983): 7–8, 15. Darrell D. Henning, "Norwegians," *America's Architectural Roots,* 149. Gritzner also noted the prevalence of double notching in Hispanic buildings in New Mexico, attributing it to the availability of saws. Gritzner, "Spanish Log Construction," 62.

57. Thomas Carter, "Northern European Horizontal Log Construction in the Sanpete-Sevier Valleys, *Utah Historical Quarterly* 52, no. 1 (1984): 57. Young cited on 51n2. Larsen cited on 58.

58. Terry G. Jordan, "Log Corner-Timbering in Texas," *Pioneer America* 8, no. 1 (January 1976): 9. Attebery, *Building with Logs*, 53, 64, argues that this shift occurred by 1900; Barrick, "Log Cabin," 7, says 1930. Williams, *Homeplace*, 31, 47. Martin, *Hollybush*, 71–79.

2. PRESIDENTIAL TIMBER

1. Presidents born in log cabins are Millard Fillmore (b. 1800 in New York), Franklin Pierce (b. 1804 in New Hampshire), James Buchanan (b. 1791 in Pennsylvania), Abraham Lincoln (b. 1809 in Kentucky), Andrew Johnson (b. 1808 in North Carolina), and James A. Garfield (b. 1831 in Ohio). Presidents who might have been born in log cabins are Andrew Jackson (b. 1767 in North or South Carolina) and James K. Polk (b. 1795 in North Carolina). Presidents who subsequently lived in log cabins are Andrew Jackson (see chapter 2), William Henry Harrison, Zachary Taylor, U.S. Grant, and Theodore Roosevelt (see chapter 4).

2. John Bach McMaster, *Daniel Webster* (New York: Century, 1902), 252. Mark Leibovich discusses present-day politicians' bent for citing past hardship—if not their own, then their parents' or even grandparents'. Mark Leibovich, "Did Anyone Wash Dishes in This Family?" *New York Times Sunday Magazine,* April 13, 2014, pp. 13–15.

3. Lincoln's log cabins, considered below, were often exhibited. Other presidents' houses received the same treatment, such as the log cabin that U. S. Grant built for himself in Missouri in 1858 and called Hardscrabble, which was dismantled and displayed at the St. Louis World's Fair in 1904.

4. The elections with higher turnout were in 1860 and 1876. Daniel Walker Howe, *What Hath God Wrought: The Transformation of America, 1815–1848* (New York: Oxford University Press, 2007), 576.

5. Adams cited by Robert Gray Gunderson, *The Log Cabin Campaign* (Lexington: University of Kentucky Press, 1957), 112. James A. Green, *William Henry Harrison: His Life and Times* (Richmond, Va.: Garrett and Massie, 1941), 419–20. Edward Pessen, *The Log Cabin Myth: The Social Backgrounds of Presidents* (New Haven: Yale University Press, 1984), 84. The Northwest Territory included modern-day Ohio, Indiana, Illinois, Michigan, Wisconsin, and part of Minnesota. It was formed in 1787 when Virginia ceded its claim to the area, and dissolved in 1803 when the State of Ohio was admitted to the Union. Harrison also served one term in Congress, one term in the Ohio state senate, and a long reign as clerk of the Court of Common Pleas in Hamilton County, Ohio. His career alternated between military and government service, and he was by most accounts a modest, friendly man. Gunderson, *Log Cabin Campaign*, 111–12.

6. Michael F. Holt, *The Rise and Fall of the American Whig Party* (New York: Oxford University Press, 1999), 107. Ronald P. Formisano, "The New Political History and the Election of 1840," *Journal of Interdisciplinary History* 23, no. 4 (Spring 1993): 666. Howe, *What Hath God Wrought,* 583.

7. *North American and Daily Advertiser* (Philadelphia), April 17, 1840, citing *Washington Globe.*

8. Holt, *Rise and Fall,* 89–90. Howe, *What Hath God Wrought*, 574. Elizabeth R. Varon,

"Tippecanoe and the Ladies, Too: White Women and Party Politics in Antebellum Virginia," *Journal of American History* 82, no. 2 (September 1995): 495. Ronald J. Zboray and Mary Saracino Zboray, "White Women, Politics, and Culture in the Campaign of 1840: Three Perspectives from Massachusetts," *Journal of the Early Republic* 17, no. 2 (Summer 1997): 278. Richard Carwardine, "Evangelicals, Whigs and the Election of William Henry Harrison," *Journal of American Studies* 17, no. 1 (April 1983): 48.

9. "The Log Cabin Candidate," *Log Cabin,* May 2, 1840, p. 2.

10. Barbara Burlison Mooney, *Prodigy Houses of Virginia: Architecture and the Native Elite* (Charlottesville: University of Virginia Press, 2008), 283–88. Green, *William Henry Harrison,* 407–11, 420. Fire destroyed the house in 1858. Harrison's father, Benjamin Harrison V, was a signer of the Declaration of Independence and a governor of Virginia.

11. Harrison's speech at Columbus reported in *Ohio Confederate* of June 11, 1840, recorded by A. B. Norton, *The Great Revolution of 1840: Reminiscences of the Log Cabin and Hard Cider Campaign* (privately printed, 1888), 176–77. Harrison's speech at Fort Greenville reported in *Eaton (Ohio) Register,* August 1840, recorded in Norton, *Great Revolution,* 245. Description of the house in "Correspondence of the Express," *Connecticut Courant* (Hartford), February 8, 1840, p. 1. Another description by a supporter said that the log building, dating from about 1800, was one story, two rooms, each "about 15 feet square." Harrison added a log second story in about 1820, then two frame wings and hyphens in 1828, extending the front to about 90 feet across. "General Harrison's House," *Log Cabin* 1, no. 12 (July 18, 1840). As Barbara Burlison Mooney has pointed out, the additions transformed the building into a Palladian "paragon of gentility." Mooney, *Prodigy Houses,* 288. "Definition," *Rhode-Island Republican* (Newport), April 1, 1840, p. 3.

12. "Politics of the Day," *National Intelligencer,* January 14, 1840. *The Tippecanoe and Log Cabin Almanac, 1841* (New York: H. A. Chapin, 1841), 46–48.

13. *Tippecanoe and Log Cabin Almanac, 1841,* 48.

14. "To the Friends of Harrison and Reform," *Log Cabin Advocate* 1, no. 1 (March 21, 1840): 2. This campaign also marked the first time the Pilgrims were associated with log cabins. See the Historiographical Note in this volume. *Ohio State Journal* (Columbus), March 20, 1840, p. 4. Why the landowner specified a log cabin—whether he thought it superior or just the most likely—is unclear.

15. Charles Ogle, *The Regal Splendor of the President's Palace* (Boston: Weeks, Jordan, 1840). *Log Cabin Advocate* 1, no. 1 (March 21, 1840): 2.

16. Diary entry for April 10, 1840, cited in Wilcomb E. Washburn, "The Great Autumnal Madness: Political Symbolism in Mid-Nineteenth-Century America," *Quarterly Journal of Speech* 49, no. 4 (1963): 419.

17. *North American and Daily Advertiser* (Philadelphia), November 9, 1840. "Great Harrison Meeting," *Connecticut Courant (Hartford),* February 1, 1840, p. 1. Gunderson, *Log Cabin Campaign,* 129.

18. One exception was a two-story cabin on a pitcher, which Roger A. Fischer attributed to an English artist unfamiliar with American log cabins. Roger A. Fischer, *Tippecanoe and Trinkets*

Too: The Material Culture of American Presidential Campaigns, 1828–1984 (Urbana: University of Illinois Press, 1988), 42.

19. "The Convention," *Ohio State Journal* (Columbus), February 26, 1840, p. 3. Cobbs cited in S. Allen Chambers Jr., *Poplar Forest and Thomas Jefferson* (privately printed, 1993), 178. Brockway letter, July 17, 1840, reproduced in Anna Brockway Gray, comp., "Letters from the Long Ago," *Michigan History Magazine* 13 (1929): 484. My thanks to Larry Lankton for this last reference.

20. Gunderson, *Log Cabin Campaign,* 142. *Daily National Intelligencer*, October 7, 1840, and October 2, 1840. "Log Cabin," *Connecticut Courant* (Hartford), April 25, 1840, p. 3. *Painesville (Ohio) Telegraph*, April 2, 1840, p. 2. *Cleveland Daily Herald*, March 19, 1840. *North American and Daily Advertiser* (Philadelphia), May 2, 1840.

21. "Correspondence of the Albany Evening Journal," *Albany (N.Y.) Evening Journal,* May 5, 1840, p. 2. The pro-Harrison paper the *Log Cabin*, in an article titled "Log Cabin Raisings," enumerated a half dozen. *Log Cabin* 1, no. 11 (July 11, 1840): 3. In addition, the domestic aspect of the log cabin counteracted the masculine world of hard cider. The sentimental attachment to home, and especially log cabins, attracted women to the campaign. Their presence demanded civil behavior at Whig gatherings and conferred moral standing on the party. Varon, "Tippecanoe and the Ladies," 495.

22. Gunderson, *The Log Cabin Campaign,* 254–56. Others attribute his death to enteric fever contracted from Washington's water supply. Jane McHugh and Philip A. Mackowiak, "What Really Killed the President?" *New York Times* April 1, 2014.

23. "Deeds of Lincoln Sway All Chicago," *Chicago Daily Tribune,* February 13, 1909, p. 1.

24. The two-story clapboard-covered house attracted tourists in the years after Lincoln's death. Although it remained in Lincoln's family, none of his family lived there again. In 1887 Lincoln's son, Robert, donated the house to the state to operate it as a house museum; the National Park Service acquired it in 1972.

25. "'Honest Old Abe,'" *Chicago Press and Tribune,* May 19, 1860, p. 2. Lincoln cited in Merrill D. Peterson, *Lincoln in American Memory* (New York: Oxford University Press, 1994), 89.

26. Barry Schwartz, *Abraham Lincoln and the Forge of National Memory* (Chicago: University of Chicago Press, 2000), 155. Peterson, *Lincoln in American Memory,* 144. "Abraham Lincoln's Log Cabin," *New York Times*, July 21, 1865, p. 2. "Lincoln Cabin Vanished in Thin Air After Leaving Boston Common," *Boston Sunday Globe*, April 13, 1930, p. 22.

27. A wide variety of George Washington memorabilia was available at the 1893 Chicago World's Fair, but very little of Lincoln. Between 1875 and 1899 the *New York Times* published 678 articles on Washington versus 256 on Lincoln. Schwartz, *Abraham Lincoln,* 101–2. Ida M. Tarbell, *The Early Life of Abraham Lincoln* (New York: S. S. McClure, 1896), 4.

28. Robert W. Blythe, Maureen Carroll, and Steven Moffson, "Abraham Lincoln Birthplace National Historic Site: Historic Resource Study" (Atlanta: Southwest Regional Office, National Park Service, 2001), 51–52.

29. "Lincoln and Davis Cabin," *New York Times,* March 23, 1903, p. 14.

30. For examples of ads, see *New York Evening World,* February 12, 1906, and *Breckenridge (Ky.) News*, June 20, 1906, p. 1. Philip B. Kunhardt III, Peter W. Kunhardt, and Peter W. Kun-

hardt Jr., *Looking for Lincoln: The Making of an American Icon* (New York: Alfred A. Knopf, 2008), 404. Governor Joseph W. Folk of Missouri presided over the board of trustees, which included such luminaries as Samuel Clemens, Augustus Saint-Gaudens, Ida Tarbell, and William H. Taft. "Make Lincoln Birthplace Nation's Park," *New York Evening World*, February 12, 1906, p. 6. Barry Schwartz and Howard Schuman, "History, Commemoration, and Belief: Abraham Lincoln in American Memory, 1945–2001," *American Sociological Review* 70, no. 2 (April 2005): 193.

31. "Make Lincoln Birthplace Nation's Park," *New York Evening World,* February 12, 1906, p. 6. Photo shows up in *World* article as well as "The Old Lincoln Cabin," *Breckenridge (Ky.) News*, June 20, 1906, p. 1, and "The Lincoln Cabin," *Berea (Ky.) Citizen*, June 21, 1906, p. 1.

32. "Lincoln Cabin Goes," *New-York Daily Tribune,* June 7, 1906, p. 4. "Lincoln Cabin Due Today," *Baltimore Sun*, June 8, 1906, p. 7. "Lincoln's Cabin at Columbus," *Baltimore Sun*, June 12, 1897. "Stevenson at Louisville," *Washington Post*, June 17, 1906. Blythe et al., "Abraham Lincoln Birthplace," 53–55.

33. Kunhardt et al., *Looking for Lincoln,* 308. Peterson, *Lincoln in American Memory,* 178. "Lincoln's Father's Cabin," *New York Times*, August 16, 1891, p. 8. "'Abe' Lincoln's Cabin," *Chicago Daily Tribune*, August 22, 1891, p. 1. "Arabs at the Log Cabin," *Chicago Daily Tribune*, November 9, 1891, p. 3. "Tires of Lincoln Cabin," *Chicago Daily Tribune*, June 12, 1897, p. 13.

34. Schwartz, *Abraham Lincoln,* 283. Dwight T. Pitcaithley, "Abraham Lincoln's Birthplace Cabin: The Making of an American Icon," in *Myth, Memory and the Making of an American Landscape,* ed. Paul Shackel (Gainesville: University of Florida Press, 2001), 252.

35. Blythe et al., "Abraham Lincoln Birthplace," 55–57.

36. It may also reflect the reputation of the cabin, which, of course, had to be *small* if it were to represent a humble birth. Schwartz, *Abraham Lincoln,* 281.

37. Tarbell, *Early Life,* 37. A biography of Nancy Hanks appeared shortly thereafter: Caroline Hanks Hitchcock, *Nancy Hanks: The Story of Abraham Lincoln's Mother* (New York: Doubleday and McClure, 1899).

38. Much of Olmsted's work involved removal—a branch line of a railroad, a state highway, the elaborate iron gates, and a number of buildings. He also planted more than 22,000 trees and 15,000 shrubs to reforest what had become farmland. Marla McEnaney, "A Noble Avenue: Lincoln Boyhood National Memorial Cultural Landscape Report" (Omaha, Neb.: Midwest Regional Office, National Park Service, 2001), 11, 17; HRA Gray & Pape, "The Evolution of a Sanctified Landscape: A Historic Resource Study of the Lincoln Boyhood National Memorial," (Omaha, Neb.: Midwest Regional Office, National Park Service, 2002), ch. 8.

39. Hibben cited in McEnaney, "A Noble Avenue," 22–23. "Stones Taken from Scenes . . . ," *Evansville Courier and Journal,* January 1, 1933, cited in McEnaney, "A Noble Avenue," 17. The memorial building, completed in 1943, was designed by NPS architect Richard Bishop. The sculptures were designed by Indiana sculptor Elmer H. Daniels.

40. Peterson, *Lincoln in American Memory,* 78, 232–43.

41. William D. Moore, "'United We Commemorate': The Kentucky Pioneer Memorial Association, James Isenberg, and Early Twentieth-Century Tourism," *Public Historian* 30, no. 3

(August 2008), 56–58, 70–73. *The Lincoln Marriage Temple* (privately printed, 1931). Soon after, the courtship cabins were also celebrated. Beginning in 1933, the Washington County Historical Society assembled several buildings associated with Thomas Lincoln and Nancy Hanks near Springfield, Kentucky. There is even a log cabin memorializing Nancy Hanks in West Virginia. Constructed in 1933, it marks her birthplace. S. Allen Chambers Jr., *Buildings of West Virginia* (New York: Oxford University Press, 2004), 506.

42. The idea of shrines was a popular one. In an article in *Munsey's Magazine,* Harry Thurston Peck wrote about "Famous American Shrines," concluding with Lincoln's birthplace, whose commemoration had obviously sparked the 1909 article. Other American shrines included Bunker Hill, Plymouth Rock, Faneuil Hall, Independence Hall, Mount Vernon, Monticello, Arlington House, the Alamo, Gettysburg battlefield, and Grant's Tomb. Harry Thurston Peck, "Famous American Shrines," *Munsey's Magazine* 41, no. 1 (April 1909): 2–17.

43. Keith A. Sculle, "Interpreting the Lincoln Memorial Landscape at Hodgenville, Kentucky: The Howell Family Heritage," *Journal of the Abraham Lincoln Association* 24, no. 2 (Summer 2003): 67, 73–74. The site now receives more than 150,000 visitors annually.

44. After county prohibition went into effect, the tavern served as a museum and gift shop. Joseph K. Opperman, "Abraham Lincoln Birthplace National Historic Site, Boyhood Home Unit, Lincoln Cabin, Historic Structure Report" (Washington, D.C.: National Park Service, 2005), I.A.9–10. Alterations described by Karen E. Hudson in Appendix D of that report.

45. Tarbell, *Early Life,* 116. In 1898, a Presbyterian Chautauqua, a recreational and educational gathering, had begun meeting here. In 1906, the Old Salem Chautauqua Association convinced William Randolph Hearst to purchase the site and deed it to them. *Lincoln's New Salem: A Village Reborn* (Petersburg, Ill.: New Salem Lincoln League, 1994), unpaginated. Richard S. Taylor and Mark L. Johnson, "A Fragile Illusion: The Reconstruction of Lincoln's New Salem," *Journal of Illinois History* 7, no. 4 (Winter 2004): 255, 259. The state acquired and moved in one log cabin that had been moved away in 1840.

46. Robert L. Burns, column printed in the *Dale News,* January 15, 1965, reprinted in *The Slate,* special 50th anniversary publication of the Lincoln Boyhood National Memorial (2012), 14.

47. *Abraham Lincoln: A Living Legacy: A Guide to Three Abraham Lincoln National Park Sites* (2008), 70.

48. Richard West Sellars, "Lincoln's Logs," Opinionator Blog, *New York Times,* February 12, 2013, opinionator.blogs.nytimes.com, accessed March 12, 2013. In 2004 dendrochronology established that the logs date from the 1840s and 1850s. Henri D. Grissino-Mayer and Dwight T. Pitcaithley, "Forensic Dendroarchaeology and the Strange Case of Abraham Lincoln's Birthplace Cabin," http://slideplayer.com/slide/5849394/, accessed April 23, 2017. Danny Scheidt, "Abraham Lincoln Birthplace Memorial Building, Historic Structure Report" (Atlanta: Southeast Region, National Park Service, 2001), 3.

49. Mooney discusses the restoration, portraying it as a product of late 1920s modernism, in Barbara Burlison Mooney, "Lincoln's New Salem: Or, the Trigonometric Theorem of Vernacular Restoration," *Perspectives in Vernacular Architecture* 11 (2004): 19–39. Taylor and Johnson, "A Fragile Illusion," 276, 280. The state built a new visitors center in 1992, replacing the limestone

building constructed in 1921 as a museum and custodian's residence, which now serves as a gift shop.

50. Schwartz, *Abraham Lincoln,* 117, 146–49. Peterson, *Abraham Lincoln in American Memory,* 27. Pessen, *The Log Cabin Myth,* 3. Whether Americans believe that their presidents come from modest backgrounds has been called into question. Ralph Ketcham, review of Pessen's book, *Journal of American History* 71, no. 4 (March 1985): 481–82. Blythe et al., "Abraham Lincoln Birthplace," 17.

51. Schwartz and Schuman, "History, Commemoration, and Belief," 189. In the case of his mother, an image was needed. Although no picture of her survives, a local inn operator commissioned a drawing in 1963 that shows her as a pretty young woman. Imagining a mother in abstract terms was no longer adequate; she had to be pictured for visitors to understand her, and this image reappears at several Lincoln sites and in park service publications.

52. Sally Kitt Chappell and Ann van Zanten, "John Lloyd Wright" (Chicago Historical Society, 1982), available at http://www.incredibleart.org/links/jlwright/lloyd_wright.html. Erin K. Cho, "Lincoln Logs: Toying with the Frontier Myth," *History Today* (April 1993). Jay P. Pederson, "Lincoln Logs," *Encyclopedia of Consumer Brands,* vol. 3: *Durable Goods* (Detroit: St. James Press, 1994) 297.

53. Chappell and van Zanten, "John Lloyd Wright." Pederson, "Lincoln Logs," 297. "Toy Cabin Construction," Patent No. 1,351,086, August 31, 1920. Strong Museum online catalog. Early sets contained instructions for building not only a Lincoln cabin but also Uncle Tom's cabin. Sharon M. Scott, *Toys and American Culture: An Encyclopedia* (Santa Barbara: Clio, 2010), 177. There were also some precursors to Wright's invention. Joel Ellis developed a "Log Cabin Playhouse" in 1866 in which the logs were more slender, compared to their length, and metal rods stabilized the logs at the door openings. Montgomery County Historical Society, http://afinecollection.files.wordpress.com/2010/10/r2112acr-2.jpg, accessed September 3, 2013.

54. Milton Bradley acquired Playskool in 1968, then merged with Hasbro in 1984. Pederson, "Lincoln Logs," 298. Cho, "Lincoln Logs." Lincoln Logs were inducted into the National Toy Hall of Fame in 1999.

55. One explicitly political connection is that of the Log Cabin Republicans, whose name readily relates the organization to the famous Republican and Emancipator. Formed in 1977, the group consists of gay Republicans who found the name "Lincoln Club" already taken and thought that "Log Cabin" was a recognizable substitute for "Lincoln." Log Cabin Republicans website, http://www.logcabin.org/about-us/our-history/, accessed September 3, 2013.

3. HOVELS AND COTTAGES

1. Harriet Beecher Stowe, *Uncle Tom's Cabin* (New York: Signet Classics, 2008), 25, 118, 497. The book was serialized in a Washington abolitionist newspaper beginning June 5, 1851. The book came out in March 1852. E. Bruce Kirkham, *The Building of Uncle Tom's Cabin* (Knoxville: University of Tennessee Press, 1977), 71, 80.

2. Stowe, *Uncle Tom's Cabin,* 27. Harriet Beecher Stowe, *The Annotated Uncle Tom's Cabin,*

ed. Henry Louis Gates Jr. and Hollis Robbins (New York: W. W. Norton, 2007), 27n4. The definition of a cottage as a comfortable small house is explored in John E. Crowley, "'In Happier Mansions, Warm and Dry': The Invention of the Cottage as the Comfortable Anglo-American House," *Winterthur Portfolio* 32, no. 2/3 (Summer-Autumn 1997): esp. 169–72. The term "cottage" is discussed in terms of race by William A. Gleason, *Sites Unseen: Architecture, Race, and American Literature* (New York: New York University Press, 2011), 39–45.

3. J. P. Kennedy, *Swallow Barn, or A Sojourn in the Old Dominion* (New York: George P. Putnam, 1852), 449–50.

4. Other types of slave quarters did exist. In some places, no separate housing was provided for slaves, who lived in buildings that served other functions: kitchens, barns, sheds, and other outbuildings. The 1798 direct tax, which enumerated buildings and materials, was frustratingly vague when describing outbuildings, in places characterizing surprisingly few as slave quarters. Ashli White, "The Character of a Landscape: Domestic Architecture and Community in Late Eighteenth-Century Berkeley Parish, Virginia," *Winterthur Portfolio* 34, no. 2/3 (Summer–Autumn 1999): 129–31. Philip D. Morgan, *Slave Counterpoint: Black Culture in the Eighteenth-Century Chesapeake and Lowcountry* (Chapel Hill: University of North Carolina Press, 1998), 108. John Michael Vlach, *Back of the Big House: The Architecture of Plantation Slavery* (Chapel Hill: University of North Carolina Press, 1993), 155. The common provision of dual-purpose spaces for slaves in the seventeenth and early eighteenth centuries gave way to more provision of separate accommodations in the nineteenth century. George W. McDaniel, *Hearth and Home: Preserving a People's Culture* (Philadelphia: Temple University Press, 1982), 42–43. Also in the seventeenth and eighteenth centuries, large, barracks-like structures would house a number of unrelated slaves together. Edward A. Chappell, "Housing Slavery," in *The Chesapeake House: Architectural Investigations by Colonial Williamsburg*, ed. Cary Carson and Carl R. Lounsbury (Chapel Hill: University of North Carolina Press, 2013), 158.

5. Harry Toulmin, *The Western Country in 1793: Reports on Kentucky and Virginia* (privately printed, 1948), 17. Frederick Law Olmsted, *Journey in the Seaboard States, with Remarks on Their Economy* (New York: Dix and Edwards, 1856), 111–12. On log as the dominant material, see Dell Upton, "White and Black Landscapes in Eighteenth-Century Virginia," in *Cabin, Quarter, Plantation: Architecture and Landscapes of North American Slavery*, ed. Clifton Ellis and Rebecca Ginsburg (New Haven: Yale University Press, 2010), 123. McDaniel, *Hearth and Home*, 47. Morgan, *Slave Counterpoint,* 109. The 1798 direct tax described these buildings too unevenly to provide quantification.

6. Dennis J. Pogue, "The Domestic Architecture of Slavery at George Washington's Mount Vernon," *Winterthur Portfolio* 37, no. 1 (Spring 2002): 3, 16, 18. The 1788 quote from J. P. Brissot de Warville, *New Travels in the United States of America, 1788*, ed. Durand Echeverria (Cambridge: Harvard University Press, 1964), 343, cited in Pogue, "Domestic Architecture," 16. The ad from John C. Fitzpatrick, ed., *The Writings of George Washington* (Washington, D.C.: GPO, 1931–44), 34:433–41, 33:196, cited in Pogue, "Domestic Architecture," 15. The French quote from Louis-Philippe, *Diary of My Travels in America, Louis-Philippe, King of France, 1830–1848* (New York: Delacorte Press, 1977), 53–55, cited in Pogue, "Domestic Architecture," 18. The

Polish quote from Julian Ursyn Niemcewicz, *Under Their Vine and Fig Tree: Travels through America in 1797–1799, 1805* (Elizabeth, N.J.: Grassman, 1965), 100, cited in Pogue, "Domestic Architecture," 18.

7. Nicholas King maps, Map and Geographic Division, Library of Congress. Widow Young is Peter Force no. 784. Abraham Young is Peter Force no. 788. George Walker is Peter Force no. 789. Robert Peter is Peter Force no. 794. Notley Young's property depicted on two plats: Peter Force no. 783 identifies uses; Peter Force no. 801 identifies building materials and sizes. Certainly the most extensive, Young's estate, in addition to his own 42 by 52–foot house and the slave quarters, had two stables, two barns, a coach house, and a pigeon house. Federal Direct Tax of 1798 for District of Columbia, Particular List of Slaves, Maryland Historical Society, Baltimore. Allen C. Clark, "The Abraham Young Mansion," *Records of the Columbia Historical Society* 12 (1909): 60.

8. Morgan, *Slave Counterpoint,* 111, estimated the smallest typical dwellings and fewest number of inhabitants: "Most cabins probably housed three or four slaves and were typically 150 to 250 square feet in size." Camille Wells, "The Planter's Prospect: Houses, Outbuildings, and Rural Landscapes in Eighteenth-Century Virginia," *Winterthur Portfolio* 28, no. 1 (Spring 1993): 16, found an average of 345 square feet in the eighteenth century, but Barbara Heath, "Space and Place within Plantations Quarters in Virginia, 1700–1825," in *Cabin, Quarter, Plantation: Architecture and Landscapes of North American Slavery*, ed. Clifton Ellis and Rebecca Ginsburg (New Haven: Yale University Press, 2010), 164, found that slave quarters were getting smaller through the eighteenth century, averaging 192 square feet in 1800. Liz Gallow, "Observations from the 1798 Tax Record for Anne Arundel, Baltimore, Prince George, and Somerset Counties, Maryland" (Williamsburg, Va.: Colonial Williamsburg Foundation, Architectural Research Department, 2005), unpaginated, studying the 1798 tax lists for Prince Georges County, Maryland, found the median size of quarters was 18 by 12 feet, or 216 square feet. Mark L. Walston, "'Uncle Tom's Cabin' Revisited: Origins and the Interpretations of Slave Housing in the American South," *Southern Studies* 24, no. 4 (1985): 367. Eugene D. Genovese, *Roll, Jordan, Roll: The World the Slaves Made* (New York: Pantheon Books, 1974), 524. Vlach, *Back of the Big House,* 22, 158–59.

9. James O. Breeden, ed., *Advice among Masters: The Ideal in Slave Management in the Old South* (Westport, Conn.: Greenwood Press, 1980), 115–34. These journals were the primary source for Genovese, *Roll, Jordan, Roll.* Breeden's book is a compilation of this advice, sorted thematically.

10. "Management of Negroes upon Southern Estates," *DeBow's Review* 10, no. 6 (June 1851): 621. Omo, "Negro Houses—Plantation Hospitals," *Southern Cultivator* 1 (January 1856): 17–18, cited in Breeden, *Advice among Masters,* 127. "Management of Slaves, Etc.," *Farmer's Register* 5, no. 1 (May 1, 1837), 32. W. C. Handy, *Father of the Blues: An Autobiography* (1941; repr., Cambridge, Mass.: DaCapo Press, 1969), 1.

11. "Management of Slaves, Etc.," *Farmer's Register* 5, no. 1 (May 1, 1837), 32. Arator, "Negro Houses," *Soil of the South* 2 (March 1852): 220, cited in Breeden, *Advice among Masters,* 124–25. A Southron, "Hints in Relation to the Dwellings and Clothing of Slaves," *Farmer's Register* 2,

no. 11 (April 1835): 703. A Mississippi Planter, "Management of Negroes upon Southern Estates," *DeBow's Review* 10 (June 1851): 621–27, cited in Breeden, *Advice among Masters*, 122. Tattler, "Management of Negroes," *Southern Cultivator* 8 (November 1850): 162–64, cited in Breeden, *Advice among Masters*, 121. The one writer who recommended unhewn logs: R. J. Gage, "Plantation Hygiene," *Farmer and Planter* 8 (February 1857): 24–31, cited in Breeden, *Advice among Masters*, 132. "Management of Negroes," *DeBow's Review* 11, no. 4 (October 1851): 369.

12. Josiah Henson, *The Life of Josiah Henson, Formerly a Slave, Now an Inhabitant of Canada, as Narrated by Himself* (Boston: Arthur D. Phelps, 1849), 7. Henson was not, however, the model for Uncle Tom, as has been suggested. In Harriet Beecher Stowe, *A Key to Uncle Tom's Cabin: Presenting the Original Facts and Documents upon Which the Story Is Founded* (Seattle: Inkling Books, 2005, facsimile of 1853 edition), 26, which she wrote to fend off critics by documenting her allegations about slavery, Stowe cited Henson, among others, as inspiration for Uncle Tom. But it appears that she did not read Henson's autobiography before she wrote *Uncle Tom's Cabin*, so she did not model Tom on Henson; she cited the book merely as evidence that slave conditions were as she stated. Kirkham, *Building of Uncle Tom's Cabin*, 88–91. The Henson–Uncle Tom connection was further complicated by a log cabin near Rockville, Maryland, that was allegedly occupied by Henson and therefore the prototype for Uncle Tom's cabin. After Montgomery County acquired the site, the cabin was dated through dendrochronology to 1850, some twenty years after Henson had left. Annys Shin, "Confusion over History of Md. Cabin Museum," *Washington Post*, October 4, 2010.

13. Information in this paragraph and the next from Elizabeth Hughes, "Slave House at Sotterley," Maryland Historical Trust State Historic Sites Inventory Form, SM-7A, 1996, based on Jeffrey Bostetter, Edward Chappell, Willie Graham, and Mark R. Wenger, "The Slave House at Sotterley near Hollywood, St. Mary's County, Maryland: Architectural Investigations and Recommendations" (Williamsburg, Va.: Colonial Williamsburg Foundation, September 27, 1995). Chappell, "Housing Slavery," 174. Also discussed by McDaniel, *Hearth and Home*, 64–67.

14. It appears that two preexisting buildings were brought together to form this two-pen cabin, and the numbering of the pegged rafters might also indicate it was moved, but it is unclear when this might have occurred.

15. Virginia Price, "The Hermitage, West Cabin," Historic American Buildings Survey, National Park Service, Library of Congress, 1999. Robbie D. Jones, "First Hermitage Restoration: Historic Structure Report" (Hermitage, Tenn.: The Hermitage, 2006.

16. Virginia Price, "The Hermitage, Alfred's Cabin," Historic American Buildings Survey, National Park Service, Library of Congress, 1999. Like most log slave cabins, though, this one, as well as the other log buildings at the Hermitage, has been altered. Foundations, sill logs, and roofs have all been replaced.

17. Chappell, "Housing Slavery," 160. Edward A. Chappell, "Social Responsibility and the American History Museum," *Winterthur Portfolio* 24, no. 4 (Winter 1989): 259–64. Eric Gable, Richard Handler, and Anna Lawson, "On the Uses of Relativism: Fact, Conjecture, and Black and White Histories at Colonial Williamsburg," *American Ethnologist* 19, no. 4 (November 1992): 801–2. Mark P. Leone, "Carter's Grove," *Journal of American History* 79, no. 3 (December

1992): 1083. Edward A. Chappell, "Museums and American Slavery," in *"I, Too, Am America": Archeological Studies of African-American Life*, ed. Theresa A. Singleton (Charlottesville: University Press of Virginia, 1999), 241–49.

18. Booker T. Washington, *Up from Slavery: An Autobiography* (New York: Doubleday, Page, 1907), 3–4. Booker T. Washington, "Negro Homes," *Century Magazine* 76, no. 1 (May 1908): 71.

19. Washington's accommodationist views were more politically palatable than those of Frederick Douglass, whose home the National Park Service had recently refused to take on. Patricia West, *Domesticating History: The Political Origins of America's House Museums* (Washington, D.C.: Smithsonian Institution Press, 1999), 145–46, 153.

20. Lisa Nowak, H. Eliot Foulds, and Phillip D. Troutman, "Cultural Landscape Report for Booker T. Washington National Monument" (Brookline, Mass.: Olmsted Center for Landscape Preservation, National Park Service, [2003?]), 62, 74.

21. Genovese, *Roll, Jordan, Roll,* 526. Avery O. Craven, "Poor Whites and Negroes in the Antebellum South," *Journal of Negro History* 15, no. 1 (January 1930): 16–17. Upton, "White and Black Landscapes," 126.

22. Walston, "'Uncle Tom's Cabin' Revisited," 357.

23. Washington, "Negro Homes," 71. W. E. Burghardt Du Bois, *The Negro American Family* (Atlanta: Atlanta University Press, 1908), 51, 52.

24. Washington, "Negro Homes," 73–79. Barbara Burlison Mooney, "The Comfortable Tasty Framed Cottage: An African American Architectural Iconography," *Journal of the Society of Architectural Historians* 61, no. 1 (March 2003): 57–58, 64.

25. Carl Fleischhauer and Beverly W. Brannan, eds. *Documenting America, 1935–1943* (Berkeley: University of California Press, 1988), 148. John Temple Graves II, "The Big World at Last Reaches Gee's Bend," *New York Times Magazine,* August 22, 1937, p. 12.

26. Allen W. Batteau, *The Invention of Appalachia* (Tucson: University of Arizona Press, 1990). Porte Crayon [David Hunter Strother], "A Winter in the South," *Harper's New Monthly Magazine* 15, no. 90 (November 1857): 721–40, and 16, no. 92 (January 1858): 167–83. Will Wallace Harney, "A Strange Land and a Peculiar People," *Lippincott's Magazine of Popular Literature and Science* 12 (October 1873): 431. Strother was John Pendleton Kennedy's cousin and illustrated the 1851 edition of *Swallow Barn.*

27. Mary Noailles Murfree, *In the Tennessee Mountains* (Knoxville: University of Tennessee Press, 2008), 23. Murfree had grown up in central Tennessee and had summered at a resort in the Cumberland Mountains in central Tennessee, although she placed her stories in the Great Smoky Mountains at the eastern end of the state.

28. In an address to the Woman's Meeting of the American Missionary Association, one missionary called the mountaineers "peculiar" and contrasted them to former slaves, Indians, and Chinese, who had all been the focus of missionary efforts, but these "poor people" had been neglected. Mrs. A. A. Myers, *Mountain White Work in Kentucky* (New York: American Missionary Association, 1883), 3, 6. Henry D. Shapiro, *Appalachia on Our Mind: The Southern Mountains and Mountaineers in the American Consciousness, 1870–1920* (Chapel Hill: University of North Carolina Press, 1978), 5, 55. Presbyterians established 31 schools between 1885 and 1895 and

another 34 in the next decade. By 1921 churches and independent settlement workers sponsored 193 schools. Olive D. Campbell, comp., *Southern Highland Schools Maintained by Denominational and Independent Agencies* (New York: Russell Sage Foundation, 1921). Karen E. Hudson has also looked at reformers' buildings in Appalachia in her article "The Model Appalachian Home: A Fitting Environment for the Region's Arts and Crafts 'Revival,'" *Journal of the Appalachian Studies Association* 4 (1992): 124–32, and dissertation, "'God Held the Torch That Brought the Old House Down': Class, Gender, and the Built Environment of the Appalachian Kentucky Social Settlement Movement, 1880s-1930s" (Ph.D. diss., University of Pennsylvania, 1995).

29. Ellen Churchill Semple, "The Anglo-Saxons of the Kentucky Mountains: A Study in Anthropogeography," *Geographical Journal,* June 1901, 9, 10, 6. The idea that most Appalachian residents had British origins is questioned today; some note that many had central and northern European origins. Michael Ann Williams, *Great Smoky Mountains Folklife* (Jackson: University Press of Mississippi, 1995), 5.

30. Batteau, *Invention of Appalachia,* 74, credits Frost. William Goodell Frost, "Our Contemporary Ancestors in the Southern Mountains," *Atlantic Monthly* 83, no. 497 (March 1899): 311, 312, 319. Frost's reputation has risen and fallen over the past century. While he was a strong advocate of Appalachia, he also disparaged the people he was trying to save. Discussion in Batteau, *Invention of Appalachia,* 75–81. At Berea, he is remembered as the president who took an integrated college and shifted its focus to whites, abandoning the original mission of the institution. Shannon Wilson, "William Goodell Frost: Race and Region at Berea College," paper from Berea College website, no date, http://libraryguides.berea.edu/frostessay, accessed March 11, 2015).

31. Not much is known about Lyman's effort; it seems to have decreased its activity, maybe even as early as 1900, and seems to have ceased operations by 1910. Lyman died under mysterious circumstances in 1917 and perhaps suffered from a mental illness. Most of the information on this settlement is from an unpublished paper by David E. Whisnant, "Susan G. Chester and the Log Cabin Settlement: First Social Settlement Institution in the Southern Mountains," University of North Carolina at Chapel Hill, Wilson Special Collections Library, David E. Whisnant Papers, Collection #14326, Folder 3. "A Log-Cabin Settlement," *Outlook* 51, no. 2 (January 12, 1895): 64. Lizabeth A. Cohen, "Embellishing a Life of Labor: An Interpretation of the Material Culture of American Working-Class Homes, 1885–1915," in *Common Places: Readings in American Vernacular Architecture,* ed. Dell Upton and John Michael Vlach (Athens: University of Georgia Press, 1986), 265.

32. Jess Stoddart, *Challenge and Change in Appalachia: The Story of Hindman Settlement School* (Lexington: University Press of Kentucky, 2002), 62–63. Lucy Furman, *The Glass Window: A Story of the Quare Women* (Boston: Little, Brown, 1925), 29–30.

33. Furman, *Glass Window,* 184, 185, 193. Stoddart, *Challenge and Change,* 65.

34. Ellen C. Semple, "A New Departure in Social Settlements," *Annals of the American Academy of Political and Social Science* 15 (March 1900): 158.

35. Jess Stoddart, ed., *The Quare Women's Journals: May Stone and Katherine Pettit's Summers in the Kentucky Mountains and the Founding of the Hindman Settlement School* (Ashland, Ky.: Jesse Stuart Foundation, 1997), 62.

36. The novel went through four editions: 1925, 1926, 1929, 1937. David E. Whisnant, *All That Is Native and Fine: The Politics of Culture in an American Region* (Chapel Hill: University of North Carolina Press, 1983, repr., 25th anniversary ed., 2009), 85.

37. Allen H. Eaton, *Handicrafts of the Southern Highlands* (New York: Russell Sage Foundation, 1937), 71. Today the cabin serves as a craft shop. Other log buildings have been moved in, and compatible modern architecture completes the campus.

38. Williams, *Great Smoky Mountains,* 65–66, 70–71. Michael Ann Williams, "Pride and Prejudice: The Appalachian Boxed House in Southwestern North Carolina," *Winterthur Portfolio* 25, no. 4 (Winter 1990): 219.

39. Fannie W. Dunn, "Missionary and Philanthropic Schools," in *Religion in the Highlands: Native Churches and Missionary Enterprises in the Southern Appalachian Area,* ed. Elizabeth R. Hooker (New York: Home Missions Council, 1933).

40. Eaton, *Handicrafts of the Southern Highlands,* 257. Campbell, *Southern Highland Schools,* xv, 195–96.

41. Lucy Morgan, *Gift from the Hills* (Penland, N.C.: Penland School of Crafts, 2005), 50. Eaton, *Handicrafts,* 238.

42. Morgan, *Gift from the Hills,* 99–106, 151–52. Catherine W. Bishir, Michael T. Southern, and Jennifer F. Martin, *A Guide to the Historic Architecture of Western North Carolina* (Chapel Hill: University of North Carolina Press, 1999), 233–34. Jane S. Becker, *Selling Tradition: Appalachia and the Construction of an American Folk, 1930–1940* (Chapel Hill: University of North Carolina Press, 1998), 205–6.

43. The eviction numbers were 450 families in Shenandoah and 1,200 landowners in Great Smokies, per the parks' respective websites. No numbers for Blue Ridge. Anne Mitchell Whisnant, *Super-Scenic Motorway: A Blue Ridge Parkway History* (Chapel Hill: University of North Carolina Press, 2006), 243–45. Williams, "Pride and Prejudice," 220–21.

44. Phil Noblitt, "The Blue Ridge Parkway and Myths of the Pioneer," *Appalachian Journal* 21 (1994): 395. A. M. Whisnant, *Super-Scenic Motorway,* 243–44.

45. Jean Haskell Speer, Frances H. Russell, and Gibson Worsham, "The Johnson Farm at Peaks of Otter: Historic Resources Study, Historic Structures Report" (Asheville, N.C.: Blue Ridge Parkway, National Park Service, 1990), 50, 56, 67, 74.

46. Speer, Russell, and Worsham, "Johnson Farm," 75. This story is also told by A. M. Whisnant, *Super-Scenic Motorway,* 245–255. Interpretive Prospectus of 1972 cited in Speer, Russell, and Worsham, "Johnson Farm," 75. "Historic Structures Report, Part I, Johnson Farm Group" (Asheville, N.C.: Blue Ridge Parkway, National Park Service, 1964), 1.

47. "Historic Areas" (Gatlinburg, Tenn.: Great Smoky Mountains National Park, National Park Service, 2001; rev. ed., 2012). "Mountain Farm Museum Self-Guiding Tour" (Gatlinburg, Tenn.: Great Smoky Mountains National Park, National Park Service, n.d.). Morgan, *Gift from the Hills,* 84.

48. A. Randolph Shields, *The Cades Cove Story* (Gatlinburg, Tenn.: Great Smoky Mountains Association, 1977), 11.

49. Durwood Dunn, *Cades Cove: The Life and Death of a Southern Appalachian Community,*

1818–1937 (Knoxville: University of Tennessee Press, 1988), 251. Secretary of the interior cited in Williams, *Great Smoky Mountains*, 128. Also see A. Randolph Shields, "Cades Cove in the Great Smoky Mountains National Park," *Tennessee Historical Quarterly* 24 (Summer 1965): 103–20.

50. Henry Caudill, *Night Comes to the Cumberlands: A Biography of a Depressed Area* (Boston: Little, Brown, 1962). See also Michael Harrington, *The Other America: Poverty in the United States* (1962; repr., New York: Scribner, 2012). Anthony Harkins, *Hillbilly: A Cultural History of an American Icon* (New York: Oxford University Press, 2004), 184–85. Marjorie Hunter, "President Hailed on 5-State Tour of Poverty Areas," *New York Times* April 25, 1964. Jerome Ellison, "The Plight of the Hill People," *Saturday Evening Post,* June 4, 1960, p. 46.

4. ROMANCING THE WILDERNESS

1. Roderick Nash, *Wilderness and the American Mind* (New Haven: Yale University Press, 1967), describes this shift in two chapters, 23–66. He also pinpoints Henry David Thoreau as leading the change in attitude. As Thoreau wrote in 1851, "From the forest and wilderness come the tonics and barks which brace mankind," cited by Nash, 84. Also see David Lowenthal, "The Pioneer Landscape: An American Dream," *Great Plains Quarterly* 2, no. 1 (1982): 6. Unfortunately for our story, Thoreau's cabin at Walden Pond was wood frame, not log. Henry David Thoreau, *Walden* (New York: Library of America, paperback classic ed., 2010), 36.

2. Edward Ellis, *From the Ranch to the White House: Life of Theodore Roosevelt* (New York: Hurst, 1906).

3. John Nerber, introduction to Mrs. Caroline Matilda Kirkland, *A New Home, or Life in the Clearings,* ed. John Nerber (New York: G. P. Putnam's Sons, 1953), 13–15. William S. Osborne, *Caroline M. Kirkland* (New York: Twayne, 1972), 18–24.

4. Mrs. Mary Clavers [Caroline Kirkland], *A New Home: Who'll Follow? or, Glimpses of Western Life* (New York: C. S. Francis, 1839). Mrs. Mary Clavers [Caroline Kirkland], *Forest Life* (New York: C. S. Francis, 1842). Some of her other articles are discussed in Scott Peeples, "'The Servant Is As His Master': Western Exceptionalism in Caroline Kirkland's Short Fiction," *American Transcendental Quarterly* 13, no. 4 (December 1999): 305–16. She also published a collection of stories: Mrs. C. M. Kirkland, *Western Clearings* (New York: Wiley and Putnam, 1846). She died in 1864, eighteen years after her husband.

5. Annette Kolodny, *The Land before Her: Fantasy and Experience of the American Frontiers, 1630–1860* (Chapel Hill: University of North Carolina Press, 1984), 133, called her first book "the first realistic depiction of frontier life in American letters." Noreen Groover Lape, "The Frontier Origins of North American Realism: Metarealism and the Travel Writings of Susanna Moodie and Caroline Kirkland," *Western American Literature* 42, no. 4 (Winter 2008): 363. Henry Nash Smith, *Virgin Land: The American West as Symbol and Myth* (Cambridge: Harvard University Press, 1970), 184. Kirkland, *New Home,* v, 125.

6. Kirkland, *New Home,* 54, 38. Kirkland, *Forest Life*, 27–28. Wildcat banks were state banks not subject to federal regulation.

7. Kirkland, *New Home,* 317.

8. The Editor [Caroline Kirkland], "The Log-House," *Union Magazine of Literature and Art* 2 (June 1848): 274–75. Kirkland, *New Home*, 83.

9. Kirkland, "Log-House," 274–75.

10. Smith, *Virgin Land*, 177. Kirkland, *New Home*, 48.

11. Kirkland, *New Home*, 244. Kirkland, *Forest Life*, 57. Her preferences can also be discerned in politics so that the rough Jacksonian Democrat was much less preferable to the cultured Whig—and the Log Cabin Campaign of 1840 even garnered a mention. Kirkland, *Forest Life*, 203. See also John C. McCloskey, "Jacksonian Democracy in Mrs. Kirkland's *A New Home—Who'll Follow?*" *Michigan History* 45 (December 1961): 347–52.

12. Lori Merish, "'The Hand of Refined Taste' in the Frontier Landscape: Caroline Kirkland's *A New Home, Who'll Follow?* and the Feminization of American Consumerism," *American Quarterly* 45, no. 4 (December 1993): 494. Kirkland, *New Home*, 246.

13. Kirkland, *New Home*, 73–4, 18–19.

14. Kirkland, *Forest Life*, 58.

15. The South Dakota books by Wilder were *By the Shores of Silver Lake* (1939), *The Long Winter* (1940), *Little Town on the Prairie* (1941), and *These Happy Golden Years* (1943). *The First Four Years*, about her married life, was published posthumously in 1971.

16. Anita Clair Fellman, "The Little House Books in American Culture," in *Laura Ingalls Wilder and the American Frontier: Five Perspectives*, ed. Dwight M. Miller (Lanham, Md.: University Press of America, 2002), 45, 63. Brian Q. Cannon, "Homesteading Remembered: A Sesquicentennial Perspective," *Agricultural History* 87, no. 1 (Winter 2013): 9. Pamela Smith Hill, *Laura Ingalls Wilder: A Writer's Life* (Pierre: South Dakota State Historical Society Press, 2007), 145, 170, 177. Judith Thurman, "Wilder Women: The Mother and Daughter behind the Little House Stories," *New Yorker*, August 10, 2009. In recent decades, critics and devotees have been concerned with how accurately the books portray Wilder's life. Although the books are sold as fiction, the immediacy of the writing and the similarity to Wilder's life lead readers to expect that the books are more memoir than fiction. Complicating the picture is the fact that Rose Wilder Lane, Wilder's only child and a prominent journalist in her own right, heavily edited her mother's work and served as an intermediary with her publisher. Lane's staunchly libertarian views emerge in the novels, but it is not known to what extant Wilder shared her daughter's politics. Elizabeth Jameson, "Laura Ingalls Wilder and the American Frontier," in Miller, *Laura Ingalls Wilder*, 6. As Wendy McClure, *The Wilder Life: My Adventures in the Lost World of Little House on the Prairie* (New York: Riverhead Books, 2011), 214, described the TV show: "Walnut Grove is *Walnut Grove*, the legendary TV town that took most of the 'prairie' out of *Little House on the Prairie* and instead gave viewers a community of folks in old-timey clothing who bravely endure blizzards, droughts, epidemics, racism, drug abuse, gang violence, and franchise restaurant encroachment."

17. Laura Ingalls Wilder, *Little House in the Big Woods* (1932; rev. ed., 1953), New York: HarperCollins, 2004, 3, 166.

18. Laura Ingalls Wilder, *Little House on the Prairie* (1935; rev. ed., 1953), New York: HarperCollins, 1971), 1, 57. Although Pa heard that the land was soon to be opened to settlers, the book

ends with the threat of soldiers enforcing the sovereignty of the Indian reservation and dispossessing them from their land, so the Ingallses move on again after a year.

19. Ibid., 64.

20. Ibid., 125, 126.

21. Wilder, *Little House in the Big Woods,* 1–2. Wilder, *Little House on the Prairie,* 40–41. Hill, *Laura Ingalls Wilder,* 14, 16. Elizabeth Jameson, "Unconscious Inheritance and Conscious Striving: Laura Ingalls Wilder and the Frontier Narrative," in Miller, *Laura Ingalls Wilder,* 73. Wilder emphasized isolation even at the expense of Indians. Two lines in the first chapter of *Little House on the Prairie* read: "There the wild animals wandered and fed as though they were in a pasture that stretched much farther than a man could see, and there were no people. Only Indians lived there." After a reader objected, "people" was changed to "settlers" in the 1953 edition. Hill, *Laura Ingalls Wilder,* 190–91.

22. The title of *Little House in the Big Woods* was suggested by her publisher. Hill, *Laura Ingalls Wilder,* 142. William Anderson, *Laura Ingalls Wilder: A Biography* (New York: HarperCollins, 1992), 56. William Holtz, "Closing the Circle: The American Optimism of Laura Ingalls Wilder," *Great Plains Quarterly* 4, no. 2 (1984): 84. The Ingallses lost the house when the crop failed. They moved to Burr Oak, Iowa, where they lived in a hotel that they helped operate. Anderson, *Laura Ingalls Wilder,* 61, 67.

23. Quoted in Anderson, *Laura Ingalls Wilder,* 14. Holtz, "Closing the Circle," 82.

24. Wilder, *Little House on the Prairie,* 129.

25. Wilder, *Little House in the Big Woods,* 128.

26. Fellman, "Little House Books," 49. Jameson, "Unconscious Inheritance," 73. Holtz, "Closing the Circle," 82–87. Cannon, "Homesteading Remembered," 12.

27. Hill, *Laura Ingalls Wilder,* 183–84. Ann Romines, "The Frontier of the Little House," in Miller, *Laura Ingalls Wilder,* 32.

28. Theodore Roosevelt, *The Winning of the West,* vol. 1: *From the Alleghanies to the Mississippi, 1769–1776* (New York: G. P. Putnam's Sons, 1900), xxii.

29. Theodore Roosevelt, *An Autobiography* (New York: Macmillan, 1914), 95.

30. Mike Thompson, *The Travels and Tribulations of Theodore Roosevelt's Cabin* (privately printed, 2004), 4.

31. Louis Torres, "Theodore Roosevelt National Park Historic Structure Report: CCC Structures/Peaceful Valley Ranch/Maltese Cross Cabin/Elkhorn Ranch" (Medora, N.D.: Theodore Roosevelt National Park, National Park Service, 1980), 58. Roosevelt, *Autobiography,* 96–97.

32. Theodore Roosevelt, *Hunting Trips of a Ranchman: Sketches of Sport on the Northern Plains* (New York: G. P. Putnam's Sons, 1885), 11–12.

33. Theodore Roosevelt, *Ranch Life and the Hunting-Trail* (New York: Century, 1902), 6. Theodore Roosevelt, *The Wilderness Hunter: An Account of the Big Game of the United States and Its Chase with Horse, Hound, and Rifle* (New York: G. P. Putnam's Sons, 1902), 19, xv.

34. Grinnell cited, among the club's accomplishments, the preservation of Yellowstone National Park through the passage of the Park Protection Act in 1894, as well as the establishment of forest reserves (renamed National Forests in 1907), Glacier National Park, and state

game refuges. In addition the society ensured the enactment of laws to protect game in Alaska and to regulate the hunting of deer in New York State. Even closer to home, the group helped establish the New York Zoological Society. George Bird Grinnell, "Brief History of the Boone and Crockett Club," in *Hunting at High Altitudes: The Book of the Boone and Crockett Club,* ed. George Bird Grinnell (New York: Harper and Brothers, 1913), 438–41. Douglas Brinkley, *The Wilderness Hunter: Theodore Roosevelt and the Crusade for America* (New York: HarperCollins, 2009), 201–7, 238.

35. *The Dream City: A Portfolio of Photographic Views of the World's Columbian Exposition* (St. Louis: N. D. Thompson, 1893), unpaginated.

36. Roosevelt identified a type of manliness to which urban men, victims of an industrialized society that kept them indoors and in jobs that were not physically demanding, should aspire. Gail Bederman, *Manliness and Civilization: A Cultural History of Gender and Race in the United States, 1880–1917* (Chicago: University of Chicago Press, 1995), 15.

37. Roosevelt's history *The Winning of the West,* the first volume of which was published in 1889, glorified the white frontiersmen who fought the Indians, wresting control of the land and making it safe for settlement. His harsh view of humanity easily divided people into civilized and savage, and he had no doubt that the civilized were destined to prevail. He also believed that this process helped forge American character, and on this he shared a philosophy with Frederick Jackson Turner, who presented his seminal paper "The Significance of the Frontier in American History" at the Chicago World's Fair. He and Turner admired each other and cited each other's work. Brinkley, *Wilderness Hunter,* 241. Turner saw less of a racial component to the process of civilization building, though; he credited the frontier environment, not the triumph of "civilized" over "savage," with shaping American character. Edmund Morris, *The Rise of Theodore Roosevelt* (New York: Modern Library, 2001), 474–78. Jameson, "Unconscious Inheritance," 76.

When he was not ranching and hunting in the West, Roosevelt continued to build his political career in the East. He served as U.S. Civil Service commissioner and then presided over the Board of Police Commissioners of New York City. He was assistant secretary of the U.S. Navy, a post from which he resigned to volunteer to serve in Cuba during the U.S. invasion of that island in 1898. With the publicity and popularity he gained there, he was elected governor of New York. He was elected McKinley's vice president and assumed the presidency when McKinley was assassinated in September 1901. Brinkley, *Wilderness Hunter,* 825–30.

38. Thompson, *Travels and Tribulations,* 29–32. Torres, "Theodore Roosevelt National Park," 47. Brinkley, *Wilderness Hunter,* 578.

39. Thompson, *Travels and Tribulations,* 35–41. Torres, "Theodore Roosevelt National Park," 47–51.

40. Thompson, *Travels and Tribulations,* 46–53. Torres, "Theodore Roosevelt National Park," 49–51. Congressional action changed the name to Theodore Roosevelt National Park in 1978.

41. Morris, *Rise of Theodore Roosevelt,* 378.

42. *Alone in the Wilderness,* Bob Swerer Productions, 2003. Sam Keith and Richard Proenneke, *One Man's Wilderness: An Alaskan Odyssey* (1973; repr., Anchorage: Alaska Northwest Books, 1999).

43. John Branson, ed., *More Readings from One Man's Wilderness: The Journals of Richard L. Proenneke, 1974–1980* (Port Alsworth, Alas.: Lake Clark National Park and Preserve, National Park Service, n.d.), xiii–xxi. Richard Proenneke, interviewed by Theodore Karamanski (transcript, Lake Clark National Park, 1990). Proenneke staked out his own five acres, but by the time he went to file his claim BLM had closed the land to new claims. Thus he never owned the land on which his cabin sat. Karamanski interview, 14.

44. In 1974 the National Park Service employed Proenneke to film wildlife. Branson, *More Readings,* viii. John Branson, ed., *The Early Years: The Journals of Richard L. Proenneke, 1967–1973* (Anchorage: Alaska Geographic Association, 2010), xi.

45. Branson, *Early Years,* 4–51. Raymond Proenneke, telephone interview by author, August 15, 2013.

46. Branson, *Early Years,* 53.

47. Ibid., 88–90. It was actually white spruce that he was working. See 184nn5–6.

48. Ibid., 94.

49. Ibid., 94, 100, 95, 136. John B. Branson, "National Register of Historic Places Registration Form: Proenneke, Richard L., Site" (National Park Service, 2005).

50. Branson, *Early Years,* 99, 122. Keith's rendering of Proenneke's journals displayed some remorse over the use of nonnative material: "I feel guilty about the tar paper and polyethylene because they are not true wilderness cabin materials, but I am convinced that they will do a better job of keeping the weather out." Keith, *One Man's Wilderness,* 48. Proenneke did not express this regret in his journal.

51. Branson, *Early Years,* 105, 115, 116. His written description of making the hinges pales in comparison to the film, which articulates the process better.

52. Ibid., 112, 103.

53. Ibid., 69, 140 141, 144, 148.

54. Richard Proenneke interview, 24. Branson, *More Readings,* iii. Raymond Proenneke interview. White had encouraged Proenneke to keep a journal and supplied him with notebooks and ink. Proenneke's filming was more directly concerned with a public audience. At one point he explained his process, noting that three days after his return to Twin Lakes in May 1968 he reenacted it for his camera. Branson, *Early Years*, 88. Branson, *More Readings*, vii, xvi. John Branson, telephone interview by author, August 7, 2013. As Keith explained it, he used Proenneke's journals "as a guide, and knowing him as well as I did, I have tried to get into his mind and reveal the 'flavor' of the man." Keith, *One Man's Wilderness,* 9. Proenneke charged that "He tried to put words in my mouth." Richard Proenneke interview, 30.

55. Keith, *One Man's Wilderness,* 21. Proenneke echoed the idea of a test when he said: "I had seen and examined lots of cabins and I just wondered what kind of job I could do building a cabin on my own, you know, and just—and do it all the time too—no chain saw, just an axe and one of them bow saw chisels and knots and whatever." Richard Proenneke interview, 16. After he cut his logs in 1967, Babe Alsworth told him that "a lot of guys drop wood." Proenneke said "I took that as a challenge" and completed his cabin. Richard Proenneke interview, 18.

56. Branson, *Early Years,* 86. Richard Proenneke interview, 21. Keith, *One Man's Wilderness,* 21.

57. Keith, *One Man's Wilderness,* 22.

58. Branson, *More Readings,* xix, xvii. Keith, *One Man's Wilderness,* 221. In 2000, Proenneke donated his journals—ninety pounds worth—to Lake Clark National Park. Branson, *More Readings,* vii. Proenneke's brother Raymond, called Jake, also agreed to these donations.

59. Branson interview. In the early 2000s, Lake Clark National Park staff replaced the sill logs and placed concrete piers under the new logs. They also replaced roofing material and added flashing. Windows that Proenneke had left as plastic sheeting were replaced with glass and steel mullions to deter bears. Branson, "National Register Form."

5. TWENTIETH-CENTURY LEISURE

1. Warren James Belasco, *Americans on the Road: From Autocamp to Motel, 1910–1945* (Cambridge: MIT Press, 1979), 7. James J. Flink, *The Automobile Age* (Cambridge: MIT Press, 1998), 129. A study of a group of skilled workers in the 1920s revealed that more than half of them took vacations away from home. Daniel Horowitz, *The Morality of Spending: Attitudes toward the Consumer Society in America, 1875–1940* (Baltimore: Johns Hopkins University Press, 1985), 140. The Fair Labor Standards Act of 1938 mandated the forty-hour work week, and the full two-day weekend became the norm in the mid-twentieth century. David E. Kyvig, *Daily Life in the United States, 1920–1939: Decades of Promise and Pain* (Westport, Conn.: Greenwood Press, 2002), 132, 37–38. Orvar Lofgren, *On Holiday: A History of Vacationing* (Berkeley: University of California Press, 1999), 63. Anthony D. King, "A Time for Space and a Space for Time: The Social Production of the Vacation House," in *Buildings and Society: Essays on the Social Development of the Built Environment*, ed. Anthony D. King (London: Routledge and Kegan Paul, 1980), 200, 204, 212.

2. Donald G. Mitchell, "In and About the Fair," *Scribner's Monthly* 12, no. 5 (September 1876): 747. J. S. Ingram, *The Centennial Exposition Described and Illustrated* (Philadelphia: Hubbard Brothers, 1876), 706, 707. James D. McCabe, *The Illustrated History of the Centennial Exhibition* (Philadelphia: National, 1876), 645–46. William B. Rhoads, *The Colonial Revival* (New York: Garland, 1977), 1:62–63. Rodris Roth, "The New England, or 'Olde Tyme,' Kitchen Exhibit at Nineteenth-Century Fairs," in *The Colonial Revival in America,* ed. Alan Axelrod (New York: W. W. Norton, 1985), 173–79. Karal Ann Marling, *George Washington Slept Here: Colonial Revivals and American Culture, 1876–1986* (Cambridge: Harvard University Press, 1988), 37–40. New England Kitchens also appeared at the Sanitary Fairs of the 1860s, but these were not housed in purpose-built buildings. Roth, "New England," 160. On the centennial as a catalyst for the Colonial Revival, see Vincent J. Scully Jr., *The Shingle Style and the Stick Style: Architectural Theory and Design from Downing to the Origins of Wright* (New Haven: Yale University Press, 1955; rev. ed., 1971), 30. Alan Gowans, *Styles and Types of North American Architecture: Social Function and Cultural Expression* (New York: HarperCollins, 1992), 325. Mark Gelernter, *A History of American Architecture: Buildings in Their Cultural and Technological Context* (Hanover, N.H.: University Press of New England, 1999), 180.

3. McCabe, *Illustrated History,* 646.

4. Roth, "New England," 178. The Lincoln cabin was from Goose Nest Prairie, Illinois, built by his father, allegedly with Lincoln's help, after Lincoln had grown up and moved away. See chapter 2 above. The cabin associated with Sitting Bull was the one in which he had been killed three years earlier at the Standing Rock Indian Agency.

5. Rev. Alexander Young, *Chronicles of the Pilgrim Fathers* (1841), 179n., cited in Shurtleff, *Log Cabin Myth,* 188–89. Frank M. Gregg to Arthur Emond, May 7, 1921, in collection of Virginia Emond Davis, Plymouth, Mass. The log building was a popular attraction, and at the end of the summer Gregg donated it to Plymouth's Pilgrim Society. Trustees of the Pilgrim Society, meeting of August 27, 1921, Pilgrim Society Archives, Box 4, Trustees' meetings, vol. 2, 1912–1944. The cabin did not stand for long, however; it had disappeared by 1927, according to Sanborn maps. See also L. J. T. Biese, "The Pilgrim Tercentenary (1920)," pamphlet, undated [late 1960s?], in collection of Pilgrim Hall, Plymouth Tercentenary Celebration, Box 2. *Plymouth Tercentenary Illustrated, with a brief history of the life and struggles of the Pilgrim Fathers* (New Bedford, Mass., 1921), in Plymouth Plantation Library. Newspaper clipping titled "Modern Pilgrims Greet President: Throngs from Everywhere Jam the Streets of Plymouth: Visitors Exceed Fifty Thousand," Plymouth Antiquarian Society Archives, Series 1, Hedge Family Papers, Box 4, scrapbooks. Anne Reilly, "The Pilgrimization of Plymouth: Creating a Landscape of Memory in Plymouth, Massachusetts, during the Pilgrim Tercentenary of 1920–21," in *We Are What We Remember: The American Past through Commemoration*, ed. Jeffrey Lee Meriwether and Laura Mattoon D'Amore (Newcastle-Upon-Tyne, U.K.: Cambridge Scholars, 2012), 244–66.

6. Groups other than Anglo-Americans also used the log cabin to assert ethnic heritage. See Matti E. Kaups, "Cultural Landscape—Log Structures as Symbols of Ethnic Identity," *Material Culture* 27, no. 2 (1995): 1–19.

7. Richard Guy Wilson, "American Arts and Crafts Architecture: Radical though Dedicated to the Cause Conservative," in *"The Art That Is Life": The Arts & Crafts Movement in America, 1875–1920,* ed. Wendy Kaplan (Boston: Little, Brown, 1987), 114–17.

8. "Three Craftsman Log Houses," *Craftsman* 11, no. 6 (March 1907): 742.

9. Natalie Curtis, "The New Log House at Craftsman Farms: An Architectural Development of the Log Cabin," *Craftsman* 21, no. 2 (November 1911): 196–203. Notches on both tops and bottoms of the logs aligned the courses, instead of staggering them. These aligned courses, unusual in log construction, resembled masonry coursing and added a quirkiness to the corners. Vertical pins set a few inches back from the intersections further secured the double notches. Philetus H. Holt, "A Different Perspective on Log Construction," undated paper available at Craftsman Farms. Mark Alan Hewitt has written extensively about this building. Mark Alan Hewitt, "Words, Deeds, Artifice: Gustav Stickley's Club House at Craftsman Farms," *Winterthur Portfolio* 31, no. 1 (Spring, 1996): 23–51. Mark Alan Hewitt, *Gustav Stickley's Craftsman Farms: The Quest for an Arts and Crafts Utopia* (Syracuse: Syracuse University Press, 2001).

10. Montgomery Schuyler, "American Domestic Architecture: Old Types and Modern Instances, I: The Log Cabin," *Art and Progress* 3, no. 10 (August 1912): 677.

11. Wilson, "American Arts and Crafts," 109. William B. Rhoads, "The Colonial Revival and

American Nationalism," *Journal of the Society of Architectural Historians* 35, no. 4 (December 1976): 242. Curtis, "New Log House," 196.

12. Chester H. Liebs, *Main Street to Miracle Mile: American Roadside Architecture* (Baltimore: Johns Hopkins University Press, 1985, 1995), 43, 44, 47, called these conspicuous buildings "a blend of building and sign."

13. Born in 1732, Washington moved away from this site when he was three years old, and the house where he was born was destroyed by fire in 1779. By the time people sought to recognize the site in some fashion, no visible trace of the house remained. In 1896, the U.S. government placed a granite obelisk, one-tenth the scale of the Washington Monument, on the spot where his house was thought to have been. Information on this site from Seth Bruggeman, *George Washington Birthplace National Monument: Administrative History, 1930–2000* (Philadelphia: Northeast Region, National Park Service, 2006). Seth Bruggeman, *Here, George Washington Was Born: Memory, Material Culture, and the Public History of a National Monument* (Athens: University of Georgia Press, 2008). *George Washington Birthplace National Monument: Cultural Landscape Report* ([Washington, D.C.]: National Park Service, 1999). Files at George Washington Birthplace National Monument. See also Elizabeth Sargent, "George Washington Birthplace National Monument: Provenance of a Colonial Revival Commemorative Landscape," in *Re-creating the American Past: Essays on the Colonial Revival*, ed. Richard Guy Wilson, Shaun Eyring, and Kenny Marotta (Charlottesville: University of Virginia Press, 2006), 216–34. Joy Beasley, "The Birthplace of a Chief: Archaeology and Meaning at George Washington Birthplace National Monument," in *Myth, Memory, and the Making of an American Landscape,* ed. Paul A. Shackel (Gainesville: University Press of Florida, 2001), 197–220. Charles B. Hosmer Jr., *Preservation Comes of Age: From Williamsburg to the National Trust, 1926–1949* (Charlottesville: University Press of Virginia, 1981), 1: 478–86.

14. Bruggeman, *George Washington Birthplace,* 18. Mrs. Harry Lee Rust, "Restoration of George Washington's Birthplace," December 15, 1930, George Washington Birthplace National Monument files. The tract was Duck Hall, adjacent to the Washingtons' property. The Commission of Fine Arts approved the Log House in concept in December. The association then put its efforts toward funding and constructing the birthplace home, which was completed in 1931, in time for the commemoration of the bicentennial of Washington's birth in February 1932. The park's first superintendent, Philip Hough, began work just a week before the birthday observances. Construction of the Log House cost $32,000.

15. Jan Whitaker, *Tea at the Blue Lantern Inn: A Social History of the Tea Room Craze in America* (New York: St. Martin's Press, 2002), 2, 4–5, 9, 34, 67, 85. Cynthia A. Brandimarte, "'To Make the Whole World Homelike': Gender, Space, and America's Tea Room Movement," *Winterthur Portfolio* 30, no. 1 (Spring 1995): 1–19. William B. Rhoads, "Roadside Colonial: Early American Designs for the Automobile Age, 1900–1940," *Winterthur Portfolio* 21, no. 2/3 (Summer-Autumn 1986): 140–42. Liebs, *Main Street,* 197. Quote from August 1922, cited in Whitaker, *Tea at the Blue Lantern,* 85. Like the tea room at Washington's birthplace, many also failed to succeed financially.

16. "Quick Lunch in California," *Fortune,* 16, no. 1 (July 1937): 93, 122. Rhoads, "Roadside Colonial," 146–47. Although most of these are defunct, victims of the rise of fast food places, one survives in Los Angeles. After a stint as a blue-painted Tony's Burgers, it is now El Comedor Mexican Grill with a beige and red color scheme.

17. Information on this site from Virginia Price, "Historic American Buildings Survey: Old Fort Rosalie Gift Shop" (Library of Congress, 2006). Tommy H. Jones, "Old Fort Rosalie Gift Shop Historic Structures Report" (Atlanta: Southeast Regional Office, National Park Service, 2006). Ann Beha Associates, "Natchez National Historical Park: Historic Structure Report: Old Fort Rosalie Gift Shop," (Atlanta: Southeast Regional Office, National Park Service, 1997). At the time, the success of the Spring Pilgrimage, a tour of historic houses and gardens sponsored by the Natchez Garden Club, indicated that heritage tourism might be a worthwhile industry for this Mississippi River town. The French had occupied Fort Rosalie from 1716 until 1729, when the Natchez Indians destroyed it; then the French rebuilt it in 1731.

18. Instead of the lower part of the upper log being notched, the upper part of the lower log was, which was a less sound method. Dickson enlisted in the army soon after Fort Rosalie opened; he was killed over Germany in 1943.

19. Carl R. Crego, *Fort Ticonderoga* (Charleston, S.C.: Arcadia, 2004), 119. Christopher Fox, phone interview, September 29, 2014. There were also two other log buildings on the site. Near the ticket office, Stephen Pell encouraged the development of the Fort Ticonderoga Pottery Works and built a small log cabin to serve as its sales office. Like the ticket office, the cabin had round logs, saddle-notched at the corners, and a side-gable roof. Near the house, the Dicksons built a playhouse, discussed in the next section.

20. Alfred C. Bossom, "The Restoration of Fort Ticonderoga," *Architecture* 52, no. 2 (August 1925): 275. Note that Bossom was referring to "trappers and huntsmen." There was no indication that any of the troops stationed at the fort had built log buildings to house themselves; although several thousand Americans occupied the fort in 1776 and 1777 and built hundreds of huts outside the walls, it appears that these were wood frame covered with planks.

21. Paul LaVanway, a local historian who has been researching roads and roadside projects in Keweenaw County, has shared information on this building in several discussions with me and through his lectures. Today the building serves as a shop for local crafts.

22. The Chamber of Commerce and the business community funded the information center, which architect Edwin B. Crittenden designed. Alison K. Hoagland, *Buildings of Alaska* (New York: Oxford University Press, 1993), 83.

23. Quote from M. L. Blumenthal, "Antiqueering," *Saturday Evening Post,* February 16, 1924, p. 18. Anecdote from "The Junk Snupper," *Saturday Evening Post,* April 19, 1924, p. 25. See also Kenneth L. Roberts, "Antiquamania," *Saturday Evening Post,* March 14, 1925, pp. 12–13, 193. Marling, *George Washington Slept Here,* 220.

24. Caneta S. Hankins, "National Register of Historic Places Inventory Nomination Form: Womack House" (National Park Service, 1983). Cynthia B. Campen, current owner of the log building, interviewed by author in McMinnville, Tennessee, October 9, 2013. Although the

National Register form dates the beginning of the business at 1927, clippings provided by Mrs. Campen dated it as 1929. Womack's parents died in 1927 and 1928, and it seems likely that she undertook this venture with her inheritance.

25. Alexis de Tocqueville, *Democracy in America* (New York: J. and H. D. Langley, 1840), 2:106. Gerald Gamm and Robert D. Putnam, "The Growth of Voluntary Associations in America, 1840–1940," *Journal of Interdisciplinary History* 29 (Spring 1999): 523, 528–29. Kyvig, *Daily Life,* 134.

26. William Pencak, *For God and Country: The American Legion, 1919–1941* (Boston: Northeastern University Press, 1989), 279–81.

27. Korral Broschinsky, "National Register of Historic Places Registration: Fillmore American Legion Hall" (National Park Service, 2010).

28. Patrick Zollner, "National Register of Historic Places Registration Form: American Legion Post #121" (National Park Service, 1995). The seven were in Augusta, Des Arc, Eudora, Newport, Paris, Rison, and Yellville.

29. Donna Sink, "National Register of Historic Places Registration Form: Woodlynne Log Cabin" (National Park Service, 1997). Similarly, on the other side of the country, a log cabin used by Scouts stands in a park in the middle of Santa Ana in southern California.

30. Cited in Erin St. John Kelly, "Built in a Church, Log Cabin Isn't Near Its End. Scout's Honor," *New York Times* April 17, 2013.

31. Paul Liberatore, "Lib at Large: Novato Contractor Supplies Century-Old Log Cabins for New Twitter Headquarters," *Marin Independent Journal* (San Rafael, Calif.), March 2, 2014. Jillian Wong, "Twitter Installs 19th Century Log Cabins in Its San Francisco Headquarters," *Taxi,* March 5, 2014.

32. Dean Boyer, "Log Cabin Syrup," *Encyclopedia of Consumer Brands,* vol. 1: *Consumable Products,* ed. Janice Jorgensen (Detroit: St. James Press, 1994), 344–46. Juliann Sivulka, *Soap, Sex, and Cigarettes: A Cultural History of American Advertising* (1998; rev. ed., Boston: Wadsworth, 2012), 50. The syrup tin was designed by James William Fuller, Patent No. 26,936, dated April 20, 1897. Towle sold his label to Postum in 1927; General Foods Corporation bought Postum in 1929. General Foods merged with Kraft in 1990, and Kraft sold Log Cabin Syrup to Aurora Foods in 1997. Aurora went bankrupt, and Pinnacle Foods acquired Log Cabin in 2003. Pinnacle also owns Mrs. Butterworth's, one of Log Cabin's major competitors (Aunt Jemima is the other).

33. Boyer, "Log Cabin Syrup," 344. *Products of General Foods: Brief Biographies of 29 Famous Products Issued by General Foods* (ca. 1934–46), 15. Andrew W. Higgs and Robert A. Sattler, "Cabin Comforts: The Archaeology of Bachelor Cabins on Fish Creek, Alaska," in *Eldorado! The Archaeology of Gold Mining in the Far North,* ed. Catherine Holder Spude, Robin O. Mills, Karl Gurcke, and Roderick Sprague (Lincoln: University of Nebraska Press, 2011), 294. The archaeologists determined that the cabin was occupied some time between 1906 and 1915.

6. "ALL THE PLEASURES OF PRIMITIVE LIVING"

1. Craig Gilborn, *Adirondack Camps: Homes Away from Home, 1850–1950* (Syracuse: Syracuse University Press, 2000), 87. August D. Shepard, *Camps in the Woods*, comp. and ed. R. W. Sexton (New York: Architectural Book, 1931). Roger Yepsen, "'Our Forest Home': Camp and Lodge Life," in *The Adirondack League Club, 1890–1990*, ed. Edward Comstock Jr. (privately printed, 1990), 34.

2. "A Vanderbilt Log Cabin," *Boston Daily Globe,* September 27, 1903, p. 45. Gilborn, *Adirondack Camps,* 221. Harvey H. Kaiser, *Great Camps of the Adirondacks* (Boston: David R. Godine, 1982), 64.

3. Robert Engel, Howard Kirschenbaum, and Paul Malo, *Santanoni: From Japanese Temple to Life at an Adirondack Great Camp* (privately printed, 2000), 69–86. Gilborn, *Adirondack Camps*, 227–29.

4. William S. Wicks, *Log Cabins: How to Build and Furnish Them* (New York: Forest and Stream, 1889), 7, 22, 29, 25, 14, 32, 10; (rev. ed., 1908) 14, 29. The 1889 edition of Wicks's book, on Google Books, from the Harvard College Library, was once owned by local colorist Sarah Orne Jewett. Gilborn, *Adirondack Camps*, 105–6, 249, 252.

5. Aaron Shapiro, *The Lure of the North Woods: Cultivating Tourism in the Upper Midwest* (Minneapolis: University of Minnesota Press, 2013), 46. Lofgren, *On Holiday,* 138. Melanie Shellenbarger, *High Country Summers: The Early Second Homes of Colorado, 1880–1940* (Tucson: University of Arizona Press, 2012), 55, 49–50, 51. An interesting example of an early retreat was architect Benjamin Henry Latrobe's sojourn in a log house in rural Delaware, as discussed by W. Barksdale Maynard, "A Log House for an Architect: Benjamin Henry Latrobe at Iron Hill," *Delaware History* 31, no. 2 (Fall-Winter 2005–2006): 97–124.

6. William Allen White, *The Autobiography of William Allen White* (New York: Macmillan, 1946), 461. "Historic American Buildings Survey: William Allen White Cabins" (Library of Congress, n.d.). Shellenbarger, *High Country Summers*, 2, 96–100.

7. December 15, 1914, cited in Shellenbarger, *High Country Summers,* 209.

8. Thomas Carter, "Together for the Summer: Architecture and Seasonal Community," *Perspectives in Vernacular Architecture* 11 (2004): 71–89.

9. Mary K. Otto, ed., *Rusticators in Sprucewold: Preserving the Legacy* (privately printed, 2007), 60, 65, 6. See also Christi A. Mitchell, "National Register of Historic Places Registration Form: Sprucewold Lodge" (National Park Service, 2014). The community survived as a place of privately owned vacation homes, and individuals bought up the rental cabins in 1970.

10. Early residents recalled hand pumps at the kitchen sink and outhouses in the yards, consistent with rustic vacations, but within a few years, Medford Lakes began the shift from a resort area to one of year-round residents. The area incorporated as a municipality in 1939, and city services began to be provided. The requirement for log construction began to be relaxed, and by the 1940s wood-frame houses with log veneer were permitted; by the 1960s houses without any log references were built. In the 1970s new guidelines called for all houses on the lakefronts to have

"the appearance of logs," and others "must be rustic in appearance." Robert W. Craig, ed., "Down Jersey: From Bayshore to Seashore" (Vernacular Architecture Forum guide, 2014), 316. Medford Lakes Colony Club, *The Medford Lakes Story, 1927–1977* (privately printed, 1977), 21, 13.

11. Medford Lakes Colony Club, *Medford Lakes Story,* 24, 40. Craig, "Down Jersey," 313. The lodge was destroyed by fire in 1998.

12. Chilson D. Aldrich, *The Real Log Cabin* (New York: Macmillan, 1935), vii, xi, 33. Aldrich also finished third place in a competition held by the *Western Architect* for a design for a log cabin to be used as a fishing retreat. "A Fishing Line," *Western Architect* 20 (June 1914): 60–61.

13. Aldrich, *Real Log Cabin,* 111, 38, 114. Ad for Page and Hill Real Log Houses, 1937, clipping in author's collection. One of these Page and Hill houses stands in Glenwood Springs, Colorado. In 1935 George Sumers ordered the two-story, 7,000-square-foot building, which was constructed in Minneapolis, then dismantled and reerected in Colorado. Kae McDonald, "National Register of Historic Places Registration Form: Sumers Lodge" (National Park Service, 1996).

14. Abigail Van Slyck, *A Manufactured Wilderness: Summer Camps and the Shaping of American Youth, 1890–1960* (Minneapolis: University of Minnesota Press, 2006), 25.

15. The camp was for white girls and was not integrated until 1968. W. Scott Breckinridge Smith, "National Register of Historic Places Registration Form: Hansill" (National Park Service, 2011). Melvin Lester and Travis McDonald, "Ivey Lodge, Camp Ruthers: Historic Structure Report" (typescript compiled for Thomas Jefferson's Poplar Forest, Forest, Va., 2004).

16. Struthers Burt, *The Diary of a Dude-Wrangler* (1924; New York: Charles Scribner's Sons, 1938), 52.

17. John Daugherty, *A Place Called Jackson Hole: A Historic Resource Study of Grand Teton National Park* (Moose, Wyo.: Grand Teton National Park, National Park Service, 1999), ch. 14. Mildred Adams, "Wild West De Luxe on the Dude Ranch," *New York Times,* June 29, 1930, p. 74. Lawrence R. Borne, *Dude Ranching: A Complete History* (Albuquerque: University of New Mexico Press, 1983), 51. Hal Borland, "Dudes at Home on the Range," *New York Times,* August 18, 1940, p. 90. A rebound after World War II was aided by TV westerns, such as *Gunsmoke,* in the 1950s. Ed Christopherson, "Western Dude Ranches Head for a Big Year," *New York Times,* May 24, 1959, p. XX27.

18. Fanny Kemble Wister, ed. *Owen Wister Out West: His Journals and Letters* (Chicago: University of Chicago Press, 1958), xv. W. Hudson Kensel, *Dude Ranching in the Yellowstone Country: Larry Larom and Valley Ranch, 1915–1969* (Norman, Okla.: Arthur H. Clark, 2010), 102.

19. Burt, *Diary,* 49. Kensel, *Dude Ranching,* 36, 83. Wister, *Owen Wister,* xv. Through his popular novel *The Virginian,* her father, Owen Wister, also helped to frame the country's understanding of the West in a way that emphasized difference.

20. Burt, *Diary,* 50, 89. Electricity and running water were rare amenities in guest cabins in the 1920s, but gradually they became widespread. Christopherson, "Western Dude Ranches."

21. Burt, *Diary,* 128, 90–92.

22. Although the industry slowed down during the war, it picked up again afterward; twenty-five dude ranches were in operation in the East in 1946. John Markland, "Ranges in the East,"

New York Times, May 26, 1940. John Markland, "The East Goes West," *New York Times*, May 25, 1941. Lee McCabe, "Dude Ranches Near By," *New York Times*, June 16, 1946.

23. Walter was quite involved in the process, as his memoir, written after he retired, makes clear. Walter H. Isaacson, "The Painted Pony" (typescript in Hadley-Luzerne Historical Society, Luzerne, N.Y., n.d.), 40–41, 29, 52, 71, 72–73, 75, 82.

24. Isaacson, "Painted Pony," 125, 190. Pete Ruggiero, interview by author, September 14, 2014.

25. In 1970 the Isaacsons sold out and retired to Florida.

26. Belasco, *Americans on the Road,* 3, 131–37. Liebs, *Main Street,* 174–82.

27. Mary Ann Carlson and Rheba Massey, "National Register of Historic Places Registration Form: Log Cabin Motel" (National Park Service, 1993).

28. Bishir, Southern, and Martin, *Guide to the Historic Architecture,* 299. Sara Amy Leach, "By the 'Way: Places to Stay," *SCA Journal,* Spring 1997, 32–33. The motel in Gallup was demolished in 2004. For a discussion of the hardscrabble origins of the wildly successful Log Cabin Farms in Armonk, N.Y., see "The Great American Roadside," *Fortune* 10, no. 3 (September 1934): 62–63, 172.

29. Initially the founders thought the directors could stay in the main house, as the regents of Mount Vernon did, but they soon discarded this idea. Ethel Armes to Mrs. Charles D. Lanier, May 24, 1928, cited in exhibit in the Preservation Gallery at Stratford Hall, visited October 2014. The foundation renamed itself the Robert E. Lee Memorial Association in 1971.

30. Minutes of the Fifth Council of the Robert E. Lee Memorial Foundation, Inc., Oct. 12–19, 1933. Appendix XXIII, May Field (Mrs. Charles D.) Lanier, "Informal Report on Directors' Quarters," October 1933. Another dozen or so cabins have been built since the war, some as replacements.

31. The dining room burned in 1944 and was replaced by a new log dining room. Also in the midst of the cabins is a tall brick Council House, designed by prominent Colonial Revival architect Fiske Kimball to resemble an eighteenth-century church. The Council House provided space for the directors' meetings. Jonathan A. Farris, "Fiske Kimball, the Robert E. Lee Memorial Foundation, and the Museumification of Stratford Hall," paper delivered at *Fiske Kimball: Creator of an American Architecture,* symposium at University of Virginia School of Architecture, November 19, 1995, http://www.stratalum.org/Farris.html, accessed July 22, 2014.

32. Caroline Gordon Brown to B. F. Cheatham, January 16, 1934, cited by Judy Henson, "History of the Directors' Cabins on the Cabin Tour," n.d. It is not known where the bulk of the slave cabins were located. The foundation built two stone double quarters near the main house in 1939, but these were atypical. The foundation also built a cabin for William Wesley Payne, a descendant of slaves who had lived and worked at Stratford Hall his whole life. The 1941 cabin had hewn horizontal logs with corner boards and a wooden chimney; it was intended to resemble the cabin in which Payne was born, but it is not known if he advised on the design.

33. Kimble A. David, "National Register of Historic Places Registration Form: Westmoreland State Park Historic District" (National Park Service, 2005). The next chapter addresses Westmoreland and other state parks more fully.

7. PARKS AND FORESTS

1. Some use the term "Park Service Rustic." See, for example, Ethan Carr, *Wilderness by Design: Landscape Architecture and the National Park Service* (Lincoln: University of Nebraska Press, 1998), 132. Also see Wikipedia entry for "National Park Service rustic." Another term is "Parkitecture."

2. Laura Soullière Harrison, "National Register of Historic Places Inventory—Nomination Form: Old Faithful Inn" (National Park Service, 1985). Karen Wildung Reinhart, "Old Faithful Inn: Centennial of a Beloved Landmark," *Yellowstone Science* 12, no. 2 (Spring 2004): 5–22.

3. William C. Tweed, Laura E. Soullière, and Henry G. Law, "Rustic Architecture, 1916–1942" (National Park Service, 1977), Part II: "The Landscape Influence: 1916–1918." Laura Soullière Harrison, "National Register of Historic Places Inventory—Nomination Form: Rangers' Club" (National Park Service, 1986).

4. Linda Flint McClelland, *Building the National Parks: Historic Landscape Design and Construction* (Baltimore: Johns Hopkins University Press, 1998), 197, 330. Laura Soullière Harrison, *Architecture in the Parks National Historic Landmark Theme Study* (Washington, D.C.: National Park Service, 1986), 6.

5. Norman T. Newton, *Design on the Land: The Development of Landscape Architecture* (Cambridge: Harvard University Press, 1971), 579, 540. Carr, *Wilderness by Design*, 257, 264. From 1933 to 1937, the NPS received $82 million from the CCC, $40 million from the PWA, and $24 million from the WPA. Harold D. Unrau and G. Frank Williss, *Administrative History: Expansion of the National Park Service in the 1930s* (Washington, D.C.: National Park Service, 1983), ch. 3.

6. Arno B. Cammerer, foreword to *Park Structures and Facilities,* comp. and ed. Albert H. Good (Washington, D.C.: National Park Service, 1935), 1.

7. Good, "Apologia," *Park Structures,* 3–4.

8. Ibid., 5, 6, 4.

9. Ibid., 7–8. Albert H. Good, comp. and ed., *Park and Recreation Structures* (Washington: GPO, 1938), 1: 3.

10. Good, *Park Structures,* 157. Maier cited in McClelland, *Building the National Parks,* 396.

11. There were more explicit precedents as well. Thomas Vint, for example, had assembled a portfolio of model designs in 1932. McClelland, *Building the National Parks,* 247–48. Herbert Maier compiled a handbook of photographs for the use of district inspectors in 1934. McClelland, *Building the National Parks,* 406. Ethan Carr attributed most of the ideas in Good's work to Maier. Carr, *Wilderness by Design,* 283.

12. Laura Soullière Harrison, "National Register of Historic Places Inventory—Nomination Form: Paradise Inn" (National Park Service, 1986). Harrison's National Register nominations were compiled into a National Historic Landmark theme study, "Architecture in the Parks." Also useful for Mount Rainier is Stephanie Toothman, Susan Begley, and Ethan Carr, "Mount Rainier National Park," National Historic Landmark nomination (National Park Service, 1996).

13. Good, *Park Structures,* 148, 107. Good, *Park and Recreation,* 1: 69.

14. Ernest A. Davidson cited in Laura Soullière Harrison, "National Register of Historic Places Inventory—Nomination Form: Yakima Park Stockade Group" (National Park Service, 1985).

15. Good, *Park Structures,* 108. Good, *Park and Recreation,* 1: 64. Harrison, "National Register Nomination: Yakima Park." See Carr, *Wilderness by Design,* for more on MORA (Mount Rainier National Park). A Pratt truss is one in which the diagonals slope toward the center.

16. Good, *Park and Recreation,* 3: 17.

17. Harry Karstens cited in Olmsted Center for Landscape Preservation, *Cultural Landscape Report for Park Headquarters, Denali National Park and Preserve: Site History, Existing Conditions, Analysis & Treatment* (Boston: Northeast Region, National Park Service, 2008), 20. Gail Evans, "National Register of Historic Places Inventory—Nomination Form: Mount McKinley National Park Headquarters" (National Park Service, 1985). This is Building 22.

18. Harry Karstens cited in Gail Evans, "National Register of Historic Places Inventory—Nomination Form: Patrol Cabins, Mount McKinley National Park" (National Park Service, 1985). This is the Pearson Cabin, No. 4.

19. Arno B. Cammerer cited in Olmsted, *Cultural Landscape Report,"* 28. The ranger's quarters does not survive. The warehouse is now Building 101, and the barn, Building 106.

20. Olmsted, *Cultural Landscape Report,* 37, 40, 45–47. Frame residences are Buildings 12 and 13. The machine shop and garage is Building 102. The log-veneered residence is Building 23.

21. Newton, *Design on the Land,* 562–65.

22. Unrau and Williss, *Administrative History,"* ch. 3, pt. A. Mark R. Edwards, Lucy Ann Lawliss, Susan Begley, and Ethan Carr, "National Historic Landmark Nomination: Pine Mountain State Park" (National Park Service, 1997).

23. Rolf T. Anderson, "National Register of Historic Places Multiple Property Documentation Form: Minnesota State Park CCC/WPA/Rustic Style Historic Resources" (National Park Service, 1988), E14, E4, E25, E27.

24. Diana Mitchell, "National Register of Historic Places Inventory—Nomination Form: Itasca State Park" (National Park Service, 1973, with additional documentation submitted in 1992). The log kitchen wing added to Douglas Lodge by 1914 was replaced in 1984–85 with one that was wood frame clad in log siding.

25. Good, *Park Structures,* 226. Good, *Park and Recreation,* 3: 17.

26. Edwards et al., "National Landmark Nomination: Pine Mountain." Ann McCleary, Gail A. D'Avino, Michael V. Jacobs, Lucy Lawliss, and Julie Turner, "The New Deal," in *Cotton Mills, Planned Communities, and the New Deal: Vernacular Architecture and Landscapes of the New South,* ed. Debbie Curtis Toole, Vernacular Architecture Forum Guidebook (Athens, Ga.: Green Berry Press, 1999), 116.

27. These historic sites are discussed in chapters 5 and 6.

28. Good, *Park and Recreation,* 3:35. See also Kimble A. David, "National Register of Historic Places Registration Form: Westmoreland State Park Historic District" (National Park Service, 2005).

29. Horace Lydick to Gifford Pinchot, October 29, 1909, transcription in "Minnesota Na-

tional Forest Personnel File—Horace S. Lydick," Chippewa National Forest, Walker, Minnesota. Elizabeth Canfield Flint described her year living here with her ranger-husband in 1911–12 in a novel, *The Pine Tree Shield: A Novel Based on the Life of a Forester* (Garden City, N.J.: Doubleday, Doran, 1943). The building was heavily restored in 1994–98. Clifford B. Senn, "National Register of Historic Places Inventory—Nomination Form: Old Cut Foot Sioux Ranger Station" (National Park Service, 1973). John R. Grosvenor, *A History of the Architecture of the USDA Forest Service* (Washington, D.C.: U.S. Forest Service, 1999), chapters 1 and 2.

30. E. G. Throop, "National Register of Historic Places Nomination: USDA Forest Service Administrative Buildings in the States of Oregon and Washington Built by the Civilian Conservation Corps" (National Park Service, 1984), FIII: 1, E:2. C. P. Fickes, comp., *Region One Handbook: Construction and Maintenance of Forest Improvements* (Washington, D.C.: U.S. Forest Service, 1935), R-35, R-1, R-40, R-43, R-37.

31. W. Ellis Groben, "Architectural Trend of Future Forest Service Buildings" (Washington, D.C.: U.S. Forest Service, 1940), 1–5.

32. Stanley A. Johnson, "National Register of Historic Places Inventory—Nomination Form: Supervisor's Office, Chippewa National Forest" (National Park Service, 1975). Also in this mode, and not far away, is the Norway Beach Visitor Center, built by the same CCC workers and completed in 1938. The building is a smaller version of the Chippewa Supervisor's Office with equally impressive craftsmanship.

33. William C. Tweed, "Recreation Site Planning and Improvement in National Forests, 1891–1942" (Washington, D.C.: U.S. Forest Service, 1980), 21–22. Leland Roth, "Building at the End of the Oregon Trail" (Vernacular Architecture Forum guidebook, 1997), 2.6.5–18.

34. See Ethan Carr, *Mission 66: Modernism and the National Park Dilemma* (Amherst: University of Massachusetts Press, 2007).

35. George Nason, "Architecture and Its Relationship to the Design of Parks," in *1940 Yearbook: Park and Recreation Progress* (Washington: GPO, 1940), 56. Harrison, "Architecture in the Parks," 9. A robust defense of rustic architecture was given by Devereux Bucher, "For a Return to Harmony in Park Architecture," *National Parks Magazine* 26, no. 111 (October 1952): 150–57.

36. Tweed, Soullière, and Law, "Rustic Architecture," ch. 6. Richard West Sellars, *Preserving Nature in the National Parks: A History* (1997; rev. ed., New Haven: Yale University Press, 2009, orig. pub. 1997), 187. Carr, *Mission 66*, 137.

EPILOGUE

1. Gary Bufe, Hiawatha Log Homes, interview by author, September 7, 2012.

2. Mark and Carol Plichta, interview by author, July 31, 2014.

3. Jeremy Bertrand of Log Homes of America, Inc., noted that the industry shies away from the term "cabin," thinking that it has a vacation-only connotation. Bertrand, telephone interview by author, November 17, 2014. There are currently about 200 log home companies. The industry, like the rest of the home building industry, was hard hit in the 2008 recession. The number of log home companies dropped from 600 in 2003 to 200 ten years later. The market has also shifted

from mostly vacation homes twenty years ago to a growth in primary homes until the recession, then mostly vacation/retirement homes now. Donna Peak, Log Homes Council, telephone interview by author, November 17, 2014. Larry Roos, Northwest Log Homes, interview by author, October 27, 2012. Pamela Johnson, Highlands Log Structures, interview by author, October 27, 2012. NAHB Log Homes Council, "Log Building Systems: A Uniquely American Tradition, and the Original 'Green' and Sustainable Way to Build," brochure, 2014. Log and Timber Home Living Institute, "Log Home Industry Insights 2013," PowerPoint. The organization polled 200 log home companies; the 72 that responded reported sales of 6,770 in 2013. The figure of 26,000 homes produced in 2015 is from Rory S. Coakley, "Not Your Great-Grandfather's Great-Grandfather's Log House," *Washington Post,* Real Estate section, June 11, 2016, p. 14.

4. According to the companies who reported data, more than half of their houses fit into the 1,600 to 2,399-square-foot range. Log and Timber Home Living Institute, "Log Home Industry Insights 2013," PowerPoint.

5. Looking ahead, it is appropriate to look abroad, where there are new markets for log cabins. Southland Log Homes, based in South Carolina, has shipped log houses to China. Fitting into four or five shipping containers, a log house can be shipped to the other side of the world relatively inexpensively. Why the Chinese want log houses is a matter for speculation, but they may appeal to wealthy Chinese who have vacationed in the western United States. The log house, imported to America more than four centuries ago, is being exported across the world. Bill Olson, Southland Log Homes, interview October 27, 2012. "Southland Log Homes Exports to the People's Republic of China," *Columbia (South Carolina) Business Monthly,* May 8, 2014.

6. Charles McRaven, *The Classic Hewn-Log House: A Step-By-Step Guide to Building and Restoring* (North Adams, Mass.: Storey, 2005), 1. The first edition was *Building the Hewn-Log House*, 1978, while the second edition was *Building and Restoring the Hewn-Log House*, 1994. See also, for example, "Recycling: The Adaptive Restoration Process," in *Muir's Original Log Structures Restoration Guide* (1993?), 48D-50. Alan Pape formed Adaptive Restoration in the late 1970s to acquire deteriorating log farm buildings in northern Wisconsin and the Upper Peninsula of Michigan, sell them to new owners, and move them to new sites. He estimates that he has relocated fifty buildings in this way. Pape, interview by author, September 1, 2011.

7. By the end of the 1970s, there were more than one million back-to-the-landers. Eleanor Agnew, *Back from the Land: How Young Americans Went to Nature in the 1970s, and Why They Came Back* (Chicago: Ivan R. Dee, 2004), 5.

HISTORIOGRAPHICAL NOTE

1. Fiske Kimball, *Domestic Architecture of the American Colonies and of the Early Republic* (1922; repr., New York: Dover, 1966), 3, 8. Henry Mercer, "The Origin of Log Houses in the United States," *Old-Time New England* 18, no. 2 (October 1927): 63.

2. Harold R. Shurtleff, *The Log Cabin Myth: A Study of the Early Dwellings of the English Colonists in North America* (Cambridge: Harvard University Press, 1939), 163–66. In 1934, at the age of fifty-one, Shurtleff entered graduate studies in history at Harvard University, half-time, where

he studied with the renowned American historian Samuel Eliot Morison. Intrigued by the log cabin question through his work in Williamsburg, Shurtleff had developed a detailed outline for his book before his untimely death in 1938. Morison picked up where Shurtleff had left off, with two chapters drafted, five chapters with extensive notes, and one chapter only outlined, and he completed the book, publishing it under Shurtleff's name in 1939. S. E. Morison, introduction to Shurtleff, *Log Cabin Myth,* xiii–xviii.

3. C. A. Weslager, *The Log Cabin in America: From Pioneer Days to the Present* (New Brunswick: Rutgers University Press, 1969), 150, 152–53, 156, 164–65, 190–96.

4. Fred B. Kniffen, "Folk Housing: Key to Diffusion," in *Common Places: Readings in American Vernacular Architecture,* ed. Dell Upton and John Michael Vlach (Athens: University of Georgia Press, 1986), 10. Fred B. Kniffen and Henry Glassie, "Building in Wood in the Eastern United States: A Time-Place Perspective," in Upton and Vlach, *Common Places,* 175.

5. Terry G. Jordan, *American Log Buildings: An Old World Heritage* (Chapel Hill: University of North Carolina Press, 1985). Terry G. Jordan and Matti Kaups, *The American Backwoods Frontier: An Ethnic and Ecological Interpretation* (Baltimore: Johns Hopkins University Press, 1989), 146.

6. Patricia Irvin Cooper, "Some Misconceptions in American Log-Building Studies," *Material Culture* 23, no. 2 (1991): 56. Patricia Irvin Cooper, "Migration and Log Building in Eastern North Carolina," *Material Culture* 31, no. 2 (Summer 1999): 27. She also attributed the gable-end cantilevered roof, used in the coastal South to protect exterior mud chimneys, to Swiss Mennonites who initially settled in Pennsylvania. She noted that the Swiss in Pennsylvania did not build these cantilevers, but they revived the tradition when they migrated south. Cooper, "Some Misconceptions," 53–55. Later, she attributed the cantilevered roof to the Swede-Finns. Cooper, "Migration," 45. Carl Lounsbury, "Log Building in the Chesapeake," *Vernacular Architecture* 41 (2010): 76, 77.

7. Garrison houses dismissed by Mercer, "Origin of Log Houses," 63; Shurtleff, *Log Cabin Myth,* 15–16; and Weslager, *Log Cabin in America,* 110, 122. Arguing for their consideration included Appleton, cited in Scott H. Suter, "'The Clapboards Lifted:' Henry Chapman Mercer and the Origin of an American Log Building Style," *Folklore Historian* 6, no. 2 (Fall 1989): 78; Abbott Lowell Cummings, *The Framed Houses of Massachusetts Bay, 1625–1725* (Cambridge: Harvard University Press, 1979), 92–94; Richard McAlpin Candee, "Wooden Buildings in Early Maine and New Hampshire: A Technological and Cultural History, 1600–1720" (Ph.D. diss., University of Pennsylvania, 1976), 257–58, 248, 268.

8. Amos Rapaport, *House Form and Culture* (Englewood Cliffs, N.J.: Prentice Hall, 1969), 24–26. J. B. Jackson, "First Comes the House," *Landscape: Magazine of Human Geography* 9, no. 2 (Winter 1959–60): 27–28. Fred Kniffen, "To Know the Land and Its People," *Landscape: Magazine of Human Geography* 9, no. 3 (Spring 1960): 22. Henry Glassie, *Pattern in the Material Folk Culture of the Eastern United States* (Philadelphia: University of Pennsylvania Press, 1968), 8.

9. Terry G. Jordan, Jon T. Kilpinen, and Charles F. Gritzner, *The Mountain West: Interpreting the Folk Landscape* (Baltimore: Johns Hopkins University Press, 1997), 8.

INDEX

Italicized page numbers refer to illustrations, and CP followed by a number denotes plates in the color gallery following page 126.

Adams, John Quincy, 52
Adaptive Restoration, 278n6
Adirondack League Club, 173, 175
Adirondack Mountains, New York, 173–76, 188–90, 194, 196
adobe, 43
Adventures of Huckleberry Finn, The (Twain), 5
advertising, log buildings as, 56, 59, 65, 108, 156, 162, 164, *170*, 170, 171, 191
African American people, 78–96
Alabama: Gee's Bend, 95, *96;* Greenville, *83*
Alaska: Anchorage, *163*, 163; Chisana, *5;* Eagle, *6, 7;* Fairbanks, 164, 171; Nenana, 164; Palmer, 164; Port Alsworth, 147; Sitka, *47;* Twin Lakes, *146, CP8, CP9;* Wiseman, 1, *41, 42*. *See also* Denali National Park, Alaska; Lake Clark National Park and Preserve, Alaska
Alaska Railroad, 210
Alaska Road Commission, 208
Alden, John, 150
Aldrich, Chilson D., 182, 189
Alfred's Cabin (Hermitage, Nashville, Tennessee), plan, *28*
Alone in the Wilderness (film), 139
Alsworth, Leon "Babe," 140
American Backwoods Frontier, The: An Ethnic and Ecological Interpretation (Jordan and Kaups), 237
American Legion halls, 165–66, *167*, 169
American Log Buildings: An Old-World Heritage (Jordan), 237
antique shops, 9, 148, 156, 164–65, *CP11*
Appalachia, 9, 16, 25, 27, 78, 96–114
Arkansas: Newport, 166; Paris, 166; Rison, 166
Arts and Crafts movement, 4, 9, 100, 103, 150, 152–53, 156
Atlantic Monthly, 97
Audubon Society, 136
automobiles, 9, 148–49, 159, 190–91, 198

Bagley Cabin (Island Park, Idaho), *179*
Baltimore, Lord, 24

Bar BC Ranch (Jackson Hole, Wyoming), 186, *187*
Barnum Museum (New York), 63
Bartram, William, 43
Battle of the Thames, 52
Battle of Tippecanoe, 52
Bell, Frank, 143
Bemis, Kenneth Eaton, 159
Berea College (Kentucky), 99, 103, 260n30
Bergley, Nels, 223
Berkeley plantation (Virginia), 54
Bertolet-Herbein Cabin (Oley Line, Pennsylvania), *38*, 39
Bigham, James W., 63
blockhouses, 34, 202, 206
Blue Ridge Parkway, Virginia and North Carolina, 108, 109–10; Johnson Farm (Virginia), 109, *110, 111;* Mabry Mill (Virginia), 109
Boekenoogen, Isaac, 223
Boone, Daniel, 137
Booz, E. C., 58
Bossom, Alfred C., 161
Boston Common, 63
Boyle, Mildred, 129
Boy Scouts, 166, 169; cabins, 166, *167*
Breitenbucher, George, 189
Brockway, Daniel D., 59
Brown, A. Paul, 205
Bryan, William Jennings, 178
Buchanan, James, 250n1
Buffalo Bill (William Cody), 186
Building the Hewn-Log House (McRaven), 232
Building with Logs (Forest Service publication), 222
Bureau of Land Management, 140
Burt, Struthers, 186–87
Butler, Laurence, 35
Byrd, William, 34

cabin, definition of, 16, 17
Caldwell-Hutchison Farm (Lowndesville, South Carolina), *CP1*
California, 159; El Dorado, *40;* Los Angeles, *CP10;* San Francisco, 169, *CP12;* Santa Ana, 271n29. *See also* Yosemite National Park, California
Cammerer, Arno B., 200, 210
Campbell, John C., 105–6; Folk School (Brasstown, North Carolina), 105, *106*
Campbell, Olive, 105–6, 107
"Camp of the Pines" (Pinedale, Wyoming), 191
Camp Ruthers (Lynchburg, Virginia), 184, *185*
camps: Adirondack, 9, 173–76; summer, 183–84
Camp Sagamore (Raquette Lake, New York), 174, *175*
Camp Santanoni (Newcomb, New York), 174–75, *CP13*
Canada, 7, 37
Candee, Richard, 237
Carncross, Horace, 186
Carrithers, Spike and Hope, 140, 141
Carter's Grove (James City County, Virginia), 91, 94, *CP6*
Caudill, Henry, 113
Cavelier, René-Robert, 37
Centennial Exposition (Philadelphia, 1876), 150; New England Farmer's Home and Modern Kitchen, 150, *151*
Central Market (Washington, DC), 59
Century of Progress Exposition (Chicago, 1933), 108
Cheatham, Benjamin Franklin, Jr., 192–93
Cheatham, Frank, 193
Cherokee people, 43, 249n51
Chicago World's Fair (1893). *See* World's Columbian Exposition (Chicago, 1893)
Chickasaw people, 43
Child, Harry, 196
Children's Home Society, 138
chimneys, 2, 11, 16, 17, 21, 25, 28, 38, 40, 42, 51, 58, 84, 88, 91, 156; wooden, 2, 11, 25, 63, 81–82, 86, 95, 97, 105, 121, 126, 136, 176, 274n32, 279n6; masonry, 13, 21, 86, 87, 93, 105, 112, 129, 143–44, 161, 163, 164, 166, 169, 174, 176, 178, 182, 194, 203, 205, 214, 218, 220, 223, 246n28. *See also* fireplaces

chinking, 21, *23*, 23, 245n16
Chippewa National Forest, Minnesota, 220–24; Cut Foot Ranger Station, 220, *221;* Norway Beach Visitor Center, 277n32; Supervisor's Office Building, 222–24, *223, CP16*
Choctaw people, 43
Civilian Conservation Corps (CCC), 74, 194, 200, 214, 216–18, 220, 223, 224, 226, 275n5, 277n32
Classic Hewn-Log House, The: A Step-By Step Guide to Building and Restoring (McRaven), 232
Clay, Henry, 52
clubhouses, 9, 148, *154*, 154, *155*, 165–69
Cobbs, Marian, 59
Collier, Robert J., 64
Collier's Magazine, 64
Colonial Coffee Shops (San Francisco, California), 159
Colonial Revival movement, 4, 9, 103, 150, 152, 156, 157, 158, 162, 191, 192, 274n31
Colonial Williamsburg (Virginia), 91, 235
Colorado: Estes Park, 177; Glenwood Springs, 273n13
Comedor Mexican Grill, El (Los Angeles, California), 270n16
Connecticut: Hartford, 59, *60;* Redding, 32
Cooper, Patricia Irvin, 237
corner men, 18
Craftsman Farms (Morristown, New Jersey), *154*, 154, *155*
Craftsman magazine, 153–54
Creek people, 43; House, *44*
Crenshaw (Will) Plantation (Greenville, Alabama), *83*
Crisis (NAACP publication), 95
Crockett, Davy, 137
Currier and Ives, 2, 5, 11, 17; "A Home in the Wilderness," *3*
Curtis, Natalie, 154–55, 156

Daniel Boone and Davy Crockett Club, 136–7
Dankers, Jasper, 33–34
Darling, Charles W., 180
Darrow, Clarence, 178
Daughters of the American Revolution (DAR), 138
Davidson, Ernest A., 204, 205, 212
Davis, Jefferson, 63–64, 65
Davis, John E., 110
Delaware Agricultural Museum (Dover), 236
Denali National Park, Alaska, 208–12; employees' residence, *213;* Headquarters Buildings, 208–12; office building, *210;* Toklat River Patrol Cabin, 209–10, *211;* warehouse, *212*
Dennett, Alfred, 63
Description of the Province of New Albion, A (Plowden), 34
Dexter Pavilion (Chicago), 61
Dickson, Jefferson Davis, 160
Doddridge, Joseph, 35
Domestic Architecture of the American Colonies and of the Early Republic (Kimball), 235
Donn, Edward W., Jr., 157
Douglass, Frederick, 259n19
Dow, Wilmot, 134
Du Bois, W. E. B., 95
Duck Hall (Virginia), 269n14
dude ranches, 9, 184–90, *188, 189,* 194
DuPont, Alfred I., 193
DuPont, Jessie Ball, 193–94
Durant, William West, 173, 174
Dutch people, 32–33

Early Life of Abraham Lincoln, The (Tarbell), 63
Eaton, Allen, 105, 106
Eaton, Howard, 184–85
Ecole des Beaux Arts, 175
Elkhorn Ranch (north of Medora, North Dakota), 134–35, *134*, 138
Emergency Conservation Works Act, 200
Emond, Arthur, 152
English people, 3, 4, 25, 34, 38, 44–46, 98–99, 103, 150, 152, 235, 237
Etholen, Adolph, 249n55
Everidge, Solomon, 104

Fair Labor Standards Act of 1938, 267n1
Farmer Boy (L. Ingalls Wilder), 124
Ferris, Joe, 131, 133
Ferris, Sylvane, 131, 138
Fickes, C. P., 221–22
Fillmore, Millard, 51, 250n1
Finnish people, 32, 46, 236–37, 249n55
fireplaces, 1, 25, 27, 28, 30–31, 38, 40, 42, 44, 48, 68, 87, 88, 91, 92, 94, 103, 107, 126, 135, 137, 141–44, 158, 161, 163, 166, 168, 169, 174, 177–78, 179, 181, 182, 184, 187, 190, 193, 194, 196, 203, 204, *205*, 210, 214, 218, 220, 223, 231, 236. *See also* chimneys
Fireside Industries, 103
Folk, Joseph W., 253n30
Forest and Stream magazine, 136
Forest Life (C. Kirkland), 119
forests, national, 10, 220–24, 264n34. *See also* Chippewa National Forest, Minnesota; Mount Hood National Forest, Oregon
Fort Rosalie (Natchez, Mississippi), 160; gift shop, *160*
Fort Ross (California), 46
Fort Ticonderoga (Ticonderoga, New York), 161, 168; gift shop, *161;* Pottery Works, 270n19
foundations, 17, 24, 29, 73, 81, 88, 155, 206, 217, 227
French people, 4, 16, 37, 238
Froebel blocks, 77
From Log Cabin to White House (book series), 117
Frost, William G., 99, 103, 260n30
Fuller, James William, 271n32
Furman, Lucy, 104

Garfield, James A., 51, 250n1
garrison houses, 17, 34, 237, 279n7
General Foods, 170
Georgia, *17*
German settlers, 4, 25, 34–35, 37–38, 45, 235, 237, 246n34, 248n38
gift shops, 9, 148, 156, 160–62, *160, 161,* 165
Girl Scouts, 166, 194
Glacier National Park, Montana, 264n34
Glassie, Henry, 237
Glass Window, The: A Story of the Quare Women (Furman), 104
Good, Albert, 200–202, 206
Goode, Patrick G., 55–56
Grandfather's House, My (antique shop, McMinnville, Tennessee), 164, *CP11*
Grant, U. S., 250n1, 250n3
Great Plains, 17, 41
Great Smoky Mountains National Park, Tennessee and North Carolina, 108, 110–13, 261n43; Cades Cove (Tennessee), 110, 111–13, *113;* Mountain Farm Museum (North Carolina), 110, *112;* Walker Farm (Tennessee), *114*
Greek Revival style, 13
Green and Wicks, 175
Gregg, Frank M., 152
Grinnell, George Bird, 136
Gritzner, Charles F., 238
Groben, W. Ellis, 222

Hall, Basil, "Log Cabin in the Forests of Georgia," *17*
Hamilton College (Clinton, New York), 118
Hampton (Towson, Maryland), 88, *89,* 94
Handy, W. C., 85
Hanks, John, 62, 63
Harney, Will Wallace, 97
Harper's New Monthly Magazine, 97
Harris, Thaddeus Mason, 16, 17
Harrison, William Henry, 8, 50–61, 117, 152, 250n1; campaign textile, *CP2;* "General Harrison's Log Cabin March and Quick Step" (sheet music), *52;* "Harrison and Reform" (silk handkerchief), *57*
Harrodsburg Herald, 70
Harrodsburg Historical Society, 70
Hart, Howard Hamilton, 27
Harte, Bret, 97
Harvey (Fred) Company, 197
Hearst, William Randolph, 254n45
Heath, Gove, and Bell, 203

Henson, Josiah, 87
Hermitage (Nashville, Tennessee), *28,* 89, *90,* 94, 169, 258n16
Hermitage Ladies' Association, 169
Herndon, William H., 69
Hiawatha Log Homes, 227–31; "Norway" plans and perspective, *230*
Hibben, Thomas, 68
Hindman School (Hindman, Kentucky), 100–104, *102*
historical societies, 10
Hone, Philip, 57
Howard, Hattie Howell, 70–71
Howell, James Richard, 70
Howells, William Cooper, 1
Howells, William Dean, 1, 27
Hudson's Bay Company, 37
Hunter's Cabin (World's Columbian Exposition), 136–37, 151
Huntington, Collis, 173
Hunting Trips of a Ranchman (T. Roosevelt), 135

Idaho, Island Park, *179*
Illinois: Charleston, 66; Decatur, 62, 66; Goose Nest Prairie, 66, 74, 268n4; New Salem, 62, 71–72, *73,* 74; Petersburg, 71–72, *73;* Springfield, 62
Illinois Republican Convention (1860), 62
Imperial Hotel (Tokyo, Japan), 77
Indiana: Little Pigeon Creek, 62, 68, 73; Lincoln City, *69, 75*
Indiana Lincoln Union, 68, 69
Indian Territory, 43
Ingersoll, Ernest, 39–40
In the Tennessee Mountains (Murfree), 97
Isaacson, Betty, 188–90
Isaacson, Walter, 188–90
Itasca State Park, Minnesota, 214–17; Cabin 8, *215;* Douglas Lodge, 214, *215;* Forest Inn, 217, *218;* Old Timer's Cabin, *216,* 216–17

jacal, 16, 43
Jackson, Andrew, 51, 53, 89–91, 169, 250n1
Jackson, Rachel, 89–90
jails, 17, 34
Jefferson, Thomas, 177, 246n28
Jewett, Sarah Orne, 97, 272n4
Johnson, Amandus, 236
Johnson, Andrew, 250n1
Johnson, Lyndon, 113
Johnson Farm (Blue Ridge Parkway, Virginia), 109, *110, 111*
Jordan, Terry G., 237–38
Joutel, Henri, 37
JY Ranch (Jackson Hole, Wyoming), 185

Kalm, Peter, 25, 35
Kansas: Emporia, 177; Independence, 129, *130*
Karstens, Harry, 208–10
Kaups, Matti, 237
Keith, Sam, 144–45
Kenderdine, William H., 181
Kennedy, John F., 113
Kennedy, John Pendleton, 79–82, 94
Kenniston, George, 179
Kentucky: Beechland, 70; Harrodsburg, *70,* 70; Hindman, *102;* Hodgenville, 62, 63, *64, 67,* 67, 70, 74; Hollybush, 16; Knob Creek, 62, 70, *71;* Louisville, 66
Kilpinen, John T., 238
Kimball, Fiske, 235–36, 274n31
Kirkland, Caroline, 116, 117–24, *118,* 147
Kirkland, William, 118, 121
kitchens: kitchen building, 28, 83, 84, 85, 91, 92–93, 150–51, 174, 178, 184, 187; kitchen within cabin, 38, 110, 120, 121, 128, 133, 150, 155, 177, 214, 218, 227
Kniffen, Fred B., 236–37

Lafayette, Marquis de, 150
Lake Clark National Park and Preserve, Alaska, 146, 267n59
Lane, Rose Wilder, 128
La Rochefoucauld-Liancourt, duke of, 34
Larom, Larry, 186
Larsen, Oluf, 47

Larson, Gus, 1; Cabin (Wiseman, Alaska), *41, 42*
Latrobe, Benjamin Henry, 24, 272n5; "Wm. Robertson's house near his quarry on Aquia Creek," *33*
Lee (Robert E.) Memorial Foundation, 192
Lewis and Clark Exposition (Portland, Oregon, 1905), 138
Lincoln, Abraham, 6, 8, 50–51, 61–77, 117, 152, 169, 170–71, 174, 182, 232, 250n1; birthplace cabin(s), *64*, 66–67, 70; Birthplace National Historical Park (Hodgenville, Kentucky), 66–67, *67*, *CP3;* Boyhood National Memorial (Lincoln City, Indiana), *69*, 73, *75;* Marriage Cabin and Temple (Harrodsburg, Kentucky), 70, *71;* Memorial (Washington, DC), 70; New Salem State Historic Site (Petersburg, Illinois), 72, *73*
Lincoln, Mary Todd, 62, 68
Lincoln, Nancy Hanks, 62, 68, 70, 73, 254n41, 255n51; Inn (Hodgenville, Kentucky), 70; Memorial Park, Indiana, 68, 73
Lincoln, Robert, 252n24
Lincoln, Thomas, 62, 66, 70, 254n41
Lincoln Coffee Shops (northern California), 159
Lincoln Farm Association, 64, 67, 74
Lincoln Highway, 191
Lincoln Logs, 21, 76–77, 255nn53–54, *CP4*
Lincoln Tavern (Knob Creek, Kentucky), 70–71, *71*
Lippincott's Magazine of Popular Literature and Science, 97
Little House in the Big Woods (L. Ingalls Wilder), 124, 125, 126, *CP7*
Little House in the Big Woods (reconstruction; Pepin, Wisconsin), 129, *130*
Little House on the Prairie, (L. Ingalls Wilder) 124, 125, *126*, 126, 128
Little House on the Prairie (reconstruction; Independence, Kansas), 129, *130*
living history interpretation, 74, 75, 93
Log Cabin Association, 66
Log Cabin Campaign (Harrison, 1840), 8, 52–61, 164, 165, 263n11
log cabin construction, 18, 141–44; tools, 19–20, 30. *See also* chinking; foundations; *jacal;* log notching; plank construction; plans; *poteaux en coulisse; poteaux en terre; poteaux sur sole;* Red River frame; roofs
Log Cabin Farms (Armonk, New York), 274n28
Log Cabin in America, The: From Pioneer Days to the Present (Weslager), 236
Log Cabin Lodge (Medford Lakes, New Jersey), 181–82, 192, *CP15*
Log Cabin Motel (Pinedale, Wyoming), *191*, 191–92
Log Cabin Motor Court (Weaverville, North Carolina), 192
Log Cabin Myth, The (Shurtleff), 3, 235
Log Cabin Republicans, 255n55
Log Cabins: How to Build and Furnish Them (Wicks), 175, *176*, 182
Log Cabin School (now Hindman School, Kentucky), 100
Log Cabin Settlement (near Ashville, North Carolina), 100, *101*
Log Cabin Syrup, *170*, 170, *171*
Log Cabin Tea Room (Medford Lakes, New Jersey), 182
Log Cabin Tourist Camp (Hot Springs, South Dakota), 192
Log Coffee Taverns (Los Angeles, California), 159
log house, definition of, 16, 17
Log House, The (Colonial Beach, Virginia), 158–59
log joining, mortise and tenon, 16
log notching, 18–19, 20, 21, *22*, 28, 42, 101, *155*, 228, 244n13, 270n18; diamond notch, *22*, 93; double notch, 21, *22*, 44, 46, 47, 76–77, 176, 268n9; dovetailing, 3, 17, 21, *22*, 36, 37, 46, 47, 48, 104, 112, 157, 169, 222, 231, 236; half-dovetailing, *22*, 39, 88, 89, 91, 110, 134, 164, 169, 237; keyed notch, 21; lap joint, 21; saddle-notching, 1, 21, *22*, 37, 39, 42, 44, 48,

49, 58, 112, 125, 133, 136, 142, 144, 149, 160, 163, 166, 168, 169, 174, 181, 182, 189, 192, 206, 208, 209, 210, 211, 214, 217, 220, 222, 230, 231; square notch, 21, *22,* 42, 87, 149, 166, 187; tooth notch, 21, *22,* 47; V-notch, 21, *22,* 39, 176, 220, 237
Louisiana State University (Baton Rouge), 236
Lounsbury, Carl, 237
Lydick, Horace, 220
Lyman, Susan Chester, 100, 260n31

Mabry, Ed, 109
Mabry Mill (Blue Ridge Parkway, Virginia), 109
Maier, Herbert, 202, 275n11
Maine: Boothbay Harbor, 179, *180;* Yarmouth, 166
Maltese Cross Cabin (Medora, North Dakota), 131–34, *133,* 138–39
Manitoba, Selkirk, 37
Maryland: Baltimore, 66; Hollywood, *88;* Towson, *89*
Massachusetts, Plymouth, 152, *153,* 235
Mather, Stephen, 198–99, 213
Mayflower (ship), 56, 150
Mayflower Coffee Shops (Oakland and Berkeley, California), 159
McClure's magazine, 63
McIntyre Log House (Charlotte, North Carolina), plan, *26*
McKinley, William, 265n37
McRaven, Charles, 232
Medford Lakes Colony Club, New Jersey, 181, 272–73n10; design for log house, *181;* Lodge, *CP15*
Mercer, Henry Chapman, 235–36
Merrifield, William, 131
Mexican people, 43–45, 238
Michaux, François André, 36
Michigan: Ahmeek, 162, *162;* Munising, 227; Pinckney, 118, 119. *See also* Muskegon State Park, Michigan
Minnesota: Gheen, *48;* St. Paul, 170; Walnut Grove, 124, 126. *See also* Chippewa National Forest, Minnesota; Itasca State Park, Minnesota
Mission 66, 225
Mississippi, Natchez, *160,* 160
MIT (Massachusetts Institute of Technology), 175
Morehead-Gano Log House (Grapevine vicinity, Texas), elevations, *31*
Morgan, J. P., 173
Morgan, Lucy, 106, 107, 110
Morison, Samuel Eliot, 279n2
Mormons, 41, 46–47
motels, 9, 156, *191,* 191–92, 194
Mountain West, The: Interpreting the Folk Landscape (Gritzner), 238
Mount Hood National Forest, Oregon, 224; Timberline Lodge, 224
Mount McKinley National Park. *See* Denali National Park, Alaska
Mount Rainier National Park, Washington, 202–8; Longmire Community Building, *204,* 204, *205;* Paradise Inn, *203,* 203; St. Andrews Patrol Cabin, 208, *209;* Yakima (now Sunrise) Park Administration and Community Buildings, 205–6, *207, 208*
Mount Rainier National Park Company, 203
Mount Vernon (Virginia), 274n29
Mount Vernon Ladies' Association, 192
Murfree, Mary Noailles, 97
Muskegon State Park, Michigan, 202

Nason, George, 225
Natchez Garden Club, 270n17
National Association of Home Builders Log Homes Council, 231
National Conference of State Parks, 213
Native Americans, 16, 43, 264n21. *See also* Cherokee people; Chickasaw people; Choctaw people; Creek people; Seminole people
New England Coffee Shops (Los Angeles, California), 159, *CP10*
New England Farmer's Home and Modern Kitchen (Centennial Exposition), 150–51

New Home, A: Who'll Follow? or, Glimpses of Western Life (Kirkland), 118, 119, *123*
New Jersey: Burlington, 33; Medford Lakes, 180, *181, CP15;* Middlebrook, 32; Morristown, 19, 32, *154,* 154, *155;* Woodlynne, 166, *167*
New Mexico: Gallup, 192; Truchas, *45*
New York, *12, 13, 14;* Albany, 135; Buffalo, 169; Clinton, 118; College Point, *65;* Herkimer County, *176;* Lake Luzerne, *189;* Newcomb, 174, *CP13;* New York City, 118, 119, 135, 186; Oyster Bay, 135; Raquette Lake, *175;* Tontawanta, 59. *See also* Adirondack Mountains, New York
New York Times, 188
New York Times Magazine, 95
New York Zoological Society, 265n34
Nickerson, Parker, 179–80
Night Comes to the Cumberlands (Caudill), 113
North Carolina, *112;* Asheville, 100, *101,* 106; Brasstown, 105, *106;* Cataloochee, *26;* Charlotte, *26;* Penland, *107;* Weaverville, 192. *See also* Blue Ridge Parkway, Virginia and North Carolina; Great Smoky Mountains National Park, Tennessee and North Carolina
North Dakota, Medora, *133, 134,* 139. *See also* Roosevelt, Theodore: National Memorial Park, North Dakota
Northern Pacific Railroad, 133, 196
North Fork Club (Island Park, Idaho), 178, *179*
North West Company, 37
North Woods Club (Adirondacks), 173
Norwegian people, 46, 47
Norwich, England, 61

Ogle, Charles, 56
Oglesby, Richard, 62, 63
Ohio: Belmont County, 24; Columbus, 54, 56; North Bend, 53, 54; Xenia, 1
Old Salem Chautauqua Association, 254n45
Old Salem Lincoln League, 72
Old World Wisconsin (Eagle), 232; Schottler House, *233*
Oliver, Elijah, 112
Olmsted, Frederick Law, 23, 82
Olmsted, Frederick Law, Jr., 68, 69, 253n38
One Man's Wilderness (Keith), 139, 144, 145
On the Banks of Plum Creek (L. Ingalls Wilder), 124
Oregon, Portland, 159. *See also* Mount Hood National Forest, Oregon

Page and Hill, 182
Paine, Thomas, 30
Painted Pony Ranch (Lake Luzerne, New York), *189,* 189–90; Gold Nugget Dance Hall, 190; Long Horn Saloon, 190
Pan-American Exposition (Buffalo, 1901), 64
Pape, Alan, 278n6
Park and Recreation Structures (Good), 201
Park Protection Act of 1894, 264n34
parks, national, 195–212. *See also* Blue Ridge Parkway, Virginia and North Carolina; Denali National Park, Alaska; Glacier National Park, Montana; Great Smoky Mountains National Park, Tennessee and North Carolina; Lake Clark National Park and Preserve, Alaska; Mount Rainier National Park, Washington; Roosevelt, Theodore: National Memorial Park, North Dakota; Shenandoah National Park, Virginia; Yellowstone National Park, Wyoming; Yosemite National Park, California
parks, state, 10, 195–96, 201, 212–20. *See also* Itasca State Park, Minnesota; Muskegon State Park, Michigan; Lincoln, Nancy Hanks: Memorial Park, Indiana; Pine Mountain State Park, Georgia; Westmoreland State Park, Virginia
Park Structures and Facilities (Good), 200–201, 202, 204, 206, 214, 216
Payne, William Wesley, 274n32
Pell, Stephen H. P. and Sarah Gibbs Thompson, 161–62, 168
Pell Playhouse (Ticonderoga, New York), *168*
Penland School (Penland, North Carolina), 106–8, *107,* 110

Pennsylvania, *23;* Harrisburg, 58; Lancaster, 34; Oley Line, *38, 39;* Philadelphia, 36, 66; Valley Forge, 30, 32, 41, 232, 245n16
Peter, Robert, 84
Pettaway Plantation (former; Gees Bend, Alabama), *96*
Pettit, Katherine 100, 103, 104
Phillips, Sidney J., 92–93
Pierce, Franklin, 250n1
Pilgrims, 150–51, 152, 251n14; log cabin (built 1921) representing initial housing, *153*
Pilgrim Society, 268n5
Pine Mountain State Park, Georgia, 217–18
Pioneer Coffee Shops (Alameda and Oakland, California), 159
Pioneer History of the Holland Purchase (Turner), 11, *12, 13, 14*
Pioneer Playhouse (television series), 77
pit sawing, 18
plank construction, 20, 39, 84, 87, 104, 244n11
plans, *26;* dogtrot, 28, *29, 31,* 39, 99, *106;* saddlebag, 28, *28,* 88, 91, 110
playhouses, 161, 168, *168*
Playskool, 77
Plichta, Mark and Carol, 227–31; House (Little Traverse Bay, Michigan), *228, 229*
Plowden, Edmund, 34
Polk, James K., 250n1
Pope, John Russell, 66
Poplar Forest (Virginia), 177
poteaux en coulisse, 37
poteaux en terre, 37
poteaux sur sole, 37
Pownall, Thomas, "A design to represent the beginning and completion of an American Settlement or Farm," *15*
Proenneke, Richard, 116, 117, 139–47, 266n43, 266nn54–55, 267n58, *CP8;* Cabin (Twin Lakes, Alaska), 141–46, *146, CP8, CP9*
Progressive Era, 103
prospectors, 39
Pruyn, Martha Anne Williams, 174
Pruyn, Robert C., 174
Public Works Administration (PWA), 200, 275n5
puncheons, 24

"Raising, The," *19*
Ranch Life and the Hunting-Trail (T. Roosevelt), 135
Real Log Cabin, The (Aldrich), 182, *183,* 189
Reamer, Robert, 196
Red River frame, 37
Red Square (wooden toys), 77
Resettlement Administration, 95
restaurants, 148, 156, 161, 165, *CP10*
Revolutionary War, 19
Robertson, Robert H., 174
roofs, 24, 42–43, 44, 48, 266n50
Roosevelt, Alice, 131
Roosevelt, Edith, 135
Roosevelt, Franklin D., 200, 217; State Park, Georgia (now Pine Mountain State Park), 217
Roosevelt, Theodore, 67, 116, 117, 131–39, *132,* 147, 151, *171,* 171, 177, 178, 250n1; National Memorial Park, North Dakota, 139
Rothstein, Arthur, 95
Ruskin, John, 153
Russell Sage Foundation, 105, 106
Russian-American Company, 249n55
Russian Bishop's House (Sitka, Alaska), 46
Russian Orthodox Cathedral (Sitka, Alaska), 249n55
Russian people, 4, 46, 238
Rust, Josephine, 157
rustic design, 195–226

Sagamore (Camp; Raquette Lake, New York), 174, *175*
Saint-Gaudens, Augustus, 253n30
St. Louis World's Fair (1904), 138, 250n3
Sandburg, Carl, 70
Sanitary Fairs, 63, 267n2
Santa Fe Railway, 197
Santanoni (Camp; Newcomb, New York), 174–75, *CP13*

Saturday Evening Post, 164
Scandinavian people, 4, 25, 152, 176, 238, 245n22
Schuyler, Montgomery, 155–56
Scotch-Irish people, 4, 25, 35, 38, 78, 248n38
Scott, Walter, 191
Seminole people, 43
Semple, Ellen Churchill, 98–99, 102
Sewall, William, 134
Sewell, Helen, 129
Shenandoah National Park, Virginia, 108, 261n43
Shields, Carter, 112
Shurtleff, Harold R., 235–36, 278–79n2
Sinking Spring Farm (Hodgenville, Kentucky), 63, 64, 65
Sitting Bull, 152, 268n4
slave quarters, 9, *28,* 78–94, *81, 83, 86, 88, 89, 90, 93,* 114, 194, 256n4, 257n8
Sluyter, Peter, 33–34
Snyder, J. F., 138
Solomon's Temple, 20
Solo Mountain Shelter Cabin (Chisana, Alaska), *5*
Sotterley (Hollywood, Maryland), 87–88, *88,* 94
South Carolina, Lowndesville, *CP1*
South Dakota, Hot Springs, 192
Southern Highland Handicraft Guild, 107
Spanish Colonial style, 197
Spanish people, 4, 45
Sprucewold (Boothbay Harbor, Maine), 179–80, *180*
Standing Rock Indian Agency (North and South Dakota), 268n4
Stickley, Gustav, 153–55
Stone, May, 100, 103, 104
storehouses, 17, 34
stoves, 5, 28, 36, 39, 42, 48, 141, 143, 210, 220. *See also* fireplaces
stovewood wall, 16, 243n4
Stowe, Harriet Beecher, 79, 82, 87, 94, 258n12
Stratford Hall (Stratford, Virginia), 192–94, *193*
Strother, David Hunter, 97
Suhling, Mrs. W. G., 184
Sumers, George, 273n13
Sumner, Henry, 199
Sutter, John, 46
Swallow Barn, or A Sojourn in the Old Dominion (Kennedy), 79–82
Swedish people, 32–33, 34, 46, 235–37
Swedish Settlements on the Delaware, The (Amandus Johnson, publisher), 236
Swerer, Bob, 144–45
Swiss people, 4, 279n6

Taft, William H., 253n30
Tait Plantation House (Columbus, Texas), plan, *29*
Tarbell, Ida, 63, 68, 71, 253n30
Taylor, Zachary, 250n1
tea rooms, 9, 156, 159
Tea-Room Management (trade publication), 159
Tecumseh (Shawnee leader), 52–53
Tennessee, *113;* Harrogate, *98;* McMinnville, 164, *CP11;* Nashville (Hermitage), *28,* 89–90, *90,* 258n16; *See also* Great Smoky Mountains National Park, Tennessee and North Carolina
Tennessee Centennial Expo (Nashville, 1897), 63
Tennessee Park Commission, 111
Texas: Columbus, *29;* Grapevine vicinity, *31*
Thames, Battle of the, 52
Thompson, Robert, 71
Thoreau, Henry David, 115, 177, 262n1
Tippecanoe, Battle of, 52
Tippecanoe Club, 59
Tocqueville, Alexis de, 165
Todd, Leon, 180–81
Tony's Burgers (Los Angeles, California), 270n16
Towle, Patrick J., 170
Towle Maple Syrup Company (Log Cabin Syrup), *170,* 170, *171*
Transylvania College (Lexington, Kentucky), 70
"Travelog" (mobile log cabin), *107,* 107
Turner, Frederick Jackson, 128, 265n37
Turner, Orsamus, 11, 16, 17, 24, 25; drawings, *12, 13, 14*

Tuskegee Institute (Alabama), 92
Twain, Mark (Samuel Clemens), 5, 253n30
Twitter, 169; offices (San Francisco), *CP12*
Tyler, John, 53

Uncle Tom's Cabin (Stowe), 79, 81, 87, 255n1; title page, *81*
Underwood, Gilbert Stanley, 24
Union Magazine of Literature and Art, The, 119
Up from Slavery (B. T. Washington), 91
U.S. Commission of Fine Arts, 269n14
U.S. Forest Service, 196, 200, 220–24. *See also* forests, national
U.S. National Park Service, 10, 73–74, 93, 108–13, 139, 146–47, 157, 196–214, 224, 225–26, 252n24. *See also* parks, national
Utah: Circleville, 47; Fillmore, 166, *167;* Salt Lake City, 178

vacations, 148–49; vacation lodging, 9, 48, 148–49, 173–94, 267n1
Valley Ranch (Wyoming), 186
Van Buren, Martin, 50, 51, 53, 56
Vanderbilt, Alfred G., 173, 174
Vassar College (Poughkeepsie, New York), 100
Veterans Conservation Corps, 217,
Vint, Thomas, 199–200, 203–4, 210–11, 275n11
Virginia: Aquia Creek, *33;* Bedford, 109; Colonial Beach, *158;* Franklin County, *93;* Fredericksburg, 157; James City County, *CP6;* Lynchburg, 59, 183, *185;* Stratford, *193*. *See also* Blue Ridge Parkway, Virginia and North Carolina; Westmoreland State Park, Virginia
Virginian, The (Wister), 273n19
visitor centers, 10, 156, 162–64, *162, 163,* 165, 254n49

Wakefield National Memorial Association, 157
Wakefield plantation (Virginia), 157
Walker, George, 84; Property (District of Columbia), *85*
Wanamaker's (John) department store, 65
War Department, 74
War on Poverty, 113
Washington, Booker T., 91–94, 95, 232; Birthplace Memorial (Franklin County, Virginia), *93,* 93, 94
Washington, George, 30–32, 63, 82–83, 157; Birthplace National Monument (Colonial Beach, Virginia), *158,* 192; Monument (Washington, DC), 269n13
Washington: Seattle, 159; Tacoma, 203. *See also* Mount Rainier National Park, Washington
Washington, DC, 83–84, 157
Washington County Historical Society (Kentucky), 254n41
Webster, Daniel, 51
Weslager, Clinton Alfred, 236
Westmoreland State Park, Virginia, 194, 218–20; Cabin 6, *219*
whipsawing, 18
White, Helen, 144
White, William Allen, 177–78; Work Cabin (Rocky Mountain National Park, Colorado), *CP14*
Whitehead, Henry, 112
White Log Coffee Shops (Portland, Oregon, and Seattle, Washington), 159
White Log Taverns and Coffee Shops (California), 159
White Grass Dude Ranch (Jackson Hole, Wyoming), *188*
whitewashing, *86,* 86
Wickersham, James, 5; House (Eagle, Alaska), *6, 7*
Wicks, William S., 175–77, 182
Wilder, Almanzo, 124
Wilder, Laura Ingalls, 116, 117, 124–31, 147, 263nn15–16
Wilderness Hunter, The (T. Roosevelt), 135, 136
Wild West Show (Buffalo Bill's), 186
Williams, Garth, 129
Williams, John S., 24
Winning of the West, The (T. Roosevelt), 131, 265n37

Wirth, Conrad, 214
Wirth, Theodore, 214
Wisconsin: Old World Wisconsin, Eagle, 232; Pepin, 124, 125, 129, *130*
Wister, Fanny Kemble, 185, 186
Wister, Owen, 185, 273n19
Witherspoon College (Perry County, Kentucky), 105
Wollerton House (Chester County, Pennsylvania), *23*
Womack, Abner, 164
Womack, Daisy Cleopatra, 164
Women's Christian Temperance Union (WCTU), 100
Woody (Tyne)House (Cataloochee, North Carolina), plan, *26*
Works Progress Administration (WPA), 43, 163, 166, 200, 214, 223, 224, 275n5
World's Columbian Exposition (Chicago, 1893), 66, 74, 136, 151, 252n27, 265n37; Hunter's Cabin, 136, *137*
Wright, Frank Lloyd, 77
Wright, John Lloyd, 77
Wyoming: Cody, 186; Jackson Hole, 166, 185, 186–87, *187, 188,* 191. *See also* Yellowstone National Park, Wyoming

Yellowstone National Park, Wyoming, 166, 182, 185, 191, 196–97, 264n34; Old Faithful Inn, 182, 196–99, *197, 198,* 201
Yosemite National Park, California, 213; Rangers' Club, *199,* 199
Young, Abraham, 83–84, 257n7
Young, Brigham, 47
Young, Notley, 84; property (District of Columbia), *CP5*
Young, Widow, 83
YWCA, 184, 194